Refugees and the Ethics of Forced Displacement

This book is a philosophical analysis of the ethical treatment of refugees and stateless people, a group of people who, though extremely important politically, have been greatly under theorized philosophically. The limited philosophical discussion of refugees focuses narrowly on the question of whether or not we, as members of Western states, have moral obligations to admit refugees into our countries. This book reframes this debate and shows why it is important to think ethically about people who will never be resettled and who live for prolonged periods outside of all political communities. Parekh shows why philosophers ought to be concerned with ethical norms that will help stateless people mitigate the harms of statelessness even while they remain formally excluded from states.

Serena Parekh is Associate Professor in the Department of Philosophy and Religion at the Northeastern University, USA.

Routledge Research in Applied Ethics

1 Vulnerability, Autonomy and Applied Ethics
   Edited by Christine Straehle

2 Refugees and the Ethics of Forced Displacement
   Serena Parekh

Refugees and the Ethics of Forced Displacement

Serena Parekh

LONDON AND NEW YORK

First published 2017 by Routledge

2 Park Square, Milton Park, Abingdon, Oxfordshire OX14 4RN
711 Third Avenue, New York, NY 10017

Routledge is an imprint of the Taylor & Francis Group, an informa business

First issued in paperback 2018

Copyright © 2017 Taylor & Francis

The right of Serena Parekh to be identified as author of this work has been asserted by her in accordance with sections 77 and 78 of the Copyright, Designs and Patents Act 1988.

All rights reserved. No part of this book may be reprinted or reproduced or utilised in any form or by any electronic, mechanical, or other means, now known or hereafter invented, including photocopying and recording, or in any information storage or retrieval system, without permission in writing from the publishers.

Notice:
Product or corporate names may be trademarks or registered trademarks, and are used only for identification and explanation without intent to infringe.

Library of Congress Cataloging-in-Publication Data
Names: Parekh, Serena, 1974– author.
Title: Refugees and the ethics of forced displacement / by Serena Parekh.
Description: New York : Routledge, 2016. | Series: Routledge research in applied ethics ; 2 | Includes bibliographical references and index.
Identifiers: LCCN 2016029523 | ISBN 9780415712613 (hardback : alk. paper)
Subjects: LCSH: Refugees—Government policy—Moral and ethical aspects—Western countries. | Stateless persons—Government policy—Moral and ethical aspects—Western countries.
Classification: LCC JV6346 .P37 2016 | DDC 172/.2—dc23
LC record available at https://lccn.loc.gov/2016029523

ISBN: 978-0-415-71261-3 (hbk)
ISBN: 978-1-138-34677-2 (pbk)

Typeset in Sabon
by Apex CoVantage, LLC

To Auggie and Kersi, with love and gratitude

Contents

Acknowledgements ix

Introduction 1
1 The Moral Significance of the Refugee Regime 17
2 Refugees in Contemporary Political Philosophy 51
3 Hannah Arendt and the Ontological Deprivation of Statelessness 82
4 Responsibility for the Forcibly Displaced 104
Conclusion 136

Bibliography 147
Index 157

Acknowledgements

Writing can be a solitary endeavor. This is why I am so grateful for the friends and colleagues who have taken the time to read various parts of this manuscript and discuss the ideas with me. I could not have completed this project without the help and encouragement of the following people: Thom Brooks, Vittorio Buffacchi, Bat-Ami Bar-On, Eleni Coundouriotis, Scott Campbell, Hege Finholt, Carol Hay, Liz Holzer, Michael Knipper, Kathy Libal, Alice MacLachlan, Diana Meyers, Julinna Oxley, Blair Peruniak, Jan Ruzicka, Susanne Sreedhar, and Kamilla Stullerova.

I'd like to especially thank my colleagues in the Department of Philosophy and Religion at Northeastern, who have created a collegial and supportive scholarly environment and given me invaluable feedback on this book. My deep thanks to John Basl, Eric Blumenson, Liz Bucar, Kerry Dugan, Candice Delmas, Patricia Illingworth, Jung Lee, Steve Nathanson, Rory Smead, Susan Setta, and Sheila Winborne. I'd like to thank Ron Sandler and the Ethics Institute for sponsoring the lunch time workshops on my book. In 2014–2015, I received a Humanities Fellowship from the Humanities Institute at Northeastern University, which allowed me the opportunity to discuss my research with an interdisciplinary group of scholars. I'd like to thank Len Albright, Emily Artiano, James Connolly, Tim Creswell, Meghan Doran, Gretchen Heefner, Kathleen Kelly, and Bert Spector. I'd also like to thank Jeremy Paul, Kevin Murray, and other members of the Program on Human Rights and the Global Economy (PHRGE) at the Northeastern School of Law for their feedback on my work as well.

I'd like to thank all the students with whom I've talked about refugees over the years in my human rights and global justice courses. I'd like to thank my two excellent research assistants from Northeastern, Monica Mercola and Meredith Stone.

I've had the privilege of presenting parts of this book in various places around the world and have benefited tremendously from these opportunities. I'd particularly like to thank Annamari Vitikainen for her invitation to a workshop at the Artic University of Norway in Tromso, Norway. I am thankful as well to Luara Ferracioli for her invitation to a workshop at Princeton University on The Ethics and Politics of the Global Refugee

Regime. I benefited enormously from the conversations I was able to have there with Christopher Wellman, Joseph Carens, Alex Betts, Alex Aleinikoff, and others, and am very grateful to them. I'd like to thank the organizers, discussants, and audience members at the following institutions and organizations where I presented parts of this book for their questions and constructive criticism: the Centre for the Study of Global Ethics at the University of Birmingham, England; the Department of International Politics, Aberystwyth University, Wales; the Department of Philosophy at the University Helsinki, Finland; the Department of Philosophy at SUNY Binghamton; Osgoode Hall Law School and York University, Toronto; University of Connecticut's Human Rights Institute; the North American Society for Social Philosophy (NASSP); the American Philosophical Association; MIT Center for International Studies; the Canadian Society for Women in Philosophy (CSWIP); and Feminist Ethics and Social Theory (FEAST).

I'd like to extend a special thanks to the anonymous reviewers from Routledge who provided helpful feedback on the completed manuscript.

Finally, I'd like to thank my Boston friends who either patiently let me vent about the frustrations of writing or distracted me from them, Aziza Ahmed, Gal Kober, Julia Legas, Edward McGushin, Siri Nilsson, Jeff Ousborne, Kate O'Brien, Steve Riden, Mary Troxell, and Liza Weinstein. And of course, a special thanks to Auggie and Kersi, for their love and support.

Serena Parekh
Boston, MA, June 2016

Much of the material in Chapter Three is drawn from my article, "Beyond the Ethics of Admission: Stateless People, Refugee Camps and Moral Obligations." *Philosophy and Social Criticism*, Vol. 40, No. 7 (2014), pp. 645–663. © Sage. All rights reserved.

Introduction

On September 2, 2015 the body of a three-year-old boy, Aylan Kurdi, washed up on the shore of Turkey. The child, and those who died with him, including his five-year-old brother, mother, and at least 12 others, were refugees from the war in Syria trying to reach the Greek island of Kos. They are among the 2600 people who died crossing the Mediterranean Sea in 2015, and they are among the hundreds of thousands who have recently fled conflict situations in the Middle East and Africa and have tried to find asylum in Europe. It is now well known that while many people make it to Europe after horrific journeys—tortured by police along the way, chased by wolves in the night, hunted down by locals with iron bars, suffocated on tiny boats—many, like Aylan and his family, do not (Kingsley 2015). Yet the picture of this child on the beach seemed to make the numbers real, showing that there are indeed people behind the statistics that are thrown around so often. Whether it was because he was nicely dressed or appeared to be like a child peacefully napping, Aylan's picture touched something within many people. The picture marked a change in attitudes about the plight of refugees from Syria. Many people in the West, including many politicians, began to ask questions not only about our legal or political obligations to help, but about our *moral* obligations as well.

It is not a stretch to say that Aylan Kurdi, and the people who died with him, are only the tip of the iceberg of the much larger problem of forced displacement. Around the world, well over 60 million people live without formal state protection and are in the process of waiting for or seeking some form of political belonging. The moral question raised by this large group is arguably no different than the one raised by the death of one, innocent child: what do we owe victims of forced displacement? Or, to put it in terms philosophers are more familiar with: what are our moral obligations to refugees like Aylan and other people who are forced to flee their homes in search of safety and security? The refugee crisis in Europe that began in the late summer of 2015 brought this question to life, so to speak, as many of the world's liberal democracies struggled to balance the humanitarian impulse to help with contradicting political values like security and sovereignty. This book is an attempt to stand back from this situation and shed some light on how we might begin to understand what our moral obligations to the forcibly displaced are and how we might be able to ground our obligations so that when faced with what seem to be competing demands—nationalism, security, the economy—they may nonetheless be taken seriously.

Before going into detail about the problem of forced migration and the ethical complexities that surround it, let me briefly summarize the approach I present in this book. The specific problem that I focus on has to do with how the forcibly displaced are treated during their displacement, while they are outside of their home states and have not yet found a state to welcome them. More specifically, I am concerned with the problem of large-scale, protracted refugee situations and the use of refugee camps to deny the displaced basic rights and political participation, for prolonged periods of time (a problem sometimes referred to as *encampment*). These problems are distinct from questions about how many refugees a country ought to resettle or admit for asylum, which are the more standard questions philosophers and politicians have grappled with.

I argue throughout the book that we have a moral obligation to reject the policy of long-term encampment as the de facto solution to the problem of unwanted and superfluous people in the world. This is not to suggest that we should ignore long-term durable solutions such as resettlement; this is an obligation that is compatible with other obligations to refugees in the long-term but can be realized independently of them. My claim is that we cannot ignore this period when refugees are between states. This is also not to say that refugee camps are never appropriate; they may be appropriate in the short term as a way to provide emergency aid. The problem is the use of camps as a long-term measure for containing the forcibly displaced so that they do not threaten the sovereignty of other states. I discuss some of the many problems with refugee camps and argue that if, for pragmatic or political reasons, they are going to continue to be used to house refugees over the long term, they ought to at least meet the level of what John Rawls calls a decent hierarchical society. That is, they ought to minimally protect the basic human rights and dignity of their residents and allow some form of political participation and accountability (Rawls 2001). Currently this does not occur in most refugee camps. Though insisting on this minimal level of decent treatment while refugees are between homes may turn out to be as difficult as finding long-term solutions, I argue that we ought to at least see this as one of the obligations we owe refugees and orient our practices and policies towards trying to realize this end.

Though a low bar in most other contexts, when it comes to the treatment of refugees and the displaced, many would consider ensuring this basic level of rights, protection, and accountability an unaffordable and unnecessary luxury. The reason that the ethical treatment of the displaced during their displacement is often ignored is because displacement is assumed by most people to be *exceptional* and *temporary*. I argue that both of these assumptions should be abandoned. Displacement is so much a fact of every day political life that far from being exceptional, it ought to be seen as a regular part of global politics. Given that the norm for displacement is now 17 years, far from being temporary, displacement ought to be assumed to be long-term and enduring. The treatment of people during their displacement, because it is regular and enduring, not exceptional and temporary, ought to be subject to rigorous ethical consideration.

The scope of this book is fairly narrow. The focus is on the moral dimension of how the displaced are treated between the time of their exile and when they are finally able to find a permanent durable solution. This period of time is ever growing, and more and more people spend their lives here. For the vast majority of people, it is a time characterized by confinement and human rights violations. This should not be the accepted norm. We ought to be promoting policies and practices that treat the forcibly displaced as fully human and with dignity.

§ Chapter Overview

My starting point in Chapter One is that we must take seriously a number of very disheartening realities and recognize these as morally salient facts: that a population close to that of the United Kingdom—65.3 million people or one in every 100 of the world's citizens—lives more or less permanently outside the nation-state system, and no state acknowledges political or moral responsibility for this group (UNHCR 2016b). Further, most people, once they are displaced from their homes, remain in *protracted* situations, situations lasting five years or more; the *average* length of time a person will remain a refugee is 17 years. Finally, less than 1% of official refugees will ever be resettled permanently in a new country.

The majority of the world's refugees remain for years, often decades, sometimes generations, in refugee camps or informal settlements. I argue that we ought to take seriously the fact that encampment—placing refugees in camps or other places where they have little access to resources, rights, or protection for prolonged periods of time—has become the de facto way of handling refugee situations. This has supplemented and increasingly overtaken the other "durable" solutions—voluntary return to the country of origin (repatriation), local integration in the country of residence or asylum, and resettlement in a third country (most often one of the wealthy liberal democracies such as the United States, Australia, Canada, and the EU). Encampment has become the unofficial solution in the sense that Western states and the international community have come to rely on camps as the primary way of handling large numbers of displaced people. If you are a refugee in the 21st century seeking aid from the international community, you are likely to spend your life in a refugee camp or a similar space of containment, rather than being resettled, receiving asylum, being repatriated, or being integrated in your host country.

That encampment is the norm can be seen from the data. In 2014, of the 59.5 million people who were displaced from their countries, 126,800 people were able to return to their home countries and 105,200 people were resettled (data on local integration is not available). What happens to the other more than 59.2 million people who were not able to avail themselves of one of the official durable solutions? The vast majority continued to live more or less outside the bounds of the nation-state system. Roughly 60% of refugees move to urban areas with limited aid from the international community, where 85% live in private accommodation and the remaining 15% live in planned and managed camps. The other 40% live in rural areas and, for the most part, in some kind of camp setting (either planned/managed camps, self-settled camps, or reception/transit camps).[1] By some accounts, as many as 34 million people live in camps in 125 countries (Esri 2013).

The situation I have just described is sometimes referred to as "warehousing"—placing people in camps, dependent on aid, for protracted periods of time so that they do not pose problems for neighboring states or have the ability to claim asylum in the West. Those who are warehoused in refugee camps are usually deprived of the rights that are part of the 1951 UN Refugee Convention, such as the right to work, run a business, own property, move freely within the country of residence, or choose a place of residence. They are not provided travel documents that would allow them to move freely and would increase their autonomy and ability to care for their families. Refugees living in camps are often not permitted to earn their own livelihood and so remain dependent on aid, either from the international community or from their host states, in a state of enforced idleness. In short, the moral harms of being in a refugee camp include a sense of captivity as well as the denial of freedom, autonomy, and basic human rights, not merely for short exceptional periods but regularly and for extended periods of time.

Not only should we take seriously the reality of life for the forcibly displaced, but we must also take into consideration the current political consensus regarding our moral and legal obligations to refugees: states have no legal obligation to resettle refugees or other forcibly displaced people, they recognize no moral obligation to resettle refugees, and Western states are, for various political reasons, unlikely to resettle large numbers of refugees. On the contrary, most states feel entitled to exclude refugees, and this motivates many of their policies. To be clear, I agree that we have a duty to resettle and provide asylum to refugees in a much more robust way than we currently do; however, given that we are not likely to realize these obligations, it is important to ask what moral obligations flow from these circumstances. Given what Western states and their populations regard as their interests and as the limits of their duties, large-scale legally mandated resettlement is not likely to be a realistic solution to the current and growing phenomenon of forced displacement. This is in part why it becomes so crucial to take this in between period seriously. The primary focus of my book is on what can be done within these unjust constraints, that is, what can be done in a world in which there will not be extensive resettlement of refugees who cannot be repatriated within a reasonable period of time and in which the vast majority of refugees will continue to live outside of a state. Because of these conditions, we ought to identify and pay close attention to the harms caused by the actual refugee regime and ask what ought to be done to address those harms. In this sense, this book engages in non-ideal, rather than ideal theory; it asks us to take seriously what morality requires of us in actual circumstances, when we cannot meet ideal demands of justice (Stemplowska and Swift 2012).

Is it possible to morally evaluate the treatment of the displaced, or should they simply be grateful that they are getting any assistance at all? This is the subject of this book. I will argue throughout that we can and ought to morally evaluate this in between period, this period of limbo where the vast majority of the displaced will spend their lives. Living outside of a nation-state is no longer an anomaly that can be brushed aside as exceptional to contemporary political life; it has in many ways become a standard way of living for millions of people, and will increasingly be so in the future.

For many in the West, the primary moral question about refugees has to do with whether we have a moral obligation to admit them into our states, either through resettlement from refugee camps or through claims of asylum, and if so, how many. This was, for example, one of the first questions discussed during the refugee crisis in Europe in the late summer of 2015. This line of thinking is obvious in many ways—the refugees who managed to make the harrowing journey to Europe demanded, after all, residence, rights, and the ability to move around freely in search of work and to be reunited with family. The moral question about whether or not we have moral obligations to admit refugees and asylum seekers—sometimes referred to as the ethics of admission—is also the primary focus of much normative philosophical analysis, which I examine in detail in Chapter Two. Yet I argue in this chapter that we ought to expand the moral approach we take to this issue and not focus exclusively on the ethics of admission. I suggest that philosophers have been overly focused on the moral obligations of liberal democracies to admit or exclude refugees, and have not given sufficient moral consideration to the treatment of the displaced who will not be resettled. I argue throughout the book that we have obligations to ensure that the displaced live dignified lives while they are awaiting a more permanent solution. This obligation can be realized independently of any responsibilities we may have to resettle refugees.

One of the ways that I argue for an increased focus on the morality of how we treat the displaced while they are displaced is by arguing for a more nuanced understanding of refugees and forced displacement. In particular, I argue in Chapter Three that displacement—being forced outside your country of citizenship and denied political belonging in your state of residence—entails two distinct harms that must be analyzed separately. The first harm is legal/political—the loss of a political community and a legal identity in the form of citizenship. But in addition to this, statelessness entails an *ontological* deprivation, that is, the loss of something fundamental to a person's humanity. Using the work of Hannah Arendt, I show that taking seriously the ontological deprivation of statelessness has important consequences for how we think about our moral obligations.

If the only harm of statelessness is the political or legal harm that comes with a loss of citizenship, and the only way to rectify this is through resettlement in Western states, then we must acknowledge that the vast majority of the displaced will remain untouched by our moral discourse, since only a small percentage of the 65.3–72 million people who are displaced "count" as refugees and are thus eligible for resettlement.[2] However, if we take seriously the ontological deprivation as a distinct form of harm, other ways to address the situation become more evident (I discuss examples such as economic integration, disaggregated citizenship, increased political participation, and temporary local integration throughout the book). Addressing the ontological deprivation of statelessness may require that we think about ways that the forcibly displaced may be able to keep a meaningful political identity and resist a reduction to bare life, even though they may be formally bereft of citizenship or political membership. Once these two sets of harms are pulled apart, we will see that even though we have had limited success in addressing the former harm (i.e., by resettling stateless people in new political communities), there are nonetheless other ways to address the second kind of harm, the ontological deprivation. Refugee policy, supported by Western states, ought to be concerned with addressing the ontological deprivation of statelessness, and not merely the political harm.

To further this argument, I suggest in Chapter Four that the harms of the refugee regime must be understood from two different points of view. On the one hand, there are many direct injustices that we contribute to, such as our policies that make it difficult for legitimate asylum seekers to claim asylum and the violation of the legal norm of non-refoulement. Yet we should also see some of the injustices from a different perspective. I argue that many of the injustices associated with the refugee regime ought to be understood as *structural injustices*. Structural injustices are not necessarily the result of deliberate wrong-doing or explicitly unjust policies, but are the unintentional outcome of the actions of different agents each working for their own morally acceptable ends. That the displaced are often forced to live in squalid camps that systematically violate their human rights for decades is clearly a moral injustice; yet this injustice is not usually the result of the deliberate policies of a given state intended to harm the displaced nor the result of ill intentions on the part of international agencies. It arises as a result of different sovereign states acting in their own best interests. Yet it is still an injustice. Seeing encampment as a structural injustice allows us to not get lost in questions of moral culpability and focus instead on remedying the injustice.

Yet thinking of encampment as a form of structural injustice brings its own challenges. In particular, it's much harder to place responsibility if a harmful outcome is not the result of the deliberate actions and intentions of an individual. It calls for a new understanding of responsibility, one that I develop by drawing on the work of Iris Young, David Miller, and Thomas Pogge. I argue that we ought to move away from linking responsibility with our actions and instead, we ought to think about ways that we may be *remedially* responsible for an unjust outcome. We ought to understand our responsibility for global displacement as remedial in the sense that we are responsible for fixing the problem in front of us because of the various ways we are connected to the situation, even though we did not directly cause it. Remedial responsibility demands that we expand the way we think about our connection to global displacement and the refugee regime.

To summarize, in Chapter One, I address the harms created by the current arrangements of the refugee regime and the background political constraints that make their elimination so difficult. The actual experience of being a refugee in the 21st century is very different from what most people assume that it is, and I devote much of this chapter to describing and analyzing this. In Chapters Two and Three, I look at two philosophical approaches to our moral obligations to the forcibly displaced. In Chapter Two I give an overview of the Anglo-American normative framing and approach through discussing the work of six contemporary philosophers. I argue that though this approach is helpful in many ways, it does not pay sufficient attention to the harms I describe in Chapter One, namely the encampment and warehousing of refugees. In Chapter Three I take up the perspective of continental philosophy through the work of Hannah Arendt, and argue that we ought to take seriously the *ontological deprivation* that comes with being a refugee. In this chapter, I present a different perspective on the harms caused by current arrangements and what is needed to remedy those harms, even if it is not possible to eliminate them entirely because of the background political constraints. I argue that both the normative and continental approaches are necessary to understand the ethics of forced displacement. In Chapter Four I take up the pressing political question of who is responsible for the harms experienced by refugees and who must address them. I argue that some of the harms of the refugee regime must be understood as structural injustices, injustices for which Western states can be held remedially responsible. Overall, these four chapters serve to establish how we ought to approach the ethics of forced displacement in the 21st century and will, I hope, shed some light on what we owe to refugees and the forcibly displaced.

To connect my claims with the recent refugee crisis in Europe, we can say that on my view the moral obligations of, say, the United States, to Syrian refugees are not exhausted by resettling 10,000 refugees, even though this may seem like a large number to some and an insignificantly small number to others. We must continue to ask: and what happens to the other 5 million people from Syria who have been displaced by the war? Under what conditions will they be forced to live and for how long? Even if we are not willing to resettle more refugees through formal resettlement programs, we are still obliged to ask this question, and the answer to it may require that we substantially increase our funding to the UNHCR and countries that host refugees; lobby and encourage other countries to resettle more refugees; come up with other ways to aid refugees who we are not willing to resettle, such as through temporarily legal protection statuses or through increasing various kinds of visa programs (student, work, and humanitarian); and expand family reunification. We ought to provide oversight of refugee camps in Turkey, Lebanon, and Jordan and insist that these states not violate the human rights of refugees; our aid to these countries ought to be contingent upon their upholding the human rights and dignity of the displaced. We must be concerned with our ethical obligations to the millions of people who will never be resettled in the West and will spend decades living in refugee camps that are supported, at least in part, by the policies of our states. Philosophers, I suggest, must move beyond their focus on resettlement and must morally challenge the practices of containment and control currently exercised over millions of displaced people that are neither inevitable nor politically necessary. We ought to challenge states to work towards building a more just refugee regime, one that takes seriously the full human rights of the displaced (not merely their survival needs).

This book is *not* an attempt to solve any of the many complex political and economic problems that surround forced displacement. I have little to say about how we change our current practices or how we overcome xenophobia and fear of the other. As Carens has pointed out, it is important to figure out what is "right in principle before moving to the question of what we should do in practice" (Carens 2013, 201). While this book is not about solutions, I hope it will help us to find better ways to deal with the growing phenomenon of forced displacement and provide a stronger ground for our ethical obligations to the forcibly displaced.

Stephen White wrote that there are two kinds of political theory, "world revealing" and "action guiding" (quoted in Brown 2011). My book aims for the former, while perhaps only secondarily achieving the latter. In other words, it is my hope that my book is not read as a book of refugee policy. Rather, I hope this book is "world revealing" in that it makes the moral dimension of displacement clearer to theorists and others concerned with this topic. I agree with Brown that asking "what is to be done" is not the only important task of normative theory. However, I disagree with him that "the search for some kind of morally satisfying general theory which will delineate our duties to and responsibilities for refugees is almost certainly a waste of time" (Brown 2011, 166). The task of articulating our duties to refugees is a worthy one, one that many philosophers have made great strides in. I see my book as one that would complement other research on this topic by making clear the problems refugees experience and the ways they have been historically ignored or assumed to be inevitable. While I do argue that we have a set of obligations to the forcibly displaced, I by no means intend to suggest that these are our only obligations or that if we fulfill them the problems around displacement will disappear.

§ Methodology

Methodologically speaking, I move between two ways of doing philosophy and use methods traditionally associated with both continental and analytic philosophy. I am critical of some analytic normative theory around refugees because I argue that it artificially excludes the lived experience of the forcibly displaced. I try to show in this book that analytic philosophers working on theories of immigration and refugees would benefit from the more *phenomenological* description of displacement that is provided by Arendt, Agier, and Agamben. Phenomenology seeks to unearth the lived experience of refugees from within the larger context. With this deeper understanding of the meaning of statelessness and the kind of harm it engenders, we are in a better position to understand our obligations to people in this situation (regardless of how they are legally defined). By contrast, the phenomenologists I analyze do not grapple with the concrete political situation and come up with meaningful normative claims about what we—as a country or as a global community—ought to do to address this as a political problem. There are broad injunctions, but these are not made concrete. This is why the normative analytic approach is essential. But the two must work dialectically so that the phenomenological and the normative perspectives mutually enrich each other and ultimately help us to move towards a deeper understanding of our moral obligations to these most vulnerable of people.

In addition to both of these methodologies, another methodological principle I hold is the importance of interdisciplinary and empirical research. Thomas Pogge showed why it is important for philosophers to take seriously empirical work. He argued that John Rawls has an inadequate view of our moral obligations to the global poor because he misunderstands the causes of global poverty (believing that they are purely domestic and not connected to the global international order). In other words, for Rawls, an inadequate empirical view of poverty led to a moral error (Pogge 2004). Likewise I want to suggest that theorists of displacement sometimes misperceive the problem. When one thinks that the political problem is that millions of refugees want to get into countries in the West, the most important moral question is whether or not to let them in, and how many refugees morality requires us to admit. Refugees are perceived to be a problem for affluent democratic states. Yet most refugees have little hope of admission to a Western state, and it is not entirely clear that this is even the solution they would prefer (Aleinikoff 1992).[3] I incorporate empirical research on both the phenomenon of global displacement as well as the refugee regime in the hopes that it will lead to a better moral assessment of our obligations.

§ Two Points of Clarification: Who are "We" and Who are "Refugees"?

Since I am arguing about *our* moral obligations, it is important at the outset to clarify who I am referring to here. Who is it precisely that has the moral obligations that I'm discussing? That is, who is the "we" that I am speaking about? The states that I believe these obligations are most applicable to are Western liberal democracies. The reasons for including these countries—and not, say, China, India, or Brazil—are both historical and theoretical. Historically, it is Western states that have dominated the global refugee regime, in terms of creating global covenants, defining practices, and funding various institutions. They are also the countries which, by and large, resettle refugees. As I show throughout the book, Western states in many ways set the terms and policies around the refugee regime. Further, Western states in general and the US in particular are the primary funders of the refugee regime and thus have the power to influence how their money is spent.

More theoretically speaking, these are the countries whose self-identity is bound up with certain moral categories. Western states like the US and Canada see themselves as founded on moral principles such as equality, human rights, and justice. Showing that their practices are out of line with their purported values is significant. Similarly, Carens directs his arguments on moral obligations around immigration to people "committed to democratic principles," "the broad moral commitments that underlie and justify contemporary political institutions and policies throughout North America and Europe," such as the equal moral worth of all human beings and equality under the law (Carens 2013, 2). For citizens of these states, there is broad moral consensus about certain ethical principles that can, I believe, serve as a ground for thinking about our obligations to the displaced. Countries which have never claimed to be founded on these moral principles may simply reject the notion that they have obligations to those outside their states. While all signatories to the 1951 Refugee Convention have the legal obligations that they formally agreed to, my analysis suggests that those states that have a vested interest in seeing themselves as upholding justice and that are committed to broader moral principles, such as universal human equality and dignity, ought to reconsider the *moral*, as opposed to legal or political, obligations that they have.

A second and connected question is, who precisely am I talking about when I talk about refugees and the forcibly displaced? In current political dialogues, the term refugee is used in a variety of ways, and there is little consensus about to whom the term ought to refer.

Indeed, one of the most charged political questions is how to distinguish a genuine refugee—somebody who is fleeing political persecution—from an economic migrant—someone who has left their home in order to improve their economic situation.[4] The former group is thought, by many, to be deserving of help, while the latter, for the most part, is not. Though the definition of a refugee has little bearing on whether or not a particular individual is allowed to enter a refugee camp, there are other important implications. First, only those people a state considers to be genuine refugees are entitled to the legal protections that refugee status confers both in international law and in most domestic law systems, such as the right to non-refoulement when claiming asylum, as well other benefits and services.[5] Only people who meet a state's definition of a refugee will have their asylum claims accepted and be considered for resettlement from a refugee camp. Second, there is an important sense in which those who are considered to be refugees are afforded more sympathy and concern than those who are considered to be "just" economic migrants or fraudulent refugees. As Shacknove has pointed out, the concept of a refugee "has little intrinsic content" and has come to mean any subset of forced migrants who are considered worthy of preferential treatment (Shacknove 1993, 518). To be a refugee is to be worthy of sympathy and compassion, and thus it's important for generating support for state or privately sponsored humanitarian aid, both in the aftermath of a crisis and in the long term.

The final reason the definition of a refugee is important is because of the negative effects on those who are denied this categorization. Denying people refugee status can be profoundly destructive to individual lives. When an individual is displaced from her home and denied asylum or refugee status, the individual may be placed in one of the many negative categories that people seeking legal protection, national or international, receive: rejected,[6] expelled, false refugee, detained, illegal. People in these administrative categories simply have no state or international agency willing to recognize them as members or to protect their human rights.[7] They are in a unique state of vulnerability. It of course makes it easier to justify ignoring long-term encampment and the deprivations of human rights in refugee camps once individuals or groups have been placed in one of these negative categories. We ought to take seriously the power that comes with categorization and the consequent harms that come with being denied refugee status (see Barnett and Finnemore 2004).

Though the moral question of who a refugee is and hence who ought to be eligible for special protection is far from settled, I argue that we ought to interpret the term as broadly as possible. For the sake of this book, I am interested in looking at all *displaced people*, the group that Benhabib defines as those *who cannot find a state to recognize it as a member* and who remain "in a state of limbo, caught between territories, none of which desire one to be its resident" (Benhabib 2004, 55). I agree with Hannah Arendt that the people we ought to be concerned with are all those who are without any form of effective citizenship or political belonging, regardless of how they are categorized legally, since they "belong to no internationally recognizable community" and are effectively outside "of mankind as a whole" (Arendt 2003, 150). Morally speaking, we must be able to include all people in this situation into our theorizing so that less privileged subsections do not get ignored. As Chris Brown notes, though philosophers of all persuasions agree that legitimate refugees should be helped, they have very little to say "about the much larger group of individuals who are not technically fleeing a well-founded fear of persecution . . . but who are equally worthy of concern" (Brown 2011, 151). Those who have been displaced for prolonged periods of time, usually in refugee camps or in crowded urban spaces, have often failed to be recognized either morally or politically.

In this sense, my use of the terms "refugee" and "forcibly displaced" are different from the way the terms are used in international law, but closer to how they are used by the UN Higher Commissioner for Refugees. According to the 1951 Convention Relating to the Status of Refugees and 1967 Protocol (known as the "Refugee Convention"), a refugee is understood as an individual who, "owing to a well-founded fear of being persecuted for reasons of race, religion, nationality, membership in a particular social group, or political opinion, is outside the country of his nationality, and is unable to or, owing to such fear, is unwilling to avail himself of the protection of that country" (Article 1a). The three key features of this definition are that the potential refugee must (i) be individually persecuted, (ii) be persecuted on the basis of one of the five reasons given in the definition—race, religion, nationality, membership in a social group, or political opinion, and (iii) be outside his home country; that is, he must have crossed an international boarder. This definition of a refugee enshrines the idea that political persecution of a certain kind has a different moral status than other forms of harm and as such, entitles an individual to greater international protection.[8] This is the definition of a refugee that is widely used to determine whether a person is eligible for resettlement in a country such as Canada, the US, and Australia.

This definition is intentionally narrow and meant to exclude many categories of forcibly displaced people. Those who are fleeing generalized violence, war, or extreme poverty are generally, though not always, excluded.[9] To be resettled in the US, not only do you have to meet the terms of the Convention definition,[10] but you must also be of "special humanitarian concern to the United States."[11] Australia and the EU also have very restrictive interpretations of who counts as a genuine refugee or asylum seeker. States are at pains to exclude "economic migrants," people who leave their home countries as a matter of choice, not necessity, from all definitions of a refugee. Much bureaucracy and financial resources go into making sure that economic migrants are not allowed to enter as fraudulent refugees. While this is understandable—after all, the global refugee regime is not intended to be a solution to global poverty—the distinction is often hard to maintain. At the extreme, those fleeing extreme poverty and insecurity often experience as much of a threat to their lives as those fleeing political persecution. Nonetheless, the distinction between economic migrant and refugee is one that all states are committed to enforcing.

The UNHCR takes a much broader view of refugees[12] and includes under its mandate, in addition to those who would be recognized according to the Convention definition, all people who are considered "persons in refugee-like situations" (UNHCR 2014b, 44).[13] People in a "refugee-like" situation are people who face the same risks as refugees but who are unable to gain refugee status "for practical or other reasons" (UNHCR 2014b,

44). The UNHCR will also consider people who are fleeing en masse as a result of war or generalized violence to be "prima facie" refugees (Jackson 1999).[14] The UNHCR also extends protection to Internally Displaced People (IDPs)—people who have been forced to leave their homes as a result of armed conflict, situations of generalized violence, violations of human rights, or natural or human-made disasters, but who *not* crossed an international border—only when they emerge from conflict situations (UNHCR 2014b, 44).[15]

A number of philosophers are sympathetic to this more expansive understanding of refugeehood (Shacknove 1985, Gibney 2004, Ferracioli 2014). Carens, for example, has argued for a wider interpretation of the term. He argues that the Refugee Convention embodies a misplaced set of priorities when it insists that a refugee must be deliberately targeted. He writes, "what is most important is the severity of the threat to basic human rights and the degree of risk rather than the source or character of the threat" (Carens 2013, 201). He endorses a more flexible and generous reading of the Refugee Convention and argues that we ought to use the term refugee in the more expansive way that the UNHCR has come to define the term, as people who are outside their own countries and unable to return "owing to serious and indiscriminate threats to life, physical integrity or freedom resulting from generalized violence or events seriously disturbing public order" (quoted in Carens 2013, 201). Though more expansive than the Convention definition, it would still exclude people who might make a claim on states on the grounds of the "ordinary inequalities of the modern world" (Carens 2013, 195).[16]

It is this more robust understanding of refugees that I use throughout this book. As stated above, I believe we ought to consider the treatment of all *displaced people*, all those who cannot find a state to recognize them as a member and spend long periods of time outside of the nation-state system. Though the restrictive Convention definition is understandable politically—the fewer refugees eligible for aid and resettlement, the easier a state's job is—it is not morally defensible since it fails to include all those who may not be technically fleeing a "well-founded fear of persecution" but are equally vulnerable and without state protection. It is only with this more expansive understanding of refugees and forced displacement that we can begin to see the many harms associated with the current refugee regime, such as prolonged displacement and encampment.

To reiterate a point made earlier, the goal of this book is neither to provide solutions to the problem of refugees nor to put forth policy prescriptions for how an individual state ought to handle the issue. I do not attempt to provide answers for how to bridge the wide gap between what we ought to do in theory and what can be done in practice. What I hope this book will achieve is a broadening of how we think about both the problem of displacement and the role that we, as members of Western states and supporters of the international community, play in the harms that the displaced

14 *Introduction*

experience. With a better understanding of the problem, both politically and philosophically, and with an alternative way of thinking about responsibility for such complex global injustices, I hope that we will be able to agree upon better ways to treat the displaced, ways that protect their fundamental human dignity and are consistent with the liberal commitments to justice, equality, and fairness.

Notes

1. There is still a fair amount of uncertainty about where the displaced go. In 2014, the exact accommodation type for 17% of the world's refugees was unknown (UNHCR 2014, 41).
2. While the UNHCR considers 65.3 million people to be forcibly displaced, the International Federation of Red Cross and Red Crescent Societies considers 72 million people to be in this situation. The ICRC's figure encompasses people who are displaced within their home countries and who have crossed borders due to conflict, repression, persecution, disasters, environmental degradation, development projects, poverty, and poor governance. Importantly, it does not include "economic migrants," people who choose to leave their countries to pursue economic opportunities, but only people who "are forced to leave their homes due to events beyond their immediate control" (International Federation of Red Cross and Red Crescent Societies 2012, 14).
3. Aleinikoff thinks it is at least possible that the displaced would prefer some kind of temporary status that would allow them to eventually return home, rather than admission to a third country like the US. But as he points out, the displaced are rarely consulted about their needs or desires, or what solutions they think are best (Aleinikoff 1992).
4. For example, even though the ICRC uses the term "forced migrants" very broadly, even they exclude economic migrants. They use the term "forced migrants" to refer to refugees, asylum seekers, trafficked persons, others who flee conflict, repression, and persecution, as well as those displaced due to disasters, environmental degradation, development projects, poverty, and poor governance, who are displaced within their home countries or who have crossed international borders, but not those who move voluntarily to seek economic opportunities (ICRC 2012).
5. In the US, for example, benefits and services for refugees include direct assistance programs (for up to eight months from arrival), as well as social service programs that help refugees find employment, become self-sufficient, and achieve social integration (for up to five years). Refugees are eligible for citizenship after a certain period of time and are then able to resettle family members still living abroad.
6. As Agier notes, the "rejected" is one of the most rapidly growing groups of displaced people. It is a term that refers to people who are held to be in a country illegally because their claims to asylum have been denied, which effectively criminalizes their displacement (Agier 2011).
7. The same individual may occupy a different classification over a period of a few years or even a few months. A Liberian *displaced person* became a *refugee* if he fled to a UNHCR camp in Guinea, then *illegal* if he left to work in a different part of the country. If he fled to France he would become a *detainee* before being registered as an *asylum applicant* (with a 90% chance of becoming a *rejected*). If he is rejected, he will be taken to the border and detained or expelled. If he is not detained or expelled, he will be considered a *non-expellable irregular*, which

Introduction 15

is also referred to as a *sans papier* in France or *tolerated* in Poland (Agier 2011, 33). All of these statuses leave the individual in a situation of political limbo and vulnerability.

8   Refugees are distinct from asylum seekers. An asylum seeker is someone who claims he or she is fleeing a well-founded fear of persecution but whose claim has not yet been definitively assessed. The country in which an asylum seeker first lands has legal obligations to determine their status, and if they are deemed legitimate, the state must grant them legal residence. By contrast, a refugee is usually granted this status by the UN in a "third-party" country that has agreed to host the refugees temporarily. Morally speaking, should it matter where a person is located when they make their claims for help? Some writers, such as Joseph Carens, argue that we have a stronger obligation to asylum seekers since they are already within our borders and are better able to receive help from us (Carens 1992). Others, such as Peter and Renata Singer, think that there is no moral difference between refugees and asylum seekers and that we ought to help them equally. Consequently, in their view, policies that favor asylum seekers over refugees ought to be deemed illegitimate (Singer and Singer 1988).

9   The Organization for African Unity has, since 1969, used a more expansive definition of refugees to avoid this exclusion. According to their definition, a refugee may include anyone who is forced to flee their home countries "owing to external aggression, occupation, foreign domination or events seriously disturbing public order" (1969 Convention Governing the Specific Aspects of Refugee Problems in Africa).

10 In the US, the legal definition of a refugee comes from the Immigration and Nationality Act (INA), 101(a)(42), which defines the term "refugee" as: "(A) any person who is outside any country of such person's nationality or, in the case of a person having no nationality, is outside any country in which such person last habitually resided, and who is unable or unwilling to return to, and is unable or unwilling to avail himself or herself of the protection of, that country because of persecution or a well-founded fear of persecution on account of race, religion, nationality, membership in a particular social group, or political opinion, or (B) in such circumstances as the President after appropriate consultation (as defined in section 207(e) of this Act) may specify, any person who is within the country of such person's nationality or, in the case of a person having no nationality, within the country in which such person is habitually residing, and who is persecuted or who has a well-founded fear of persecution on account of race, religion, nationality, membership in a particular social group, or political opinion. The term "refugee" does not include any person who ordered, incited, assisted, or otherwise participated in the persecution of any person on account of race, religion, nationality, membership in a particular social group, or political opinion. For purposes of determinations under this Act, a person who has been forced to abort a pregnancy or to undergo involuntary sterilization, or who has been persecuted for failure or refusal to undergo such a procedure or for other resistance to a coercive population control program, shall be deemed to have been persecuted on account of political opinion, and a person who has a well-founded fear that he or she will be forced to undergo such a procedure or subject to persecution for such failure, refusal, or resistance shall be deemed to have a well-founded fear of persecution on account of political opinion."

11 http://www.uscis.gov/humanitarian/refugees-asylum/refugees. The US uses the term "special humanitarian concern" to help distinguish those who "from among the millions of people termed 'refugees' will have access to the USRAP" (U.S. Refugee Admissions Program). The USRAP has a priority system to determine who fits into this category. Priority 1: Individual cases referred to the program by virtue of their circumstances and apparent need for resettlement;

Priority 2: Groups of cases designated as having access to the program by virtue of their circumstances and apparent need for resettlement; Priority 3: Individual cases granted access because they have immediate family members in the United States who were resettled as refugees or granted asylum in the United States and whose nationality is currently eligible for processing as refugees to allow family reunification (Department of State 2006).
12 While the UNHCR's mandate includes all people "of concern," including persons who are forcibly displaced (refugees, asylum seekers, IDPs, etc.), those who have found a durable solution (returnees), as well as stateless persons (those who lack formal legal status within their countries of residence, most of whom have never been forcibly displaced), this is not synonymous with the 65.3 million forcibly displaced persons. This number includes refugees and IDPs, including those beyond UNHCR's mandate (such as the 5.1 million Palestinian refugees) but excludes returnees and stateless persons.
13 It also includes individuals who are granted complementary forms of protection and those enjoying temporary protection in a country. The concept of "complementary protection" refers to those people who do not qualify for protection under refugee law but are given some kind of other protection under national, regional, or international law.
14 They do so because in many situations, such as the current Syrian civil war, it is virtually impossible to assess individual situations, and the general circumstances are well known. "UNHCR's long-held position is that people fleeing the indiscriminate effects of conflict should be generally considered as refugees if their own state is unwilling or unable to protect them" (UNHCR 2014a, 23).
15 This is important since it excludes many of the people who experience housing insecurity due to poverty. For example, people who are forcibly evicted from slums would not count under this rubric. See Weinstein (2014).
16 Similarly, Ferracioli has argued that the Refugee Convention suffers from its "under inclusiveness" because it limits international assistance to those who suffer political persecution, and this excludes large numbers of vulnerable people (Ferracioli 2014, 125). Her examples are a Somali farmer and her children who migrate because of severe drought, or an Iranian homosexual who experiences persecution because of his sexual orientation; in both cases, they would not quality for asylum. She argues that we need a more robust refugee protection regime so that it includes those who have a *moral* right but not yet a legal right to asylum.

1 The Moral Significance of the Refugee Regime

The state of forced displacement today is historically unprecedented. Not only is a sizable proportion of the human population residing outside of a formal political community, but many people who find themselves in this situation are here for close to a generation, confined to camps or other spaces of containment that, by their very definition, impose restriction on rights, freedom, and autonomy. This situation and how we ought to respond to it—that is, large-scale, protracted refugee situations and encampment—is the subject of this book. It has not, I believe, been treated with the moral seriousness that such a fundamental and systematic degradation of human dignity ought to be. The goal of this chapter is to understand how we have arrived at this situation, why it is not given the moral and intellectual scrutiny that other global injustices have received, and ultimately, how we may develop a more meaningful normative framework in the future.

There are somewhere between 65.3 and 72 million people who live effectively outside of the protection of their home states and do not belong in any meaningful sense to a political community or have effective access to rights or state protection.[1] To put it another way, a population almost the size of the United Kingdom—one in every 100 of the world's citizens—lives more or less permanently outside the nation-state system, and no state acknowledges individual political or moral responsibility for this group. Of those the UNHCR considers to be people they are responsible for,[2] 40% live in refugee camps, where "host governments and humanitarian actors provide assistance and services in a centralized manner. The defining characteristic of a camp, however, is typically some degree of limitation on the rights and freedoms of refugees and their ability to make meaningful choices about their lives" (UNHCR 2014b, 4).[3] Further, once displaced, the average length of time that people remain in this situation is 17 years (UNHCR 2006), and two thirds of refugees live in protracted situations (US Department of State 2015).[4] Less than 1% of official refugees are likely to ever be resettled permanently in a third country, and thus the number of de facto refugees (people who are in a refugee-like situation but who fail to meet the criteria for a refugee as found in the Refugee Convention) who will be resettled is even more insignificant (UNHCR 2015).[5]

This chapter will proceed as follows. I start with a detailed examination of the refugee protection regime and the different normative obligations that states have to refugees. I then discuss the way that thinking about solutions to the problem of refugees has evolved, from resettlement to repatriation to containment. I suggest that there is a moral ideal that underlies our reliance on containment: the belief that repatriation (that refugees should be sent back to their home countries) is the best solution goes hand in hand with a belief that refugees and asylum seekers ought to be contained and controlled until this becomes possible; containment is tacitly justified as an unfortunate but necessary step to achieve this higher good. I then give a detailed explanation of how encampment—the containment and confinement of the displaced, often for prolonged periods and in ways that undermine their dignity and human rights—functions as the de facto "fourth" durable solution and explain in detail why this solution is so problematic, paying particular attention to the ways that basic human rights are violated in camps. Though it seems removed from Western foreign policy, I shed light on some ways that Western states support encampment both directly and indirectly.

My analysis shows two important facts which, I argue, ought to play a larger role in our thinking about the ethics of refugees than they currently do. First, encampment or containment has become the de facto fourth solution for involuntary migrants, one that many are reluctant to acknowledge. Second, this solution, far from in fact being a real solution for the displaced, constitutes a unique harm, one that can and ought to be avoided. As a result, encampment ought to be understood as one of the most serious global problems today. Though part of our moral failure is that we do not resettle enough refugees, another significant problem is that we support a refugee regime that systematically undermines the rights of the displaced for the sake of protecting our sovereignty, and specifically the right to control immigration and citizenship.

Understanding the harms around forced displacement in this way, as well as seeing the connection to Western states, forces us to reconsider what we owe to the forcibly displaced. I argue that my analysis gives rise to two fundamental obligations. First, given the analysis I develop, we have an obligation to reject long-term encampment as a "solution" for displacement, or to reform it so that it is in line with moral principles and protects the rights and dignity of the displaced. We must morally challenge the practices of containment and control currently exercised over millions of displaced people that are neither inevitable nor politically or economically necessary. Second, I argue that we have an obligation to work towards a just refugee regime, one that takes seriously the full human rights of the displaced (not merely their survival needs) as well as the interests of states. Philosophers, I suggest, are in a position to provide some moral clarity about how the international system in general and the refugee regime in particular ought to function, and can help to analyze the ethical norms that ought to govern the treatment of involuntary migrants who are displaced for prolonged periods.

While I outline these obligations here, Chapters Two, Three, and Four of this book develop and strengthen the ground for these obligations. This chapter concludes on a hopeful note through observing that international norms are at least beginning to change in a direction away from encampment.

Let me address a potential objection at the outset. As of 2015, the majority of forcibly displaced people no longer live in refugee camps, but either in urban areas or in rural areas without the assistance of the UNHCR (UNHCR 2014c). Given this, why focus on the morality of supporting refugee camps and policies of encampment? There are several reasons why it is still important to focus our moral analysis on refugee camps. First, until very recently, refugee camps have been the "assumed foundation of refugee policy," in the sense that this was the first mechanism the UNHCR and other aid organizations used in their attempts to help refugees (Kagan 2013). As late as 1997, the UNHCR considered refugee camps "normal and good, and refugees should be discouraged from trying to leave them" (Kagan 2013). A change in rhetoric came only in 2009 with their Policy on Refugee Protection and Solutions in Urban Areas, in which the focus has started to turn to refugee autonomy, rights, and the ability of refugees to support and sustain themselves with dignity.[6] Though there has been a change in rhetoric around the permissibility of refugee camps, they still remain the standard way that the international community approaches displacement, and are still widely believed to be necessary for security. We need only think of the many camps that have sprung up in Europe since the summer of 2015 to handle the influx of Syrian refugees to see that camps are still the primary way of dealing with refugees.

Further, when the UNHCR and other humanitarian agencies are able to help the displaced, it is primarily through camps. Often agencies cannot locate or count those in need of help when they are absorbed in urban areas. The displaced have to make a decision between receiving aid or maintaining their freedom by not registering with the UNHCR. Finally, while 40% is no longer the majority, 40% of 65.3 million is still a sizable proportion of the human population who is subject to conditions that are morally questionable and thus still a worthwhile focus of philosophical attention. Since the use of camps has only increased in Europe recently, it is fair to say that refugee camps will continue to play a role in the treatment of the displaced in the foreseeable future.

§ What Is the Refugee Regime?

Protecting refugees and other involuntary migrants is a complex task, involving a number of actors and institutions that follow various norms and rules, both formal and implicit. Specifically, the "refugee regime" refers to "the set of norms, rules, principles and decision-making procedures that regulate states' responses to refugees" (Betts 2011, 56). It is comprised of "a network of states, international organizations, and non-governmental organizations" that "govern those who are forced to flee their homes because of fear for their lives" (Barnett 2011, 106). The primary document that lays out the structure of the refugee regime is the United Nations Convention and Protocol Relating to the Status of Refugees (alternatively called the Refugee Convention).[7] The body that oversees the Refugee Convention, the United Nations High Commissioner for Refugees (UNHCR), was created at roughly the same time. It is the principle humanitarian agency responsible for implementing the Refugee Convention[8] and perhaps the most important actor in the refugee regime.

Though the UNHCR was created to oversee the 1951 Convention, its original mandate was much more limited than the one that has evolved over time as the UNHCR's moral authority grew. In 1951 the UNHCR was given a very limited mandate, "a reflection of the states' desire to limit their responsibility" (Barnett 2011, 119).[9] At first it was only permitted to aid those who became refugees before 1951, and the kind of aid it could give was very limited: it could issue travel documents, help refugees to obtain a legal status, and advocate for more precise guidelines, but it did not have the authority to provide material assistance. It had only a small budget from the UN's general operating budget, and was prohibited from raising or spending money without the approval of the UN's General Assembly (Barnett 2011, 119). This reflects the almost paradoxical nature of the UNHCR and the refugee regime in which it plays a large role. When the UNHCR was created in 1951, its mission was to protect refugees and ensure their human rights in the absence of a state; it was created from a largely humanitarian impulse. Yet it was created in such a way as to not be threatening at all to the sovereignty of states or their ability to control membership.[10] Over time, the UNHCR was able to overcome some of these limitations in part because it developed a kind of moral authority regarding refugee issues, and in part, because in the wake of post-Cold War refugee crises, the agency was expected, and needed, to play an increasingly bigger role in world affairs.

The purpose of the UNHCR, of course, is not just to protect refugees but also to find a "solution" to their situation and loss of membership in a state. The three "durable" solutions that the UNHCR aimed at were repatriation to the home country, integration in the country of asylum, and resettlement in a third country. One often neglected detail about the history of the 1951 Convention is that the drafters imagined that refugees would be integrated into the countries of asylum while they waited for a permanent solution, rather than being warehoused in camps; they thought that only exceptional "hard core" cases would require that the international community maintain them in the long term. The UN secretary general in 1950 wrote, "The refugee will lead an independent life in the countries which have given them shelter. . . . They will be integrated in the economic system of the countries of asylum and will themselves provide for their own needs and those of their families" (Smith 2004, 42).

The UNHCR has grown to become a giant institution and works with over 740 other international and national NGOs along with other UN agencies like the World Food Programme, UNICEF, and the World Health Organization, among others (UNHCR 2014a, 27). Despite its scale, it still remains dependent on the member states of the UN. The UNHCR is dependent on states both for their funding and for their cooperation in securing resources, providing security, and hosting and resettling refugees. In the view of some scholars, this structural feature limits the potential of the UNHCR to help the displaced and advocate for political solutions. That the UNHCR should require the permission of host states to carry out its operations is perhaps not surprising given the importance placed on sovereignty at the global level. But the lack of mandatory assessed contributions from states that makes the UNHCR wholly dependent on donor states for its survival is unusual, especially given that this is unique to the UNHCR of all UN organizations. The UNHCR's entire budget comes from a handful of countries, with the US, Japan, and the EU accounting for 94% of all state contributions (Loescher 2012, 6). The worry is that because it is dependent on so few states, its ability to operate independently is compromised, especially when it might go against the perceived interests of these states. The UNHCR, writes Loescher, "is in no position to challenge the policies of its funders and host governments" (Loescher 2012, 6). This is a clear limitation for an institution whose job it is to find political solutions to the global crisis of refugees.[11]

The refugee regime more broadly can be understood as containing two sets of normative obligations for states: one set of obligations has to do with what states are required to do when asylum seekers arrive on their territory, while the other set of obligations has to do with state obligations towards those seeking refuge in countries other than their own. One of the distinctive features of the refugee regime is the asymmetry of these two sets of obligations: the former set is much stronger and more widely recognized than the latter. Indeed, many claim that there is a relative absence of legal obligations by states to protect refugees who are not on their territory.

Most scholars agree that the strongest norm in the whole refugee regime is non-refoulement, which is part of the 1951 Convention. This norm holds that a state cannot send back a person who has a well-founded fear of persecution. What this has meant in practice is that people who arrive in a country and claim asylum must be given a hearing before they can be deported. Over time, a strong normative and legal framework has developed to support this norm, and most states, at least in principle, acknowledge its legitimacy. As a result, non-refoulement has become a well-accepted principle of international law and is the cornerstone of the refugee regime because of its wide acceptance. This remains true even though many states have looked for loopholes to avoid their obligations to asylum seekers—for example, by intercepting asylum seekers before they reach the shore or insisting that airlines check visas so that potential asylum seekers cannot land in their country. If anything, practices like these show how seriously states take their obligations around non-refoulement, since they would rather go to great lengths to avoid having asylum seekers arrive on their territory than be seen violating the principle of non-refoulement by deporting them upon their arrival.

On the other hand, obligations towards refugees and other involuntary migrants not already on their territory are more or less discretionary and not based on any clear moral or legal obligation.[12] In other words, there is no legal obligation in the 1951 Convention or elsewhere which requires states to resettle refugees or contribute to their protection. This has had two outcomes. First, because there is no obligation on the part of signatories to the 1951 Convention to fund the protection of refugees, contributions to the UNHCR or other refugee aid agencies are strictly voluntary. As a result, the refugee regime is chronically underfunded. The UNHCR is funded almost exclusively by a handful of countries, and even though their budget is large, it is still inadequate to the job that the UNHCR is supposed to do. In 2013, the UNHCR presented a needs-based budget of $5.3 billion dollars (US) and received $2.9 billion (US). In other words, it was only able to raise about 60% of what it estimated was needed (UNHCR 2014a, 26–27). As noted above, almost all of the UNHCR'S budget is from 10 donor countries in the North, with only 3% coming from the UN's central budget; the US funds 30% of their budget (Hammerstad 2011, 252n1). This funding structure has meant that the UNHCR has to be particularly sensitive to the needs and views of the large donor states in the West, and this has had an effect on their policies and practices.[13]

The second outcome of the absence of moral and legal obligations regarding involuntary migrants is the discrepancy in "burden sharing." This refers to the fact that countries in the Global South play a much larger role in hosting refugees than the Western democracies in the North that fund the regime; 87% of refugees are hosted in the Global South and less than 1% of the displaced are resettled in Western states.[14] This is in part because Western states have actively sought to contain refugee flows outside their own regions to avoid taking on this burden. "For the most part," writes Helton, "the relatively capable states in Europe and North America seek to contain human displacement elsewhere, particularly in Africa" (Helton 2012, 31). I return to this outcome in more detail below.

The lack of strong norms or legal obligations around the protection and support of involuntary migrants not claiming asylum results in an unequal system of burden sharing, where the poorest states host the vast majority of refugees while Western states fund the majority of aid to refugees. Some in the West believe that because Western states primarily fund the refugee regime, they bear the biggest burden for refugee protection. Yet for many in the Global South, this is not the case. As the Indian Permanent Representative to the UN argued, "it has to be recognized that refugees and mass movements are first and foremost a 'developing country' problem and the biggest 'donors' are in reality developing countries who put at risk their fragile environment, economy and society to provide refuge to millions. An international system which does not address these concerns adequately cannot be sustained in the long run" (quoted in Gorlick 2012, 81). The day to day burden of large scale mass migration is born by developing states, and this is due in part to geographical contingency but also to explicit policies by Western states in partnership with the UNHCR that discourage or make difficult the movement of migrants to Western countries (policies such as administrative detention, imposition of carrier sanctions, visa restrictions, inspection of travelers in foreign airports, use of "safe zones," as well as other policies aimed at "externalizing" borders). While Western states consider large-scale refugee flows as a security threat and an unacceptable economic burden, it is generally considered not only acceptable but required that developing countries take in large numbers of involuntary migrants, despite their limited resources.

This asymmetry of power is one of the key structural features of the refugee regime: the vast majority of the world's refugees and involuntary migrants are in developing countries in the Global South, but because there are few legal obligations for Northern states to help refugees not on their territory, aid to refugees is discretionary and largely based on how they perceive refugees to be connected to their own interests (Betts 2011). As Betts notes, there are two main reasons why states comply with international law—reciprocity and legitimacy—but neither of these two reasons are sufficient to motivate Western states to support the protection and resettlement of refugees (Betts 2011).[15]

In Betts's view, it is these features of the refugee regime that have led to the current situation of protracted displacement and long-term confinement without access to rights: Northern states have few obligations or incentives to help refugees not on their territory, but because of the strength of the principle of non-refoulement, they have strong incentives to prevent refugees from arriving on their territory; countries in the Global South lack power in the international sphere and consequently have little clout in bargaining and so must take whatever Western states or international organizations offer them.[16]

§ History of Solutions: Resettlement, Repatriation, and Containment

If the displaced turn out to be unwanted in all sovereign states—countries in the Global North do not want them to resettle in their countries and countries in the Global South which host refugees do not want them to integrate permanently—it is perhaps not surprising that we have arrived at a de facto policy of containment. This refers to the practice of keeping refugees and other displaced people in camps or other forms of temporary housing for prolonged periods of time. Refugee camps, while often the best and only way to provide aid to large numbers of displaced people in critical, emergency situations, have ended up becoming a *de facto* long-term solution, since millions of people who become displaced will end up spending their lives, sometimes generations, in these spaces. In the section below, I will outline how the international community has moved from an attempt to protect the displaced and from institutions that would substitute for their states in terms of protection of human rights, to a more or less de facto policy of containment, where the goal is to prevent the displaced from disrupting life in the developed world.

The paradoxical nature of state sovereignty is important in understanding how legitimate states can exclude refugees and consequently, how refugees can end up excluded from all political communities. On the one hand, sovereignty over admissions and membership is seen by some as the very core of sovereignty and essential for the right of self-determination of the state.[17] From this perspective, states have the right to exclude refugees; the right of states to determine membership trumps the rights of refugees, even when this means that there is no state that is willing to protect their human rights.[18] Yet on the other hand, state sovereignty has been justified, since Locke, because it is seen as the best way for states to discharge the duty to protect individual human rights. This is the normative basis of the state system: states can legitimately exercise sovereignty over their citizens because the protection of human rights that results from this ultimately makes citizens better off (Betts and Loescher 2011, 6). Refugees and other involuntary migrants problematize this because they are individuals who are not under the protection of a state, and this "calls into question the legitimacy of a system that, in practice, relegates people to the largely unfettered exercise of sovereignty of a state over its citizens" (Aleinikoff 1992, 121).[19]

This helps to explain how we have arrived at the de facto policy of containment. Because states exercise a sovereign right to control their borders, a right that for many is grounded in the state's obligation to protect the human rights of its citizens, they can prevent people from entering in order to claim asylum or can fail to acknowledge them as legitimate asylum seekers once on their territory. The strong international norm of non-refoulement means that states cannot just send individuals back to their home countries when they have a genuine fear of persecution. Yet refugees have no state that is willing to exercise its sovereignty to protect their human rights and provide political belonging. As a result, we "find literally millions of refugees around the world languishing in 'temporary' arrangement, not forced to return to their countries of origin but denied permanent resettlement in countries of asylum" (Aleinikoff 1992, 124). How have we arrived at this situation and how should the international community respond? Below, I outline the history of "solutions" to the refugee crisis in the 20th and 21st centuries before moving onto the question of how we ought to respond.

There is general agreement that following the Second World War until the end of the Cold War, the preferred solution for refugees was resettlement.[20] Aleinikoff notes at least three reasons for this: refugees from the war could not be asked to return to their war-ravaged countries; because of the nature of the Cold War, each side could claim a victory when they welcomed refugees from opposing countries; and Western states believed that refugees would be better off if they resettled in the West (Aleinikoff refers to this as "Eurocentric humanitarianism"). Once the Cold War ended, these reasons for favoring resettlement lost their force. The end of the Cold War also brought about a change in migration patterns. Refugee flows were now predominantly from Africa and Asia, rather than Europe, and were connected more to poverty and war than political persecution. The result was that people in Asia and Africa fleeing war or severe poverty were not readily seen as genuine refugees and, because of their large number, seemed to pose a particular threat to Western states. Consequently, the preference for resettling refugees in the Global North shifted towards voluntary repatriation.

In addition to these political circumstances, moral and practical objections to resettlement were raised, and this contributed to the move away from resettlement as the preferred way to secure a permanent solution for refugees. The pragmatic argument held that resettlement relieved sending states of responsibility for the refugees they created and this might create a disincentive for states to address their human rights and security challenges. The moral challenge to resettlement held that because membership in one's own state is a fundamental good, people ought to have the ability to return to the place where they are from. This idea is rooted in a kind of communitarianism that takes seriously community and belonging as fundamental to the individual. On this view, resettlement cannot be the ultimate solution for refugees since it requires that we ignore the fundamental relationship between an individual and her original community.[21]

The rejection of resettlement as the preferred option after the end of the Cold War led to a preference for voluntary repatriation as the preferred durable solution.[22] The preference for repatriation was due, in Aleinikoff's view, to the following reasons: the sheer increase in number of asylum seekers; the ethnic, religious, and cultural differences between asylum seekers and inhabitants of Western states; the fact that accepting refugees was no longer a way of demonstrating ideological victory as it was during the Cold War (Aleinikoff 1992, 130). Morally speaking, repatriation can be understood as a way of returning an individual to her state, and thus restoring the relationship between the individual and the state.[23] In this way, repatriation is a way of removing the challenge to the sovereignty of the host state that refugees pose, as well as to the international system as such.

Yet the preference for voluntary repatriation should not be understood as strictly altruistic. The preference for repatriation is grounded not only in the belief that refugees are better off returning to their home countries, but also in the view that large scale migration posed a threat to Western states. Western states could justify tighter controls of their borders and policies that prevented asylum seekers from reaching their shores with the belief that this was ultimately for the good of the migrants themselves, since keeping them closer to their home countries would allow them to be returned home sooner. In other words, the belief that the best solution to the refugee problem is that they be repatriated to their home countries went hand in hand with a belief that refugees and asylum seekers ought to be contained and controlled until this became possible. This can be understood as the implicit moral basis for our current policies of containment.

This is why the shift to a preference for repatriation went along with various practices of containment, control, and deterrence that made it more difficult for refugees and other involuntary migrants to reach the West. Aleinikoff refers to these as "source-control measures," techniques states have used to keep refugees in or close to countries of origin (Aleinikoff 1992, 130). Other source-control measures are implemented with policies such as "reception in the region of origin," "the right to remain," or "preventive protection"; Roxström and Gibney argue that even "temporary protection" can be understood as one of many concepts that provide "a battery of excuses for keeping refugees away from their territories" (Roxström and Gibney 2012, 38). All these practices, however, are justified by states as ways to provide better and more efficient humanitarian assistance and on the ground that they permit the greatest likelihood of repatriation. In practice, however, they ultimately serve to justify the containment of refugees in spaces far from Western borders and thus protect the sovereignty of Western states. Franke agrees with this assessment arguing, "states funding the UNHCR have managed to cultivate a shift in the organization's ethic from one of facilitating resettlement to one largely concerned with containing refugee flows close to the regions of displacement . . . providing mere humanitarian assistance, as opposed to rights protection" (Franke 2009, 317).[24]

Hammerstad (2011) has argued that the UNHCR has contributed to this problem by tacitly agreeing to the fears that states have about refugees as security threats. The UNHCR, in an attempt to remain relevant to Western states, has treated refugees as a matter of "securitization," which "denotes the process wherein an issue is presented as an existential threat, requiring emergency measure and justifying actions outside the normal bounds of political procedure" (Buzan 1998, 23–24, quoted in Hammerstad 2011, 238).[25] The UNHCR tacitly agreed to the view that refugees are security threats by helping Western states to ensure that refugees never reach Europe through in-country protection and other preventative activities.[26] By employing the language of security, the UNHCR risked legitimizing Western states' discourse on security to limit refugee rights and asylum protection. This also helped to confirm the repatriation thesis—that as a matter of security, repatriation was the best option.

What is clear is the way that the humanitarian discourse around repatriation masks what is in fact an assertion of state sovereignty. In the view of Aleinikoff, this policy change ought to be understood not as a mere change in views about the best way to help refugees; it is a change from a way of helping refugees, resettlement, to a way of protecting state sovereignty through a discourse which justifies policies of containment and deterrence, such as the detention of asylum seekers, visa requirements, closing opportunities for resettlement, etc. "These policies are grounded less in a desire to breach the walls of state sovereignty than an attempt to keep Third World refugee problems from inconveniencing the developed states" (Aleinikoff 1992, 133).

This assertion of state sovereignty might have been morally neutral if not for the fact that the repatriation-encampment nexus is very often not in the best interests of the displaced and often leads to further human rights violations (Aleinikoff 1992). Barnett raises the worry that voluntary repatriation undermines refugee rights in two ways. First, if refugees are asked to return to "less than ideal" conditions, they may be put in danger. Though there have been decade-long debates about how to balance refugee rights with the goal of repatriation, by the 1990s the UNHCR began to consider repatriation for post-conflict situations that were far from ideal. The idea of "safe return" indicated that conditions in home countries did not have to improve substantially, but only enough to allow refugees to return home safely, and "the UNHCR would make the assessment as to whether conditions were safe enough for refugees to return" (Loescher 2012, 10). In other words, the safety of refugees did not necessarily outweigh the interests of states or the larger goal of conflict resolution. Success was measured by the UNHCR and states in terms of repatriation, even when repatriation did not serve the interests of refugees. Loescher cites refugees returning from Bangladesh to Burma, and from Tanzania and Zaire to Rwanda, as examples of refugees being returned to countries that were not sufficiently safe because of pressure from host states (Loescher 2012, 10).

In this process, refugees were rarely, if ever consulted or explicitly asked to give consent. In this way, they were denied agency. For Barnett, this lack of consent is the second way that repatriation violates the rights of refugees, since it is now a decision the UNHCR makes for refugees without their input (Barnett 2011). Refugees' voices no longer count, as the UNHCR claims to know what is in their best interests. This, in Barnett's view, is a violation of the autonomy, and thus dignity, of refugees.

As repatriation came to be seen as the only serious option, other possible solutions were ignored. The UNHCR no longer considered other options such as local integration, educational programs, income-generating projects, and other ways to promote refugee participation in the community. The "UNHCR essentially ran long-term programs in an emergency mode" (Loescher 2012, 10). Further, the dogma around repatriation made it much less likely that the UNHCR or states could promote local integration. Countries of asylum worried that allowing refugees to integrate would make it harder for them to be repatriated in the future. Roxström and Gibney refer to this as the "integration dilemma": even though the 1951 Convention makes clear that refugee status is always provisional (it ceases to apply once the political situation that gave rise to this status changes), states resist the provisions that facilitate integration because of the fear that it will deter repatriation (Roxström and Gibney 2012).

Even with this strong preference for repatriation, this durable solution has not been able to be used on a scale that would improve the lives of the millions of involuntary migrants. To put it in perspective, in 2013, Afghanistan was the third most successful country to voluntarily repatriate its citizens, with 39,700 people repatriated that year. Yet even with this success, there are still over 2 million Afghan citizens living in Pakistan (at the end of 2013, Afghanistan was the top country of origin for refugees, with 2,556,600 refugees and people in a refugee-like situation) (UNHCR 2014a, 13). So even in a "successful" country like Afghanistan, voluntary repatriation does not even come close to providing a genuine solution.[27] Since the other two durable solutions—local integration and resettlement—have benefited even fewer people,[28] we must ask what happens to those who remain? The answer of course is that the vast majority of forced migrants are either contained in refugee camps or dispersed into urban areas in the Global South. Containment has thus become the de facto fourth durable solution for the majority of the globally displaced, and this fact is either overlooked or justified because of the importance placed on repatriation.

§ What Is Containment and Why Is It Problematic?

The containment of refugees, the de facto "fourth" durable solution, is problematic in a number of ways: refugee camps are ineffective ways to provide aid to refugees, they are economically inefficient,[29] they are largely terrible places to live, and they often make it impossible to uphold the human rights of refugees. Though they are justified for several reasons, as I argue below, these reasons are not sufficient to override the harm they do to refugees in the long term.

First, host states often insist that camps that control the movement of refugees are the best way to preserve public order and ensure the safety of refugees. Host states are concerned with the potential tension between refugees and local populations, and one way of ensuring peace, in their view, is to limit competition for scarce economic resources, such as opportunities for employment, by restricting refugees to camps. Further, preventing refugees from settling in communities and participating in the local economy makes it less likely that refugees will want to stay once the opportunity to leave becomes available (UNHCR 2014c, 4).

Second, camps serve an important bureaucratic function. International agencies like the UNHCR are often willing to go along with this because camps are seen as the most efficient way to count refugees and distribute aid. "The process of attracting donor money relies upon the visibility of the refugees, and the possibility of counting them; both are easier when they are held in confined space" (Stevens 2006, 66). The UNHCR sees camps as an essential part of its operational response to emergency situations because they can provide protection and assistance in camps better than when people are dispersed. Yet they acknowledge that because camps require limiting the rights and freedoms of refugees, they remain a compromise (UNHCR 2014c, 4).[30] Verdirame and Harrell-Bond, both critical of the UNHCR, note that long-term encampment often results from institutional inertia and lack of knowledge or experience with other ways of assisting refugees.[31]

Though these reasons may be justifiable in some circumstances in the short term, they do not hold over the long term. Refugee camps often become long-term temporary living spaces run in an emergency mode, and this is not justifiable based on the reasons given above. Refugee camps become a way to keep "people alive in secure containment facilities as if refugees are, at least temporarily, surplus humanity" (Franke 2009, 318). Below, I outline some of the harms of encampment that further undermine the use of camps as a justifiable long-term solution to the problem of forced displacement and then explain the role Western states play in supporting long-term encampment.

§ Paradox of Precariousness and a Permanent Present[32]

What precisely is a refugee camp and why is the confinement of displaced populations to them for prolonged periods of time problematic? Refugee camps are heterogeneous. There are self-organized refugee camps (informal camps, ghettos), where refugees live before they can be recognized by the UNHCR or where those who do not want to register with the UNHCR live indefinitely; sorting and holding centers that often house people for months and occasionally years (Woomera in Australia, and Sangatte in France being two of the best known);[33] and the most iconic spaces, the traditional refugee camps in host countries as well as camps within states the displaced are fleeing (camps for IDPs, internal asylum camps[34]) (Agier 2011). What all these spaces have in common is that they are distinct from traditional political communities, such as territorially bound nation-states, in the following ways.

If there is one feature that can sum up this kind of community, it's that they are *precarious* regardless of how they are organized or how efficient they are. Camps are intended to be temporary and spring up as a response to a particular crisis or emergency, with the goal of housing people only temporarily. This is why, for example, camps are often built from precarious materials that can be put up and taken down with a moment's notice. The precariousness of the refugee camp is thus grounded on its exceptionality, that it is meant to be there just as long as the emergency requires. Yet, as I've previously discussed, camps often endure for years, decades, and sometimes generations. This is why Agier claims that refugee camps have a "permanent precariousness" (Agier 2011, 13).

Refugee camps have no *present*, in Agier's view. Dwellers are torn between a past symbolized by the land that was lost and a future return on the horizon. The present is only the emergency, a time that is not infused with meaning or significance. For Agier, collective memory cannot be formed in camps because people are just waiting to leave; there is no history to be written or ruin that is kept and treasured. The present is without meaning since the camps themselves are not places where people put down roots. Life in refugee camps, as Agier describes it, is a permanent meaningless present, a "brutal entry into a state of liminal floating" (Agier 2008, 30). Yet refugees do resist this: while camps themselves are precarious, individuals are nonetheless able to build lives through available resources and transform the space into one that can be lived in. The temporality and exceptionality of refugee camps does not stop individuals from attempting to build something permanent or deal with the ordinary daily struggles of life. However, if Agier is right, then life in refugee camps can never have the meaning and texture of life in a political state.

Another feature of refugee camps is their *invisibility* from the point of view of both the state that houses it as well as the international community. Camps are often located far from populated settlements and hard to reach. While UN officials and journalists can visit them, they are usually out of the way, and access to them is supervised so that their day-to-day functioning is not visible (Agier 2011). Camps that have been in existence for long periods of time may not even appear on maps (Bauman 2007, 38).

Refugee camps must be understood as distinct forms of space: they are simultaneously within a state and outside of it. Physically of course camps are within a given state whose territory they inhabit. Yet the spaces often have an exceptional legal status making them outside of national space. For example, in France, the state declared that the first floor of the Ibis hotel at Roissy airport would be a "waiting zone," where refugees could be processed before entering French soil. This space was considered a "non-national border zone" where French national law does not apply, even though the ground floor and second floor were still considered to be part of French territory and thus under French national law (Agier 2011, 50). A refugee was considered "a foreigner who is not yet on the national territory" (Agier 2011, 50). Consequently, how refugees were treated in this waiting zone did not need to comply with French national law. They were able to process refugees in this space of exception that is nonetheless on French territory. Refugees are thus physically inside a country but legally and politically outside of it at the same moment.

The same is true of refugee camps. A camp does not belong to the state in which it is located. The UN works with, and is often at the mercy of, the host state, but camps are not subject to the same laws and norms as non-camp locations in the territorial state in which the refugee camp is located. This leads Agier to conclude that camps in all their forms (holding centers, IDP camps, etc.) ought to be understood as *heterotopias*—places outside of all places, even though they can be located. These heterotopias function to exclude masses of people from domestic and international law. This means that the displaced are doubly excluded—first from their original homes, and second, from the domain of regular life where local populations live. This remains true even though over time camps can start to resemble towns or ghettos, and the "distinction between town dwellers and refugees hangs only by a thread" (Agier 2011, 189). These spaces transform over time and complex social life develops, but exclusion—legal and political—still remains a feature of this life.

§ Problems with Refugee Camps—Human Rights

Refugee camps do not actually serve the purposes they are intended to serve. It is often assumed that refugee camps are the most economical way to spend humanitarian aid; this is often not the case. As Smith argues, assisting refugees apart from local populations in separate camps "are the most expensive ways of responding to their needs with the cost per refugee typically well over the per capita GNP of the host nation" (Smith 2004, 40). Nor are they less expensive to maintain than other forms of aid, such as development investment or integration (Verdirame and Harrell Bond 2005).[35] By contrast, Alexander Betts's and his co-authors' study confirmed that when refugees are allowed to integrate economically, they contribute positively to the host state (Betts et al. 2014).

Even if refugee camps were the most economically efficient way of handling large-scale refugee populations, their inability to protect human rights alone would give us reason to question them. They violate human rights in two ways. First, refugee camps rarely uphold the rights that refugees living in them are legally entitled to based on the 1951 Refugee Convention. Second, because refugees in camps are so vulnerable, basic human rights are routinely violated, both by other refugees and by state and NGO organizations, and refugees lack the ability to claim their rights or have violations redressed. Sexual assault provides a paradigmatic case of this point.

What kind of protection is owed refugees living in camps? The most basic standard proposed by the 1951 Convention is that host states have a duty to protect refugees residing on their territory and provide them with the *same treatment* given to other categories of aliens. That states are obliged to protect refugees living on their territory is such a well-established principle that even states that have not signed the 1951 Convention remain obliged by this principle. To emphasize, this principle holds for *all* non-nationals, regardless of how they are categorized as refugees, illegal aliens, migrants, etc. (Helton 2012, 23). In terms of treatment, though there is not a specific body of international law regarding camps, states are expected to live up to the principles found in other UN agreements, such as the Universal Declaration of Human Rights, which, though not specifically discussing non-nationals, is assumed to include them as well.[36] On top of that, states are expected to live up to the principles found in customary international law, such as the prohibition on arbitrary prolonged detention and deprivations on freedom of movement.

The 1951 Convention contains a list of human rights that refugees are supposed to have while they are outside of their states, including access to education, access to national courts, and the right to seek employment. While the states that drafted the Convention rejected the idea that they have a right to membership or asylum, they instead "opted to enumerate rights that refugees can expect in order to maintain some level of dignity and sustenance consistent with human rights conventions" (Barnett and Finnemore 2004, 85). Among the specific rights listed in the 1951 Convention there are two that are particularly important and widely violated. The first is article 26, which grants refugees "lawfully in the territory" the same freedom of movement as other aliens. Refugees have "the right to choose their place of residence and move freely within [the state's] territory." Encampment as such is a violation of this basic right, but a violation that is so commonplace that it is unremarkable. Second, the 1951 Convention requires states to grant refugees the same access to employment as other nationals (article 17). It stipulates that if restrictions are placed on refugees they need to be removed after three years, so that long-term residents of camps, at the very least, are assured the right to seek employment for wages. Again, this right is routinely violated. As Roxström and Gibney note, there is such a strong assumption that whatever rights refugees may have, the right of states to restrict refugees either admission or their right to integrate once on the territory, must supersede this. "Norms that would be rejected out of hand in other contexts on the basis of human rights suddenly seem 'reasonable' and 'realistic' in the immigration asylum realm" (Roxström and Gibney 2012, 45).

Verdirame and Harrell-Bond argue that human rights cannot as a matter of fact be implemented in refugee camps, and warehousing refugees in camps cannot be reconciled with respecting human rights.[37] They claim that this fact is well known, but continually ignored. This is not because of a few bad actors or simply lack of funding. Rather, the very structure of the camps increases the potential for abuse rather than enhances the ability of humanitarian organizations to protect refugee rights. They write, "refugee rights cannot be protected in camps and settlements" (Verdirame and Harrell-Bond 2005, 15). This is in part because in camps the law of the host country virtually ceases to apply: camps are spaces *beyond the rule of law* in which "the life of refugees was governed by an oppressive blend of customary practices and rules established by humanitarian organizations and refugees" (Verdirame and Harrell-Bond 2005, 15). Though dramatic, Verdirame and Harrell-Bond intend to suggest that refugee camps are spaces where law simply does not apply, even though in principle camps fall under the legal jurisdiction of those responsible for administering the law.

In their extensive study of refugee camps in Uganda and Kenya, Verdirame and Harrell-Bond found evidence of the full catalogue of human rights violations, and they demonstrate in detail the way that the UNHCR failed to protect the human rights of refugees in camps. They found that refugees had no voice or political agency in the decisions that were made on their behalf, were negatively stereotyped and kept at a distance, and any complaints that they had about their treatment could be easily ignored. Local police and judiciaries did not have any legal training that would allow them to take the rights of refugees seriously. The UNHCR was unable to protect refugees from human rights violations by host states, such as arbitrary arrest and detention, unfair criminal and civil proceedings, and denying the right to work. But they themselves were also complicit in violating human rights. For Verdirame and Harrell-Bond, the most basic right that was violated by a policy of encampment was the right to freedom of movement, on which, they argue, other rights are based. They stress that this is not the case for only the worst camps, but also for camps that were considered to be "models" of refugee assistance and protection (Verdirame and Harrell-Bond 2005, 333).[38] Against all sources of abuse, by the UNHCR as well as by local police or other refugees, there was very little remedy.

Verdirame and Harrell-Bond argue that one of the main problems with camps is that they constitute a unique setting for the arbitrary exercise of power. The UNHCR is supposed to oversee the treatment of the displaced by host states in developing countries, in particular, to make sure their rights are protected as much as possible. In recent years, however, because of the sheer growth of the displaced, host countries have effectively handed over control of displaced populations to the UNHCR. The UNHCR now has almost total control over status determination procedures to decide who is eligible for resettlement abroad, who qualifies for assistance, who receives crucial supplies, etc.[39] The UNHCR and other humanitarian organizations working in these camps[40] have almost complete control over the displaced. The UNHCR exercises sovereign power over the displaced who are under its care.[41]

This demonstrates what Verdirame and Harrell-Bond call the "Janus face" of humanitarianism. Humanitarianism is in part cosmopolitan and caring, and in part, "often callous, sometimes cruel, and—nearly always—ineffectual" (Verdirame and Harrell-Bond 2005, 333). What this brings to light is that "power exercised under a humanitarian guise was not so different from power in other guises" (Verdirame and Harrell-Bond 2005, 333). What is unique in this relationship is that the power of humanitarian governments is not curtailed by law nor limited by external oversight. "The very organization set up to monitor the extent to which refugees enjoyed their human rights had assumed de facto sovereignty over them. Who could monitor the monitor?" (Verdirame and Harrell-Bond 2005, 17). This is because the laws of host countries often cease to apply in refugee camps. Laws are supposed to be upheld by the UNHCR, but, because they are unable to do this, "camps are spaces that are virtually *beyond the rule of law* and in which the life of refugees ends up being governed by a highly oppressive blend of rules laid down by the humanitarian agencies and the customary practices of the various refugee communities" (Verdirame and Harrell-Bond 2005, 334). This situation leads Agier to conclude, "the humanitarian world is a totalitarianism that has power over life (to let live or survive) and death (to let die) over the individual that it views as absolute victim" (Agier 2011, 196).

It is important that there was no body that was put in place to oversee the UNHCR or the implantation of the 1951 Convention. This has led to one of most widely noted limitations of the way the UNHCR currently functions. The UNHCR is largely unaccountable to anyone for violations of its mandate. Though they exercise a tremendous amount of power over the displaced, they are subject to very little accountability. As Verdirame and Harrell-Bond note, they rarely have to submit to the due process of law in national or international courts (2005). There are no external agencies that they are legally or politically accountable to, nor are they accountable to an electorate. Unlike other global institutions grounded on international law, there is no independent monitoring mechanism for the 1951 Convention, nor any procedures for overseeing the work of the UNHCR or to make independent reports to the UN about its successes and failures. Refugees themselves are in no position to pursue legal action against the UNHCR; besides being difficult, they worry about "biting the hand that feeds them" (Verdirame and Harrell-Bond 2005). There is not even minimally an ombudsman who could hear complaints from refugees and report them to the UN or attempt to resolve them. Though Article 38 of the 1951 Convention contains provisions on the settlement of disputes and allows states' parties to bring disputes relating to the application or interpretation of the Convention to the International Court of Justice (ICJ), no state has ever invoked article 38 in order to bring a case of non-compliance to the ICJ (Verdirame and Harrell-Bond 2005, 305). While the international community is now used to the idea that global financial institutions like the World Bank can sometimes get things wrong even though they are working for positive goals, there is still resistance to thinking about the UNHCR in this way.

Among the worst forms of human rights violations in camps is sexual violence. As Pittaway and Pittaway (2004) point out, it is well known that rape and other forms of gender based violence are endemic in refugee camps, and domestic violence, sexual exploitation, and various kinds of sexual torture occur at extremely high rates; as Ben Rawlence noted in Dadaab in Kenya, "rape is routine" (Rawlence 2016, 36). The violence on the Kenya-Somali border, for example, is also well known: Somali bandits either raid refugee camps or find women who had left the camps to find firewood and gang rape whoever they find (Cohen 2000). Near the Kakuma Camp in Kenya, there are regular reports of rape and sexual mutilation by local Takrarna men (Pittaway and Pittaway 2004). Sexual assault has also been known to occur by other refugees in camps as well as by UN peacekeepers and members of the security forces (Pittaway and Bartolomei 2003). This is known to occur globally in all camp settings, and may include other forms of documented sexual violence such as child brides, forced marriages, and domestic violence. Because of their total dependence on international institutions for their survival and often inadequate access to resources, in order to survive, many refugee women are forced to prostitute themselves to other refugees, local residents, the police, and men who work for international humanitarian agencies and NGOs (Pittaway and Pittaway 2004). Victims of sexual assault often have life-long health issues that cannot be addressed in camps and are stigmatized, discriminated against, and harassed by members of their own communities. Ironically, when women become infected with HIV/AIDS as a result of rape in refugee camps, they become ineligible for resettlement in certain countries, including Australia (Pittaway and Pittaway 2004).

The UNHCR recognizes that its job is to prevent the sexual abuse and violence done to women living in refugee camps who are supposed to be under their protection. To that end, they released *Guidelines on the Protection of Refugee Women* in 1991, *Sexual Violence Against Refugees: Guidelines on Prevention and Response* in 1995, and a series of other documents in the early 2000s (see UNHCR 2001a, 2001b, 2002). Despite this well intentioned effort, there is wide spread agreement that the UNHCR and the refugee regime in general has failed to protect women in refugee camps as well as in urban refugee sites (Ward 2002, Pittaway and Pittaway 2004). Why is there so little protection available for refugee women and children (Pittaway and Pittaway 2004)? There are several elements to consider.

First, though the UNHCR has recently attempted to put in more robust legal mechanisms such as mobile courts and has been successful in prosecuting some perpetrators, the vast majority of violence continues with complete impunity (UNHCR 2001a). In Pittaway's and Pittaway's view, this occurs for two reasons. First, the UNHCR's recommendations carry no real legal consequences or authority. It is the host state that must prosecute criminal activity that occurs in its jurisdiction, even in refugee camps. It is not surprising, then, that this occurs so infrequently given that many host countries themselves have weak legal systems and may see sexual violence as too common to require prosecution.

The second reason, Pittaway and Pittaway argue, that victims of sexual violence in refugee camps cannot access either protection or redress is because of the very identity of "woman refugee." In their view, the "subliminal association between 'refugee' and 'non-citizen' creates almost absolute legal impunity for those who exploit or assault refugees" (Pittaway and Pittaway 2004). In other words, because all those who work with refugee populations know how vulnerable refugee women are, that they have virtually no legal paths for recourse if they are harmed, and that there is very little will to protect refugees, there is an implicit understanding that human rights violations like sexual assault carry very little risk of legal consequence (Chalk 1998). In other words, just being labeled a "refugee woman" becomes a marker of exploitability and thus compounds the difficulty that institutions like the UNHCR experience regarding prevention and treatment of sexual violence in refugee camps.

Another factor that is widely agreed to play a role is the general attitude around sexual violence. This is perhaps most dramatically expressed by the question posed by a UN worker, "what's so terrible about rape? You don't die from it" (Cohen 2000, 74).[42] For the person who asked this question, rape in refugee camps was unfortunate but inevitable, and tolerable as a fate better than death. In Cohen's view, this comment reflected a much deeper attitude of indifference and ignorance to the harms women refugees and IDPs experience, and this in turn, helps explain why so little was done to prevent rape in refugee camps. Similarly, Pittaway and Bartolomei note that the attitude of humanitarian workers is often that refugee women "are used to rape" and because it is so common it need not be addressed (Pittaway and Bartolomei 2003). "Although there is growing recognition, particularly since Bosnia, that rape is a crime to be punished," writes Cohen, "international staff are still not forceful enough in protesting against sexual violence or taking steps to deter it" (Cohen 2000, 77). Ward notes that though the UNHCR has adopted the *ideal* that sexual violence ought to be prevented, they have not been able to realize this goal. For Ward this is connected to the funding structure of refugee projects. Because funding is often only for short-term emergency responses, it is hard to sustain long-term programming that addresses gender based violence. In addition, Ward faults the UNHCR for not advocating more strongly to national governments to improve protection against gender based violence of refugee women (Ward 2002, 13).

Verdirame and Harrell-Bond argue that the primary reason attempts to protect women from sexual violence continually fail is the structural connection between camps and sexual violence.[43] Even the UNHCR acknowledges this reason. The reason rates of sexual violence are at epidemic levels in camps is because they are artificial communities, "characterized by unemployment, lack of future prospects, total dependence on insufficient food rations, and at times, by a preponderance of single and often young men" (Verdirame and Harrell-Bond 2005, 149). This is compounded by the fact that some of the most effective measures for protecting women from sexual violence in camps—respecting a woman's right to move away from places she finds dangerous or threatening; challenging rather than buttressing male authority in camps—were not permitted. In other words, the reason that the UNHCR is unable to protect women from sexual violence in refugee camps is because it is not possible to do so in camps where women are rendered so totally vulnerable. This, I argue, is reason to reconsider whether camps can be morally supported. If there were other institutions where sexual violence occurred on such a scale and with such unregulated impunity, and Western states were known to support the conditions which help to create and sustain it, there would likely be heavy scrutiny of the institutions. Yet regarding refugee camps, sexual violence is often tolerated and tacitly accepted.

§ How the West Supports Encampment

How do Western states specifically support encampment? Though it is host states, largely in the developing world, that ultimately make the decisions for how to treat the displaced, these decisions are often made in conjunction with funding mandates from the UNHCR as well as states in the Global North. In many cases, Western states directly fund refugee camps through funding the UNHCR. As Ben Rawlence writes about Somali refugees in Dadaab in Kenya, "those who make it to Europe are few. Millions more, the vast majority, remain in camps. And through our tax contributions to the UN, we all pay billions of dollars to keep them there" (Rawlence 2016, 5). Yet there are two other less obvious ways the West supports encampment: it is supported tacitly though policies that encourage the containment of refugee flows close to countries of origin for the sake of future repatriation, and more explicitly through funding mechanisms.

As Aleinikoff has argued, because of the nature of forced displacement since the end of the Cold War, Western states have come to view the problem of global displacement not as requiring humanitarian support as much as requiring policies of control and deterrence (Aleinikoff 1992, 130). Most Western states, he argues, have interpreted the Refugee Convention in the narrowest way possible and have established policies that make it difficult for the forcibly displaced to claim asylum—and thus have the right of non-refoulement—on their territory. "Refugee law has become immigration law, emphasizing protection of borders rather than protection of persons" (Aleinikoff 1992, 130). Tighter visa control, detention of asylum seekers, and sanctions on carriers who transport asylum seekers have made it much more difficult for asylum seekers to reach Western shores, and thus they are forced to remain closer to their countries of origin. As Gibney puts it, Western states publicly acknowledge the principle of asylum, but "use fair means and foul to prevent as many asylum seekers as possible from arriving on their territory where they could claim its protections" (Gibney 2004, 229).

Another mechanism imposed by the West that encourages the displaced to remain where they are is the "externalization of borders." This term refers to the process of transferring the management of migration beyond national borders. It's effectively a way of outsourcing immigration and asylum policy by supporting third countries, especially those countries from which migrants originate or transit, in their ability to manage migration. According to the UNHCR, "officials from these countries in effect play the role of EU border guards to prevent potential migrants from traveling to Europe" (ICRC 2012, 30). Coupled with the tightening of border controls and a highly selective immigration policy, "these partnerships are developing into an instrument of deterrence at source with respect to those who, in one capacity or the other, need to migrate" (ICRC 2012, 30).[44]

FRONTEX, the EU agency created to secure the external borders from illegal migration and human trafficking established in 2004, plays a crucial role in distancing asylum seekers from the possibility of international protection. Its interceptions in the Mediterranean Sea "are designed to prevent would-be migrants and asylum seekers from reaching the Spanish, Italian and, since 2010, Greek coasts" (ICRC 2012, 31). One ironic use of FRONTEX occurred in 2011. After the Arab Spring that was so widely praised in

Europe and around the world, the European governments deployed FRONTEX off the coast of Libya and Tunisia to prevent newly freed people, encouraged by support for them from Europe, from reaching European coasts to apply for asylum. Australia has had a policy since 1992 of detaining potential asylum seekers in detention centers that are in Papua New Guinea and the island of Nauru, which are not Australian territory. According to some reports, there are 10,000 people detained in Australian-run camps, which "are breeding grounds for rape, rioting, malaria and mental illness, and that bear the look and feel of concentration camps" (Neubauer 2014). Douglas and his coauthors note that Australia has long moved away from a policy of protection to one of militarization and deterrence, represented most notably in "Operation Sovereign Borders," which works to prevent asylum seekers from reaching Australian waters (Douglas 2014, 19–20).

What the externalization of borders in Europe and Australia shows is the interest of Western states in keeping the displaced as far as possible from their territory. To say that this distancing is the overarching concern of Western states is fairly well established. As Stevens writes, "Europe and the United States have unequivocally supported the strategy of containment" (Stevens 2006, 67). This criticism is of course not to say that Western states do nothing for asylum seekers or the displaced; far from it. The point is that as a matter of policy, aid to the displaced is always within a backdrop of ensuring what they see as security for Western states from the threat of mass migration.

When we look at how Western states fund international organizations that aid the displaced, we see that their funding priorities can lead to support of containment. In particular, developed countries prioritize humanitarian aid (immediate relief after emergency situations) and funding for processing asylum seekers already on their territory, rather than the needs of the long-term displaced. Between 2006 and 2010 only about 5% of the total official development assistance of OECD countries was dedicated to long-term refugees (USD$ 33 billion).[45] Refugees spending extended periods in camps or informal settlement are simply not a fiscal priority.

In writing about the broken refugee system, and its impact on Australia in particular, Millbank notes that "the discrepancy between what Western countries spend on their asylum systems, and what is spent on refugees in camps, has reached the point where it is raising fundamental questions about the West's responsibilities. What is spent on the world's 1.2 million asylum seekers is many times the UNHCR budget, which is supposed to meet the needs of its identified (as at end-1999) 22.3 million people of concern" (Millbank 2000, 15). In other words, for Western states, funding is primarily allocated to the treatment of the displaced most likely to impact Western states.

The problems with funding emergency humanitarian programs, rather than long-term assistance, are widely known. Perhaps the most important is that this funding structure makes it seem that the most pressing problems are the ones that are currently happening, the immediate displacements, and renders invisible long-term encampment and the problems around that. According to the ICRC, "funding priorities reflect an unwillingness to take seriously the harm that is done to the displaced who are forced to remain in limbo, in temporary settlements, either urban or rural. Funding primarily short-term emergency needs makes it harder for the displaced to restore their livelihoods, for their economic well-being, self-reliance, dignity and integrity" (ICRC 2012, 200).

Smith notes that host countries also rely on funding the displaced as emergency measures, not long-term programs (Smith 2004, 48). Many host states have offices for refugee affairs that are isolated from other departments and depend on international agencies who donate funds earmarked for refugees. "The result has been the perpetuation of a population labeled refugees, left living in limbo and dependent for their survival on relief" (Smith 2004, 48).[46] According to Smith, funding for host countries—either integration of refugees or other programs—ought to be made contingent on the protection of rights listed in the Refugee Convention. As he concludes, there is an incentive structure put in place by the international community that encourages encampment of the displaced, and at a minimum, we ought to shift "incentives from policies that treat refugees like cattle to ones that honor them as human beings" (Smith 2004, 54).

§ Moral Obligations

If we take seriously the key features of the refugee regime, described above, as well as the ways in which Western states are connected to and support it, we can begin to see what moral obligations we may have to the displaced, in addition to considering long-term solutions such as resettlement in the West. The reason I say that we "may have" these obligations is that my goal in this section is to introduce some possible ethical obligations that members of Western states have towards refugees and other forcibly displaced people that have not been discussed previously. However, since there is at least some disagreement about whether or not we have moral obligations to refugees—which has been a focus of philosophical discussion in recent years—I do not doubt that these obligations will be similarly debated.[47] My contention is merely that *if* we have moral obligations to those who do not have a state of their own, as many though not all philosophers agree, then our obligations extend beyond admitting them and must also include our obligations to treat them decently while they are between states.

One of the reasons Western states and their citizens are willing to accept refugee camps is because of the importance placed on repatriation. Refugee camps become tacitly justified as necessary places to wait, like waiting rooms at a doctor's office. They are seen as a necessary means to the ultimate positive good, repatriation. However, this view of camps allows many to see the endemic human rights violations as more tolerable than they ought to be (since on this view they are both temporary and necessary, and ultimately serve a higher good, allowing refugees to be returned home). It allows for a pragmatic acceptance of the misery of camps: why waste time and effort in making camps humane, dignified, or filled with opportunities, if refugees are just going to leave as soon as they are allowed? With an exclusive focus on repatriation, life in refugee camps becomes acceptable and inevitable rather than "the worst aspect of refugee policy" (Verdirame and Harrell-Bond 2005, 271). In other words, the hope of repatriation has clouded our view on long-term refugee camps, which, I will argue, ought to be rejected as a way of dealing with the forcibly displaced who are unwanted by any country in the world. While treating involuntary migrants with dignity and respect while they are in camps is by no means a solution to the global problem of forced displacement, it will go a long way towards protecting the human rights of those who have lost the protection of their own states. Even if one still holds that repatriation is the ultimate good, we ought to remain critical of encampment as a temporary solution.

The first moral obligation we have is to reject the policy of long-term encampment as the de facto solution to the problem of unwanted and superfluous people in the world or, at the very least, insist that refugee camps and other spaces of containment be subject to the same moral and political norms of decent hierarchical societies (in the sense that Rawls uses this term in *Law of Peoples*). While it is possible that refugee camps of short duration may be justifiable in emergency circumstances as the best way of delivering aid, long-term encampment cannot be justified as a way of containing people who are unwanted elsewhere in the world. Encampment, when it ceases to be a response to an emergency situation and becomes prolonged indefinitely, systematically violates the rights and dignity of displaced people. It ought not to be considered a morally acceptable "solution" to the problem of displacement in the 21st century as it currently is.

If I am right about this, then Western states ought not support this practice as we currently do, both directly through insisting that our aid be used to fund camps (rather than other more dignified temporary solutions) and indirectly through our refugee policies which make encampment the inevitable outcome (insisting on repatriation makes encampment justifiable and necessary). If no other alternative arrangement is possible, then refugee camps and other spaces of containment ought to be subject to the same rigorous moral and political norms as states. Given my analysis above, it is clear that long-term refugee camps function as new forms of political space outside of traditional space, and as a result, systematic human rights violations should not be ignored because they are "exceptional" or "temporary" (which they in fact are not).

What would it look like if refugee camps were guided by more stringent ethical and political norms? Minimally speaking, they ought to meet the standard of what Rawls calls a decent hierarchical society. Though we need not ask the governance of refugee camps to function as liberal democracies, they ought to contain some amount of consultation between members and the governing bodies, a commitment to at least basic human rights, and include some level of accountability (Rawls 2001). This would allow for a minimal way that politics, "the ability to decide the direction and purpose of action," could be part of the life of refugees (Bauman 2007, 2).

As Holzer has argued, it is possible to build political norms into refugee camps, and the UNHCR and the international community that supports it have a choice to make, whether we react "to the unrelenting scarcities, violence and instability of humanitarian crises with a makeshift authoritarianism or a renewed commitment to innovative participatory democracy" (Holzer 2012, 275). Though refugee camps present political challenges like no other form of political space, the international community ought to be more creative in their political solutions. Holzer's analysis suggests some ways that we can incorporate political, even democratic norms into the life of refugee camps. She suggests that in certain circumstances, "refugee camps might serve as particularly strong platforms for 'associational democracy,' a participatory reform intended to bring civil society organizations into the decision-making structure of government" (Holzer 2012, 275). If it's not possible to identify refugee community representatives, camp administrators could explore direct democracy, especially the tradition that stems from Europe and North America. Alternatively, camps may also serve as platforms for novel forms of participatory budgeting to allocate humanity aid (Holzer 2012, 275). What Holzer stresses, however, is that the decision to restrict the ability of refugees in camps to be political and exercise their political capacities is a choice, not an inevitability; if increasing the political capacities of refugees is seen as an important good, organizations can find ways to incorporate politics into camps.

Let me address what is an obvious objection to my claims above: what choice do states have besides refugee camps, given the sheer numbers of the forcibly displaced and the reality that most states do not want them? My account may seem to hinge on my ability to show that there are feasible non-camp alternatives or alternative ways of designing camps that would fulfill the basic human rights of refugees that states could employ. Though I think there are such alternatives, before I discuss them, I would like to suggest that even if this were not the case, my critique of the immorality of the current status quo nonetheless remains important.

First, as I have suggested throughout this book, my purpose is not to set out a policy agenda for changing how states house and protect refugees. Rather, the main goal of this book is to demonstrate that we must frame long-term encampment as an injustice, one which ought to concern us even if solutions aren't immediately apparent. In other words, it is a work of political and moral theory, rather than policy. Long-term encampment as a solution for unwanted human beings is rarely seen as a profound injustice or one that requires serious attention. Most people in the West are only scarcely aware of the existence of prolonged encampment, and if they are aware of it, they see it as inevitable. One of the goals of this book is to change how we see this situation. It was not so long ago that many people believed that the inequalities of the modern world—what we now call global poverty—were not a matter of justice but simply an unfortunate but unavoidable facet of how the world works. Seeing global poverty as an injustice that we ought to work towards changing, even if there is no consensus on how to do this or what a just global order would look like, is important. It shows that Western states and the international community have begun to take global poverty seriously. The result is that effort has been directed towards analyzing and overcoming it, and policies that contribute to and further global poverty are critiqued. Though this framework has not ended radical poverty or global inequality, we at least know what we should be aiming for. Similarly, the goal of this book is to show that we ought to begin to recognize warehousing and long-term encampment as profound moral injustices, injustices that we can and ought to begin to work towards changing.

As the ICRC argues, "there is no shortage of innovative approaches that could help to alleviate the trauma of extended exile. However, the difficulty lies not in the new ideas, but in escaping the old ones. Solving protracted displacement is not impossible, but it requires political will. The misery of prolonged displacement has become 'normal', because many states have effectively decided that the misery of excluded forced migrants is an unfortunate price worth paying to avoid having to confront the difficult political questions raised by the injustices and inequalities of a bordered world" (ICRC 2012, 228). One of the goals of this book is simply to insist that we must see the current "normal" as unjust, and an injustice we ought to find intolerable. This is a crucial first step before alternatives can even be considered.

Once states and their citizens see the current status quo as an injustice, we can begin to consider alternative arrangements. What are the alternatives to camps for housing refugees while they await repatriation or resettlement? One alternative is "temporary local integration" or "self-reliance." On this alternative, rather than being placed in camps where refugees are segregated from the local population, refugees would be allowed to settle temporarily within local populations and international aid would go to improving all public facilities (schools, hospitals, job training programs) and developing the skills and talents of refugees that could be put to use in a host country, rather than to just funding camps. The goal is that refugees would become increasingly self-reliant and not dependent on international aid.

What would allowing refugees to integrate temporarily in a host country look like? Alexander Betts and his coauthors studied refugee integration in Uganda, where the government allows refugees the right to work and a significant degree of freedom of movement. The Ugandan government has found ways "to offer refugees freedom of movement, the right to work, and support in the pursuit of their own economic opportunities, pending going home" (Betts et al. 2014, 6). Based on extensive quantitative and qualitative research, they found that when refugees are allowed to integrate economically in a host state, they without a doubt contribute in positive ways to the national economy and do not remain dependent on the international community. Refugees contribute to Uganda's local and national economies through buying, selling, or even training and employing Ugandan nationals; "the daily economic life of many refugees directly benefits Uganda businesses" (Betts et al. 2014, 17).

Though most refugees in Uganda continue to receive assistance, they are not dependent on this assistance for survival because of their integration into the national and local economies. Betts and his coauthors stress that the most effective kind of assistance is assistance that nurtures talents, capacities, and aspirations so that refugees are able to contribute to their host country and engage in productive and sustainable livelihoods. They conclude that the best kinds of aid to refugees is aid that provides opportunities for education, skills development, access to micro credit and financial markets, and improved access to the internet. Further, in order to make this positive contribution, displaced populations need a combination of rights and freedoms that enable them to flourish as human beings.

"When refugees are given the right to work and freedom of movement, they are capable of making a contribution to the national economy" (Betts et al. 2014, 41). What this shows is that local integration is indeed possible and clearly beneficial to both displaced populations themselves and the states which host them. This economic benefit to host states demonstrated in this study may help to address the reluctance of states to consider local integration.[48] As the study by Betts and colleagues shows, there are certainly alternatives to camps that can and ought to be used, not only because they are economically more beneficial, but also because they avoid some of the worst moral injustices associated with refugee protection.

Recently, even the UNHCR has advocated for a new policy on alternatives to camps.[49] Interestingly, the UNHCR insists that alternatives to camps need not take one specific form but can be imagined in many different ways as long as they exhibit certain characteristics. Refugees must be able to exercise their rights such as freedom of movement; they must have meaningful choices about their lives, including the ability to choose where they reside; they must be allowed to work and to access services and resources. Most importantly, refugees must have the "possibility to live with greater dignity, independence and normality *as members of communities*" (UNHCR 2014b, 9, italics added). In other words, we need not specify precisely what the alternatives to camps are or what form they must take as long as they exhibit the characteristics set out above. Most importantly, refugees must become part of the political communities in which they reside. What this means is that the UNHCR would enable refugees to reside in communities "lawfully, peacefully and without harassment, whether in urban or in rural areas" and have the ability "to take responsibility for their lives and for their families" (UNHCR 2014b, 3).[50] The goal is to remove obstacles to exercising rights and achieving self-reliance.

One way of achieving the goals set out above is to alter the way that aid is provided. Rather than deliver aid only to camps, the UNHCR would take a mainstreaming approach within national, local, and community based systems and structures to provide things like education, public health, nutrition, water, and sanitation. In other words, services are integrated into the community and camps themselves become sustainable settlements. Camps would be "anchored within the framework of national development planning and housing, land and property laws and are linked to host communities and the local economy, markets, infrastructure and service delivery systems" (UNHCR 2014b, 8). Refugees would be encouraged to build sustainable livelihoods and achieve self-reliance through education, training, and other forms of support. In order to take advantage of education and employment opportunities, refugees must be allowed mobility. The UNHCR acknowledges that in the long run alternatives to camps should be both more sustainable and more cost-effective. This is because from the point of view of aid organizations, they "harness the potential of refugees" (UNHCR 2014b, 6). This is true even though transitioning to these alternative forms may require greater initial investments.

§ Conclusion

What my chapter has showed is why it is so essential to support this nascent policy change. As the UNHCR states, moving from a camp-based system of delivering aid to an alternative will "require engagement with and by host government authorities at all levels and the full spectrum of UNHCR's partners and stakeholders" (UNHCR 2014b, 2). What my chapter has also showed is that it will require more than a mere policy change to alter the primary way that the forcibly displaced are cared for; it needs a new moral justification. What has justified encampment has been a belief that it is better for people to return to their home countries than be resettled, and this requires the use of refugee camps as a temporary measure. What the new UNHCR policy will require is a similar *moral grounding* to justify the resources and change in mentality that are necessary. The analysis above has, I believe, shown why such a change in policy is so crucial and why Western states and other international actors ought to support it to the best of our capacities.

Overall, this chapter has critically examined the refugee protection regime and the role the UNHCR and Western states have played in it. The goal was to suggest that any moral obligations we have to the displaced must include the obligation to reject long-term encampment and work towards temporary solutions that protect the dignity and rights of refugees. Having explained the necessity of these obligations in this chapter, I further my argument for them in subsequent chapters. In Chapter Three, I deepen my argument for these obligations by showing that there is a further harm to refugee camps—the ontological deprivation—that many scholars had failed to appreciate. In Chapter Four I return to the question of who is responsible for upholding these obligations and why. Before I turn to either of those topics, I examine the way that our obligations to refugees have been understood by philosophers until now and show why their analyses have been limited. It is this task that I turn to in the following chapter, Chapter Two.

Notes

1 The International Federation of Red Cross and Red Crescent Societies claims that there are over 72 million forced migrants around the world, while the UNHCR says there are 65.3 million (ICRC 2012, UNHCR 2016). The ICRC's number is higher because it includes those displaced due to disasters, environmental degradation, development projects, poverty, and poor governance. For more on who is included in which categories, see the Introduction of this book.
2 Though the UNHCR's core mandate was to protect "refugees" in the narrow sense of the term, it has expanded to include those considered to be asylum seekers, internally displaced persons (IDPs), and stateless persons. These are all considered to be "persons of concern to the UNHCR" (UNHCR 2014a). Even though economic migrants are treated differently under international law than refugees or those fleeing persecution and violence, because they often use the same routes and means of transportation as refugees, the UNHCR must also consider migrants and "mixed migration" patterns (see UNHCR 2007).
3 It's interesting to note that the UNHCR includes the limitations of rights and freedoms in the very definition of a refugee camp.
4 A protracted situation is defined by the UNHCR as "a situation in which 25,000 or more refugees of the same nationality have been in exile for five years or longer in a given asylum country" (UNHCR 2014). Though they acknowledge that this is a useful definition for monitoring purposes, it also has some limitations. For example, as long as a population remains under 25,000, it will never count as a protracted situation regardless of how long the group may have been displaced. The average duration of major refugee situations has doubled from nine years in 1993 to 17 years in 2003 (UNHCR 2006).
5 "Of the 14.4 million refugees of concern to UNHCR around the world, less than one per cent is submitted for resettlement." (UNHCR 2015).
6 Kagan notes, however, that though this 2009 policy marks a dramatic shift in the rhetoric of the UNHCR, their practices have been slow to change. "Camps are still abundant, and they are still central to UNHCR's work" (Kagan 2013). Rather than blaming the UNHCR for this, he stresses the difficult position the UNHCR is in when it mediates with local host governments. It may oppose forced encampment but may feel that it needs to be involved in refugee camps that host governments insist on for the sake of the refugees.
7 The original 1951 Convention limited the scope of the Convention to people fleeing from Europe before 1951. In 1967, the Protocol Relating to the Status of Refugees was added, which eliminated the geographic and temporal limitations.
8 The UNHCR has 8,000 staff members working in 449 locations in 123 countries. According to its reports, over the past 60 years it has provided assistance to well over 50 million people and earned Nobel Peace Prizes in 1954 and 1981. Its programs are approved by an Executive Committee comprised of members of the 94 member states along with a Standing Committee that meets several times a year (*Protecting Refugees and the Role of the UNHCR* 2014, 15).

9. Elsewhere he puts it more bluntly: in 1951, "they designed an organization to do very little and only what states told it to do" (Barnett 2004, 73).
10. The Convention leaves a lot to state discretion, including what procedures states use to determine refugee status. No international body that would assist with this and make status determinations at a supra national level was created. The UNHCR certainly assists states with this, especially in refugee camps under their supervision, but it has no authority, and states are not obliged to accept their determinations. This is key because, as Aleinikoff notes, "the adjudication of who is a refugee—upon which all the protections of the Convention turn—is left entirely to state authorities" (Aleinikoff 1992, 124).
11. Roxström and Gibney, however, deny that this funding structure is necessarily an impediment to refugee protection. While they do not deny that the need of the UNHCR to be constantly raising money from donor states limits its freedom of action, it nonetheless can still insist on the highest standards of protection for refugees. They ask us to imagine what would happen if the UNHCR stood up to donor states. Is it really plausible, they ask, that states would punish the UNHCR because it tried to fulfill its mandate and challenged states to better protect the displaced? They don't think it is. States are already incredibly reluctant to aid refugees, and "it's far-fetched to argue that this limited compassion towards refugees would be further decreased because politicians are upset with UNHCR" (Roxström and Gibney 2012, 59).
12. For Betts, this lack of legal obligation means that Western states must be persuaded and encouraged to support refugees, and the best way to do this is to link refugee protection to other issues that the West already takes seriously, such as trade and security (Betts 2011, 2009). Of course if Betts is right that the West has no intrinsic interest in refugee protection and is only motivated by self-interest, we should perhaps be less surprised to find the current situation of containment rather than protection, which, in a way, serves Western interests (their interests especially in exercising sovereign control of membership and admission) at the expense of refugees themselves.
13. Even the UNHCR itself admits that refugee protection requires being sensitive to the needs of states to manage migration and maintain border security (UNHCR 2014, 13). Balancing both the legitimate concerns of states as well as refugee protection and rights has put the UNHCR is a very difficult position, being pulled between fulfilling its mandate for refugee protection and solutions, and appeasing donor states.
14. In 2014, out of the 59.5 million people who were forcibly displaced, 105,200 were resettled (UNHCR 2014). Concerning the population hosted in the Global South, see UNDESA 2012 United Nations Department of Economic and Social Affairs, "Population Facts."
15. Reciprocity encourages states to comply with international law in order to encourage other states to do the same, thus creating conditions of global stability in the long term. States also comply with international law in order to be seen as legitimate in the international system and as such, able to exercise authority. Both of these reasons act as motivations for states to comply with the norm of non-refoulement, but are absent in regards to supporting refugees who are not on their territory (Betts 2011).
16. Between 2003 and 2005 the UN introduced the Convention Plus initiatives, whose aim was to get beyond the impasse described above. The idea behind this was that the interests of Southern states in greater burden sharing could be made compatible with the interests of Northern states in reducing the number of asylum seekers coming from the South to the North. Ultimately, for a variety of reasons, it did not succeed (Betts 2011).

17 See, for example, Walzer (1983), Miller (2007), and Wellman (2008).
18 As Aleinikoff writes, the "affirmation of the authority of states to exclude refugees may well leave the refugee virtually stateless, unable to enter a country of asylum and unable or unwilling to return to the country of origin" (Aleinikoff 1992, 121).
19 Though this is the dominant view, not all scholars agree. Haddad argues on the contrary that refugees are *necessary* for modern state sovereignty and that they are the inevitable if unintended consequence of the international states system. She claims that both sovereignty and refugees are mutually constituted insofar as refugees help to create and sustain a sense of insider and outsider; refugees are necessary for the functioning of sovereignty and consequently should be thought of as a permanent and necessary feature of the international landscape. As she puts it starkly, refugees are "victims of an international system that brings them into being then fails to take responsibility for them" (Haddad 2008, 69).
20 Though 27 states resettled refugees in 2014, over 90% were resettled in the United States, Australia, and Canada (UNHCR 2014).
21 Aleinikoff refers to this as a sociological conception of membership grounded in communitarian considerations. This view holds that human beings cannot simply cast off their belonging, roots, and ties as easily as lawyers and theorists think (Aleinikoff 1992, 127).
22 In Aleinikoff's view, once states exercise their sovereignty and deny membership to refugees, repatriation effectively becomes the only possible solution, whether or not it is in the best interests of refugees.
23 See Bradley (2013) and Long (2013) on the complexities of repatriation.
24 One response to this critique is that the UNHCR is doing its best given the political circumstances. Crisp and Slaughter argue that "humanitarian agencies in general, and UNHCR in particular, have been placed in the position of establishing and assuming responsibility for such 'sprawling camps' in order to fill gaps in the international refugee regime that were not envisaged at the time of its establishment after the Second World War." Further, "the UN's refugee agency has been limited in its ability to address the problem of protracted refugee situations, mainly because of the intractable nature of contemporary armed conflicts and the policies pursued by other actors, but also because of the other issues which the organization has chosen to prioritize and the limited amount of attention which it devoted to this issue during the 1990s" (Crisp and Slaughter 2009).
25 Hammerstad argues that we ought to see refugees through the paradigm of "desecuritization," that is, we ought to shift the issue of refugees "out of emergency mode into the normal bargaining process of the political sphere" (Buzan 1998, 24, quoted in Hammerstad 2011, 239).
26 To be sure, Hammerstad is not attributing nefarious motives to the UNHCR. Arguably they adopted the language of securitization in order to protect refugees and harness resources. "It would be a deeply unfair exaggeration to argue that UNHCR is so beholden to donor agendas as to unquestioningly mimic a xenophobia-tainted, knee-jerk reaction of panic and fear against asylum seekers just to please European states" (Hammerstad 2011, 247–248). Nonetheless, if the analysis above is correct, it did have the effect of solidifying the view that refugees are a legitimate security threat from which Western states need protection.
27 The situation in Afghanistan shows the complexity of repatriation in another way as well. Since repatriation began in 2002, about 5 million Afghans were returned. Yet the country they returned to was still largely unstable and politically volatile. "In the post 9/11 world, Afghan repatriation was needed to legitimize the US-led intervention, subsequent peace process and the fledgling government. These three factors seemed to outweigh more careful considerations

of the feasibility of return and the impact that such large numbers of returnees would have on a poor and war-stricken country that was already struggling to accommodate those who had remained. The interests of host countries (wanting to rid themselves of a long-term burden, or regain land for urban expansion as in the case of Pakistan) also overruled the best interests of the refugees and Afghanistan, and possibly even of long-term regional stability. In the search for quick success, the durability of the repatriation solution was not adequately considered" (Schmeidl 2009, 20).

28 The second durable solution, local integration, has also not been able to address the problem. Local integration refers to the process where refugees who may be admitted only temporarily gradually gain full rights and citizenship. According to the UNHCR, in the past 10 years 716,000 refugees have been granted citizenship in the country they sought asylum in, with two thirds of these occurring in the United States (UNHCR 2014, 22). This means that the number of people living in refugee camps in the Global South who have successfully integrated is very small indeed. As for resettlement, in 2013, 98,400 refugees were resettled, with over 90% of them resettling in the US, Australia, and Canada (66,200, 13,200, and 12,200, respectively) (UNHCR 2014). Though a tremendous good for those who receive this benefit, resettlement is not a good most refugees can expect.

29 Verdirame and Harrell-Bond argue that they are a bad investment for donor states, since they cost more and have a smaller return on investment than development aid or funds for integration (Verdirame and Harrell-Bond 2005). Also see Betts et al. (2014).

30 As Arafat Jamal, the former Deputy Representative of UNHCR in Jordan put it, "with refugees sequestered, concentrated, visible and presumably out of harm's way, camps represent a convergence of interests among host governments, international agencies and the refugees themselves. They are not ideal for anyone but they help focus attention and provide a safety net. Host governments in Africa . . . see camps as a means of isolating potential troublemakers and forcing the international community to assume responsibility. . . . Refugees understand that camps make them visible, and keep their plight, and the politics that underpin it, in the world's consciousness" (Smith 2004, 50).

31 As an example of the institutional inertia that perpetuates camps, Verdirame and Harrell-Bond argue that the UNHCR has two budgets—one for emergency relief and one for development—and because donors insist on funding emergency situations rather than long-term projects, the UNHCR must keep refugees in camps to satisfy this requirement (Verdirame and Harrell-Bond 2005, 288).

32 I show below that this is one of the reasons why camps have been missing from political philosophy. Their precariousness and exceptionality mean that they are not important to the past and not relevant to the future, and thus not worth considering. Their ephemeral quality is at least in part why they have been normatively invisible. Philosophers are interested in the time *before* displacement occurs, and the war, violence, and instability that often causes it; they are also interested in the time *after* refugees return home and in issues around peace, resettlement, and reconciliation. However, this time *in between*, whose duration is unknown, is hard to represent to those who theorize about it (Agier 2008 and 2011).

33 Agier has observed that for many, the waiting in the waiting zones is the most intolerable. This is in part because there are none of the distractions that life in a refugee camp has. In addition, what makes this situation intolerable is that the outcomes of decisions in the waiting zones and the logic used to explain them are often incomprehensible to the detainees (Agier 2011, 51). It is for these reasons that hunger strikes, suicides, and other "acts of despair" are not uncommon.

34 The concept of "internal asylum" in countries like Morocco, Libya, and Senegal occurred as a response by European states and UN agencies to mass displacement

in the first part of this century, and in particular to the new category of "prima facie refugee" used in emergency situations on a collective, not individual basis (Agier 2011). The principle behind this is that aid agencies can provide aid before individuals leave their home countries and thus make a return in time easier too. However, Agier argues, internal asylum can be understood as another kind of camp that functions to contain and collect individuals and, importantly, distance them from Europe. Humanitarian organizations manage the flow of refugees, keeping them at a safe distance from Western states where they could apply for asylum.

35 This is in addition to the well-known problems of camps: disease epidemics, environmental degradation, and radicalization of ethnic identity, among others (Verdirame and Harrell-Bond 2005, 270).

36 Gorlick argues that human rights law must be used to bolster refugee law. "At a time when refugee law is under attack and its very foundations are being questioned, one must rely on other binding rights norms and enforcement mechanisms to bolster the system of refugee protection" (Gorlick 2012, 98). The non-derogable legal standards of human rights law must be used when refugee law fails to protect those in need.

37 For a detailed discussion of the rights systematically violated in refugee camps, see Verdirame and Harrell-Bond (2005), chapter 4 on civil and political rights and chapter 5 on social and economic rights.

38 To this list of human rights violations, Michel Agier adds the unequal distribution of covers; food rations in disastrous quantity or quality; insult and physical violence against people who request aid; forced repatriation; and prohibition on building huts from rigid materials (Agier 2011, 215).

39 See Verdirame and Harrell-Bond (2005) for a detailed analysis of this in camps in Kenya and Uganda. Kenya and Uganda are particularly interesting examples of camps since, for the vast majority of refugees there, none of the three "durable" solutions were available (repatriation, integration, and resettlement).

40 The UNHCR works by subcontracting out its various operations to different NGOs. In 2007, it worked with approximately 575 different NGOs (Agier 2011, 203).

41 "UNHCR is the main authority that exercises power and effective control in camps; combined with its role in the status-determination process, this power means that UNHCR is not simply unable to promote respect for the rights of refugees, but is often responsible for the violation of these rights" (Verdirame and Harrell-Bond 2005, 17).

42 Though it is perhaps obvious, it is nonetheless worth mentioning that many women experience rape as among the most intolerable forms of harm a person can endure. To point out one horrendous example, take the Africa Rights Watch report from 1993. As they describe it, most of the Somali women who were raped that year in refugee camps in Kenya were gang-raped at gun point, by as many as seven men; they often had to endure this gang rape several times. The vast majority were also robbed, severely beaten, knifed or shot; if they had been circumcised, they had their vaginal openings torn or cut by their attackers. Most Somali women had undergone a kind of female genital mutilation called infibulation, where the clitoris and inner lips are removed and the woman is sewn together so that only a small opening is left to allow for the flow of urine and menstrual blood. Because of this operation, rape is excruciatingly painful. In the aftermath, they experience ongoing medical problems, sexually transmitted diseases, unwanted pregnancies, miscarriages for women raped when pregnant, inability to control urination, life-altering stigma, ostracism, death, and murder. There are also documented cases of the rape of children between 5 and 13 years old (Africa Rights Watch 1993).

43 See Verdirame and Harrell-Bond (2005, 143) for a list of failed initiatives to protect women in camps.
44 "Readmission agreements are a key tool in these collaborations. Negotiated by the EU with ever more source or transit countries, they require the countries to 'take back' not only their own nationals who have entered and/or stayed illegally in an EU member state, but also any other person in this situation, irrespective of their nationality. This means that the EU gives these countries a free hand to deal with the people sent back to them, regardless of the conditions for return in these countries" (ICRC 2012, 30–31).
45 OECD, Organization for Economic Co-operation and Development, is a group of 34 high-income countries that include many of the countries in Europe, North America, Australia, Israel, and Turkey. The largest proportion of funding by the OECD, 43%, was dedicated to humanitarian aid, and the second largest share, 41.8%, went to supporting displaced populations within donor countries (Czech Republic, France, Greece, and Turkey each spent more than 95% of their designated funding for displaced people on support for refugees at home). A much smaller amount, 13%, went to development activities in host states to fund basic service provision, strengthening governance and security, and support to productive sectors (ICRC 2012, 176).
46 Smith quotes Mark Malloch-Brown, who writes, "when a tight-fisted international community says to a very poor country it will provide help for refugees in camps . . . this evidently encourages that poor country to root out refugees who are integrated and plonk them into camps. It is probably no exaggeration to claim that without any new refugee outflows, the old donor approach might actually lead to growing refugee camp populations in many countries" (Smith 2004, 48).
47 My own position is that moral obligations can be grounded on the principle of the Good Samaritan, which I discuss in detail in Chapter Two. Further, I think that our moral obligations to refugees are rooted in the commitment of Western states to the principles of human rights, found in international Declarations (such as the Universal Declaration of Human Rights) and Conventions (such as the Convention against Torture, the Convention on the Rights of the Child, and the Convention against Racial Discrimination, among others), which contain both moral and legal principles.
48 Kagan, for example, writes, "why should we think that local governments will be willing to open their schools, their medical clinics, their employment markets, and their housing supply to refugees, especially in a climate of xenophobia or economic distress?" (Kagan 2013).
49 See UNHCR (2014c). This shift has been said to mark a "paradigm shift in refugee protection" (Hovil 2014). This new policy calls on the UNHCR to pursue integration "whenever possible, while ensuring that refugees are protected and assisted effectively and are able to achieve solutions" (UNHCR 2014c, 3). What this means in practice is that the UNHCR is going to work towards removing restrictions so that "refugees have the possibility to live with greater dignity, independence and normality as members of the community, either from the beginning of displacement or as soon as possible thereafter" (UNHCR 2014c, 4).
50 This is an extension of the UNHCR's policy surrounding "urban refugees." They try to ensure that "cities are recognized as legitimate places for refugees to reside and exercise their rights" (UNHCR 2014b, 4).

2 Refugees in Contemporary Political Philosophy

In the last chapter I outlined one of the most pressing problems of global justice—our system of responding to mass displacement and the resulting use of encampment. In this chapter, I turn to the ways that contemporary philosophers have tried to grapple with the moral issues connected to refugees and the ways that philosophers have understood our moral obligations to refugees. I provide an overview of the contemporary discussion of the refugee question through examining the work of six normative philosophers:[1] Michael Walzer, David Miller, Christopher Wellman, Seyla Benhabib, Joseph Carens, and Matthew Gibney. These theorists, though concerned about the broad question of what justice requires with respect to the treatment of refugees, focus predominantly on the obligations raised by refugees for Western states in terms of resettlement. I refer to this as the ethics of admissions. The ethics of admissions focuses on the question of what moral obligations states have to foreigners who seek admission to their countries, and refugees are thought of as one category of people seeking admission. They all agree that the fact that people are forcibly displaced from their states is an injustice that creates moral obligations for other states, yet they differ as to what precisely is entailed in our moral obligations. The six accounts that are represented here reflect different perspectives on this issue and show the lack of consensus on what moral obligations states have to refugees.

The first three authors, Walzer, Miller, and Wellman, set strong limits on our obligations to aid refugees. For Walzer, though we have some obligations to refugees based on the principle of mutual aid, these obligations are limited by the importance of creating and maintaining "communities of character" that allow individuals to be rooted in a political community. Though David Miller argues that refugees have claims to temporary sanctuary, aid, and even to a state, when these claims conflict with a state's right to self-determination, states may justifiably exclude refugees. Christopher Wellman argues that though we may have obligations to help refugees, states have no moral obligation to admit refugees for resettlement, a view that he grounds in the importance of freedom of association. Throughout the chapter I explain why I disagree with these views and suggest some reasons why they reflect a limited perspective on our obligations to refugees given the reality of forced displacement in the 21st century. I also stress that the fact that they have little or nothing to say about what happens to those who Western states justifiably or unjustifiably refuse to resettle reflects the limited nature of their view.

Benhabib, Carens, and Gibney take a much broader approach and argue for much more extensive obligations to refugees. Benhabib argues that we have robust moral obligations to non-citizens, including refugees, who want to become members of our polities. These obligations are grounded in two features of our contemporary political life: our fundamental global interdependence and the fact that human migration is not an aberration but a basic feature of human existence. For both Carens and Gibney, we have robust obligations to refugees grounded in the principle of mutual aid or humanitarianism. They both insist that Western states ought to consider resettlement a duty and not merely an act of discretion and further, that we ought to work towards reformulating the global refugee regime and establishing ways of distributing resettlement that are just and do not disproportionally burden some states. I agree in many ways with the arguments by these theorists and highlight what I think are the strongest arguments from each. In many ways, my arguments complement and enhance the work done by other philosophers who are concerned with what an ideal refugee regime would look like.

Yet I argue that even these views reflect a limited perspective in that they do not say enough about how refugees should be treated in the period during their initial displacement and their repatriation or resettlement. Carens and Gibney in particular are right that given the current state of the refugee regime, resettlement ought to be greatly expanded and classified as a duty. However, given the current status quo—that states believe they have no legal obligations to resettle refugees, they recognize no moral obligation to resettle refugees, and are very unlikely to resettle large numbers—I will go on to argue that the duty to resettle needs to be supplemented with an *ethics of the temporary*, a morally acceptable way to house refugees and allow them to live with dignity while they are waiting to be resettled or to return to their home countries. We have an obligation to explore other ways that the refugee regime might be structured so that refugees are not kept in camps and are able to maintain their dignity and autonomy. In other words, while resettlement may be the ultimate goal, we have to morally scrutinize the ways in which the global community cares for the displaced while they are waiting for something more permanent since, I as discussed in Chapter One, this "temporary" period can last decades, even generations. In other words, even among the authors who argue in favor of more robust moral obligations, the ethics of the temporary is a neglected moral question.

In short, the goal of this chapter is to show the contributions various philosophers have made towards our understanding of what morality requires of us in terms of our treatment of refugees. Yet I also aim to show what has been neglected by contemporary philosophers, namely the ethics of the temporary and the obligations we have to refugees that we are not able or willing to resettle. I aim to remedy this lack in the subsequent chapters of this book.

§ Walzer, Miller, and Wellman

Michael Walzer is among the first philosophers to discuss our moral obligations to refugees. He initiated the debate by defining them in *moral*, rather than political or legal, terms (Walzer 1983). In his view, refugees differ from migrants in general because their claims have a stronger moral dimension. Refugees, he writes, "make the most forceful claim for admission. 'If you don't take me in,' they say, 'I shall be killed, persecuted, brutally oppressed by the rulers of my own country'" (Walzer 1983, 49). Because of the way that Walzer understands refugees, he argues that our moral obligations to them can *only* be met by admitting them to our country. For him, by definition, refugees are people whose "claims cannot be met by yielding territory or exporting wealth, but *only* by taking people in" (Walzer 1983, 48). This definition is significant because it lays the foundation for the philosophical accounts that followed. His foundational principle is that our obligations to refugees can *only* be met through admission to a country; there is no other way to aid vulnerable refugees except through admission. As such, the primary moral questions become whether or not we are morally obliged to let them in and on what ground. Other questions that follow from an affirmation of this question, such as which refugees to take in and how many, become secondary. Because of the influence of Walzer's view on the nature of what it means to be a refugee, the questions that are raised in this book about the refugee regime in general and our obligations to the displaced while they are displaced have largely been ignored.

The question of our moral obligations to refugees goes to the heart of a tension in liberal political theory: how to balance treating all people equally and at the same time protecting a democracy's ability to exclude some people from citizenship. In other words, the question of how to morally justify exclusion while maintaining a commitment to universal human equality has posed a challenge for liberals, and thus any liberal position which holds that we can deny refugees admission to our country must do so in a way that does not deny the fundamental equality of refugees.[2] For these two reasons—that refugees are *defined* as people whose legitimate moral claims can be met only by admission to a state, and the challenge to a coherent liberal political philosophy—the ethics of admission has dominated the philosophical landscape. Working out the ethical parameters around admissions has sparked a lively debate.[3]

Not only did Walzer define the terms of the debate, he also provided one of the most influential answers. He argues that states have a *moral* right to control their borders, grounded in the importance of creating "communities of character" that allow individuals to be rooted in a political community. Yet we also have obligations to help needy strangers, rooted in the principle of mutual aid.[4] In his view, states have a moral obligation to take in refugees because of the sheer moral force of their claim, but it is up to states to decide which refugees and how many it is able to take without fundamentally challenging the nature of their communities. His goal was to balance moral equality with political closure. As a result, his position requires that we take the moral claims of the forcibly displaced seriously—theirs is a condition of "infinite danger"—yet it does not require states to do anything that would radically challenge their self-understanding, such as opening their borders and taking in large numbers of refugees with no affinity with the state (Walzer 1983, 32). Ultimately although refugees, like all people, have a right to membership in some state, this right does not trump the right of individual states to self-determination. Since Walzer's position on refugees has been so influential, it is worth looking at how he arrives at his conclusions in more detail.

He begins his discussion of immigration by noting that the "primary good that we distribute to one another is membership in some human community" (Walzer 1983, 31). The reason membership is so important is because it structures all other choices regarding distributive justice—who gets to determine the shape of the political community through voting or holding office, who pays taxes, who receives social benefits, goods, and services. Even if you can participate in the market without political membership, you are cut off from provisions around security and welfare. More importantly, people without membership can always be expelled. This leads Walzer to conclude that being without political membership "is a condition of infinite danger" (Walzer 1983, 32). Membership is not something that citizens distribute among themselves, but rather it is something that is given by citizens to strangers or outsiders. Deciding how to distribute this to strangers requires that citizens make decisions about strangers and determine with whom they want to share their political communities.

There is a moral question posed by "necessitous strangers," both economic migrants and the forcibly displaced: do we have a moral obligation to admit them to our countries? Walzer disagrees with what might be understood as the conventional view that holds that we only have *negative* duties to people who are not fellow citizens, duties not to kill, rob, or harm them, but no *positive* duties to provide aid since positive duties occur only among fellow citizens. He disagrees with this because there is in his view at least one positive moral principle that extends to all people regardless of citizenship: the principle of mutual aid, also known as the Good Samaritan principle. This principle holds that if two strangers meet and one is in need of help, the other person ought to help if the need is urgent and the risks and costs of helping are low.

Walzer notes that the philosophical ground of this principle is hard to specify; he thinks that Rawls is wrong to argue that this principle can be established simply by imagining what society would be like if this duty were rejected since this is not a duty that arises among citizens (who have much stronger duties to each other). It is a duty we have to people we do not share a political life with. On the international level, outside of individual societies, we already do disregard the principle of mutual aid and do not find the consequences—millions of people dying from preventable causes, for example—to be intolerable. Walzer insists that the principle of mutual aid is more coercive for political communities than for individuals because there is a broad range of actions that a community can do to provide aid that only weakly impacts the members of the community. For Walzer, despite its vagueness, mutual aid is an external principle for the distribution of membership and it requires that we at least take seriously the demands of refugees to be admitted to our country.

Recall that for Walzer, refugees must be understood as a group "of needy outsiders whose claims cannot be met by yielding territory or exporting wealth; they can be met only by taking people in" (Walzer 1983, 48). What must we do for victims of political or religious persecution, victims who say, "if you don't take me in . . . I shall be killed, persecuted, brutally oppressed by the rulers of my own country" (Walzer 1983, 49)? Given the urgency of their need and our ability to help, Walzer claims that states cannot simply refuse to let in any needy foreigners. This is based on his endorsement of the Hobbesian idea that you cannot prevent people from seeking what they need to survive just for the sake of "things superfluous," that is, anything other than what is needed for bare survival (Walzer 1983, 46–47). Does that mean we have obligations to admit refugees? Yes and no.

For Walzer, because of the principle of mutual aid, we are obliged to admit some refugees but, because of the importance of maintaining communities of character, it is up to each state to decide how many and which refugees they want to take in. He argues that one of the reasons that would obligate a country to accept refugees is *affinity*, political, religious, or cultural. "The repression of political comrades, like the persecution of co-religionists, seems to generate an obligation to help, at least to provide refuge for the most exposed and endangered people" (Walzer 1983, 49). Yet he acknowledges that the principle of mutual aid combined with affinity only works when numbers are small. When numbers are large, "we will look, rightfully, for some more direct connection with our own way of life" (Walzer 1983, 49). Since communities are based on a sense of relatedness and mutuality, refugees "must appeal to that sense" (Walzer 1983, 50). For Walzer, refugees are those people fleeing persecution, in relatively small numbers, who can appeal to states on the principle of mutual aid and based on their affinity. Of the large numbers of people who are de facto refugees, but cannot make any kind of direct appeal to more affluent countries on the grounds of political, cultural, or racial affinity, Walzer has little to say. His view would seem to justify our political indifference to this group and gives us little reason for taking seriously the harms of encampment or warehousing.

He acknowledges that his position on refugees doesn't really help us to deal with the large numbers of refugees generated by 20th century politics and the fundamental dilemma that is at the heart of it: on the one hand, everyone must have a place to live, "where a reasonably secure life is possible," yet on the other hand, this is a right that cannot be enforced against any particular state (Walzer 1983, 50). We can mitigate the "cruelty of this dilemma" via the principle of asylum, according to which any refugee who has actually made an escape and found temporary refuge can claim asylum and not be expelled from this territory. "Though he is a stranger, and newly come, the rule against expulsion applies to him as if he had already made a life where he is: for there is no other place where he can make a life" (Walzer 1983, 50).

The principle of asylum is grounded on two reasons: to deny it would require that we use force against "helpless and desperate people," and the numbers are likely to be small and easily absorbed (Walzer 1983, 51).[5] Walzer argues that when asylum seekers arrive in Western countries, states should simply not resist. When it comes to asylum, states are not actively helping refugees but simply refraining from stopping people in need from taking what is needed. Walzer goes so far as to say that the claims of these needy foreigners are so strong that if "driven by famine in the densely populated lands of Southeast Asia, thousands of people were to fight their way into an Australia otherwise closed to them, I doubt that we would want to charge the invaders with aggression" (Walzer 1983, 46). Though the principle of asylum, ultimately rooted in the principle of mutual aid, is so important as to allow the invasion of thousands of needy people into a country, it ought not to transform admission policies that are rooted in a country's understanding of itself. For Walzer, the balance between helping those in need and having sovereign control of immigration policies must always tip towards the latter.

Ultimately, states retain the right to control immigration and admissions, and this includes discretion to choose which refugees to admit and how many. The root of his argument is that political communities require *closure* in order to preserve the distinctiveness of cultures and groups. The distinctiveness of cultural or communal life is something that most people value; it is the reason people often want to immigrate to a particular country and hence why migration is an important political issue. This is why political communities must "claim authority to make its own admissions policy, to control and sometimes restrain the flow of immigrants" (Walzer 1983, 39). He goes on to say that restrictions on immigration are justifiable in order to preserve *communities of character*. "The distinctiveness of cultures and groups depends upon closure," writes Walzer, "and, without it, cannot be conceived as a stable feature of human life" (Walzer 1983, 39). Without closure there could not be *communities of character*, "historically stable, ongoing associations of men and women with some special commitment to one another and some special sense of their common life" (Walzer 1983, 62).[6] Without closure, with a global state, human beings would lose this cultural distinction and we would be left with "radically deracinated men and women" (Walzer 1983, 39). The right to control admission and to exclude some goes to the heart of communal independence and is at the core of the meaning of self-determination. This is not to say that countries are free to make decisions on immigration on any grounds—they must be subject to some constraints though Walzer acknowledges that he cannot specify fully what these might be; it ultimately remains a matter of political decision as to what kind of community citizens want to create and with what other people they want to share and exchange social goods (1983, 40).

In short, for Walzer a state's right to control borders is rooted in a moral commitment to the importance of distinct communities and the need for roots and connection. He writes, "the collective version of mutual aid might require a limited and complex redistribution of membership and/or territory. Farther than this we cannot go" (Walzer 1983, 47). Paradoxically, the importance of community is what allows us, if necessary, to exclude people from a given territory. This right to self-determination embodied in immigration policy is never absolute; it must be subject to certain moral constraints, and states are never justified in refusing entry to at least some refugees when they are able to take them in. In this respect, Walzer is arguing that the claims of refugees ought to be given much greater moral consideration than they usually receive in domestic immigration policy, requiring states to either adjust their immigration policies or to distribute wealth to alleviate some of the suffering. Nonetheless, the right to self-determination is a right that trumps the right of refugees to a state.

When the problem of our moral obligations to refugees is framed in the way that Walzer frames it—as a tension between the moral right of states to control immigration as they wish and the right of all people to a political community—it appears that our morally appropriate responses to the forcibly displaced are limited. If the primary way of aiding the displaced is by granting admission, and states are justified in not granting admission on the grounds of communal identity, then it seems that there is very little we can actually do to change this situation.

Though extremely influential, I think Walzer's account is problematic for a number of reasons. First, his view of the problem with refugees—that they need a new home—is too narrow. He excludes other ways that states may be able to aid the forcibly displaced whom we choose not to admit, namely by refusing to support policies of encampment and warehousing, by funding local integration, and by insisting that aid money be contingent on respecting the basic rights of the forcibly displaced. The question that Walzer never raised is, what happens to people who states exclude on the grounds of preserving communities of character? As discussed in Chapter One, most forcibly displaced people remain in a position of statelessness for a prolonged period of time, where they are without political rights, community, or representation. Prolonged encampment and long-term displacement, which are in many circumstances the result of uncoordinated policies of various sovereign states each acting to preserve their "communities of character," are never raised as moral issues.

In other words, for Walzer, an insufficient understanding of the global refugee regime led to an unhelpfully narrow perspective on our obligations. As described in Chapter One, the outcome of each country acting to preserve the interests and character of their states is a de facto policy of encampment and containment that systematically denies the human rights of millions of people for sustained periods of time. Because of this narrow perspective, other ways of aiding refugees besides resettlement (such as by refusing to support policies of encampment and warehousing, funding local integration, and insisting that aid money be contingent on respecting the basic rights of the forcibly displaced) are never considered.

David Miller, in taking up the issue of our responsibility to refugees, takes a similar tragic view of our obligation to help. He argues strongly for the injustice of permanent refugee camps yet does not see a way out of the situation given the "tragic choice" between the rights of refugees and the right to self-determination. He writes, "when a refugee applies to be admitted to a state that is able to guarantee her such rights, then prima facie the state in question has an obligation to let her in" (Miller 2007, 225). This, he is quick to point out, is not the same as a right to immigrate or a right to citizenship; it is only a claim to "temporary sanctuary," a place where immediate security can be guaranteed (Miller 2007, 202). States then have an obligation to admit refugees at least temporarily on the assumption that they will return to their home countries once the cause of their flight has lost its force. This he thinks is an appropriate solution for people fleeing civil wars and other temporary conflicts.

Another way to discharge the duty we have to refugees is to establish "safety zones" closer to their home. Once this is established, we can then deal with the root cause of the rights violation either by "sending in food and medical aid, or intervening to remove a genocidal regime from power" (Miller 2007, 225).[7] Miller is aware of the danger of these temporary safety zones becoming permanent and argues that this would be unacceptable since we owe refugees more than just the protection of their basic rights. Refugees, he claims, "are owed the opportunity to make a decent life for themselves in the place that they live" (Miller 2007, 225). If it is the case that a refugee residing in a given country will not be able to return to his home, that country has to give him the opportunity to acquire full citizenship. Miller insists that refugees cannot be kept in a temporary status for the long term. Refugee camps "must not become permanent settlements by default" (Miller 2007, 225). Yet Miller gives us no reason to think the displaced can challenge the state sovereignty that keeps them excluded and contained in refugee camps. As Chapter One demonstrated, this has become more or less the status quo.

Despite the injustices Miller lists above—that refugees have a right to a state, that long-term temporary status is not acceptable—he still holds that because states have a right to determine membership, there is no guarantee that "every bona fide refugee will find a state willing to take her in" (Miller

2007, 227). "At the limit," he argues, "we may face tragic cases where the human rights of the refugees clash with a legitimate claim by the receiving state that its obligation to admit refugees has already been exhausted" (Miller 2007, 227). For Miller, refugees have a strong but not absolute right to a political community. It is worth pointing out that though Miller acknowledges that permanent refugee camps and long-term exclusion and displacement ought to be rejected morally, Miller seems to treat this status quo as a less-than-ideal but nonetheless acceptable consequence of his views of immigration. For both Miller and Walzer, there is something tragic about the conflict between the right to self-determination and the rights of each person to belong to some political community; but both are willing to accept this conflict and ultimately seem to think of it as a morally serious, but marginal, situation.

Though Miller is in many ways aware of the problems with the contemporary treatment of refugees (such as refugee camps becoming permanent), he does not provide any resources for thinking about how to challenge the moral defects in the status quo. Though he acknowledges that refugees have strong claims on Western states, the moral obligations they give rise to are ultimately very weak. For him, refugees have a claim to temporary sanctuary where they can be secure until they are able to return home. Yet this solution is inadequate for a number of reasons discussed in Chapter One. First, the norm for "temporary sanctuary" is now 17 years. This challenges what refugees are owed in this temporary period—while tents might be justifiable for a few months, people cannot be expected to live like this for years or generations; yet thinking about the claims of refugees as merely those of "temporary sanctuary" makes their terrible treatment appear normal and justifiable. As I argued in Chapter One, we must reconsider what is owed to refugees who are living in "temporary" situations that in fact last for decades. Second, the assumption that repatriation is the best outcome serves to justify long-term encampment and makes it less likely that other solutions such as resettlement or local integration will be pursued. The promotion of repatriation, as I demonstrated in Chapter One, serves to give a moral foundation and thus support the practices of long-term encampment and warehousing. For these reasons, Miller's approach to the problem of what we owe to refugees remains inadequate.

Like Miller and Walzer, Christopher Wellman agrees that our obligations to refugees are limited. He has written an account of why states do not have strong—or, rather, any—obligations to admit refugees. His account differs significantly from those of Walzer and Miller because it does not endorse the partialist claim that states have obligations to their fellow citizens in virtue of their connection to each other; he puts forth a universalist understanding of rights. That is, he does not think the right to exclude refugees is grounded on the need to protect unique cultures or preserve a people's identity. On the contrary, he starts from the liberal view that holds freedom and autonomy to be the central focus of state protection. On the ground of freedom of association, Wellman is able to show that though we may have obligations to help refugees, this does not include an obligation to admit refugees into our country. This position makes him unique in the literature—he is willing to grant that the principle of the Good Samaritan requires that we help those in desperate need, including refugees, yet denies that we are required to admit refugees.

Wellman seeks to ground a state's right to exclude all potential immigrants, even refugees from its territory, by appealing to the right of freedom of association. His argument for this is straightforward: freedom of association is highly valued in society, and this right includes the right *not* to associate with people we do not want to. He argues for the right of a state to freedom of association by showing how this parallels the right for individuals. In both marriage and religion—two domains of fundamental importance to humans—freedom of association is critical. This reflects the importance for all people of being able to have "dominion over our self-regarding affairs" (Wellman 2008, 110). Yet just as an individual has a right to determine whom she should marry, citizens have the right to determine who will share their political lives and can legitimately choose to exclude anyone they don't want.

Wellman's argument hinges on the analogy between states and individuals. He responds to the criticism that there are morally relevant differences between individuals and groups that could explain why individuals possess the right to freedom of association and groups do not by noting that by and large, most people presume that states have this right. States would not have the ability to take collective action or join with other entities without this right; NAFTA and the EU would not be imaginable without the presumptive right to freedom of association.

Wellman is careful to note that he is not arguing that freedom of association is an absolute right; it is merely a *presumptive* right that may be overridden by other factors. States have a right to order their affairs as they please, and this right of autonomy entails the right to include only those members it chooses to include, but this right can be outweighed by "sufficiently compelling considerations" (Wellman 2008, 111).

If we follow Wellman in concluding that states, like individuals, have a presumptive right to freedom of association, and this right includes the right to not associate with some, then it is clear why it follows that states have a right to exclude any would-be immigrant, including refugees. We can note here how his position differs from Walzer: for Walzer, while states in general have no obligation to admit immigrants, they do have obligations to admit some refugees because of the nature of their moral claim on us and the fact that help cannot be exported in the form of food or aid. Wellman turns this idea on its head. For him, states have absolutely no obligation to admit refugees because of the right of freedom of association, but he acknowledges the Samaritan obligations that states have to "export" aid in some way. For

Wellman, this gives rise to strong obligations to help refugees, but not ones that include admission.

His argument for this position is as follows. In responding to the egalitarian objection to his view, Wellman insists that the injustice that needs to be addressed is poverty and the suffering of the poor, not merely inequality or moral luck (that citizenship is morally arbitrary since it is based on the place we happen to be born into rather than on morally relevant factors such as hard work). Our duty to aid the poor in other countries is rooted in our "natural duty to assist others when we can at no unreasonable cost to ourselves" (Wellman 2008, 124). In short, for Wellman, we have natural duties to aid the poor, Samaritan duties, but these duties do not trump the presumptive right of freedom of association and hence, do not require that we admit refugees. This remains true even when he grants that contemporary structures of globalization entail that "virtually all of the world's people now share some type of relationship" (Wellman 2008, 123). Because he endorses a view of relational egalitarianism, he is committed to the view that the more robust our relationships are, the deeper our obligations and connections are. This is because despite the close connections between apparent strangers forged by globalization, relationships between co-citizens remain of a different nature and importance. Consequently, even though he acknowledges the "stringent duties" that we may have to foreigners that are rooted in the duty to aid, these duties can be fully satisfied without allowing them to immigrate into our countries and become members.

He gives support for this conclusion by again drawing an analogy with individuals. Just as no one would require individuals to fight poverty by insisting wealthy people marry poor ones, we cannot insist that wealthy countries fight global poverty by admitting the global poor. The right to freedom of association exists in a different and separate domain from our duties of distributive justice. Because of the importance of keeping these domains separated, Wellman insists that we can discharge our duties to refugees in other ways than resettling them. In particular, he argues that we could fulfill this obligation by "exporting justice" such as through military interventions that would rectify an unjust political environment and ensure the safety of would-be refugees. The example he provides is setting up no-fly zones in Iraq to protect Kurds from a government that had lost legitimacy because it was unwilling or unable to protect the basic rights of its citizens. Though he acknowledges that such action is not always easy or the best thing to do, it shows at a minimum that states can acknowledge obligations to help refugees who are in desperate need of a home without allowing that this obligation should trump the right to freedom of association.

While Wellman makes a compelling case for the right of states to exclude refugees for asylum and resettlement, his analysis fails to acknowledge the current global reality of mass displacement and the result that *some* country or countries cannot exercise the right to freedom of association. That is, even if Wellman is right that freedom of association permits one nation to close its borders to all refugees, because the forcibly displaced must live somewhere, some other country must admit them. To point out a truism, because involuntary migrants are embodied creatures, they *must* inhabit some physical space on the earth.⁸ Because there is finite space on the earth, *some* state must forfeit its sovereign right to control its borders and exclude refugees and asylum seekers. There has to be at least one country that is not free to reject the displaced on the grounds of freedom of association.

In other words, Western states' enjoyment of the right of freedom of association and the right to refuse all refugees requires some other state or states to give up this right, since refugees—people who have fled their own country—must have some state and territory to live in. This remains true even if the state that takes in refugees is compensated financially or politically (through better terms for trade, for example) since it is still true that *some* country would have to accept these terms and allow the displaced onto their territory. If Wellman would like to preserve the right of freedom of association on universal grounds, he needs to take seriously the larger context in which this right functions.

Note that this does not apply to immigration in general. If all countries were to decide to exercise their sovereign right of freedom of association and exclude all immigrants, such people would be able to stay where they are, even if they have a strong preference for emigrating. However, this is precisely how immigrants in general differ from forced migrants like refugees and asylum seekers—they *cannot* stay where they are and continue to live a decent life and sometimes continue to live at all. If refugees are forced to return to their countries once they have left, then they may be killed, tortured, or experience other forms of intolerable suffering. The right of freedom of association as the ground for a state's right to control immigration and membership seems to hold only for immigration in general but not for forced migrants in particular.

Wellman concludes that even though the right of freedom of association means that we have no obligations to admit refugees, we nonetheless still have obligations to help. For Wellman, refugees and asylum seekers can be assisted, like "impoverished foreigners," through "exporting justice" (Wellman 2008, 129). Though not always advisable, one way to help would be to "intervene, militarily if necessary, in an unjust political environment to ensure that those currently vulnerable to the state are made safe in their homelands" (Wellman 2008, 129). This would not constitute a violation of sovereignty in the country intervened in because a country that produces asylum seekers is no longer a legitimate state. The duty to help is a "disjunctive duty": if states choose not to admit people fleeing their home countries, aid must be exported so that they no longer fear their domestic regimes. He, like Miller, is suggesting that simply shutting borders and doing nothing for the plight of refugees is not an option.

What I am suggesting is that given the 65.3 to 72 million people who lack a secure political community, military intervention to secure their states would either be impossible or mean committing ourselves to permanent and global warfare, often times with countries which in other respects are considered friends and allies (Pakistan, Iraq, etc.). Yet if we bracket his proposal for military intervention, one thing his work makes clear is that if we do have obligations to help refugees, they can extend beyond admitting them into our countries (though, as I will suggest, these aspects do not need to be mutually exclusive). I would like to suggest that we interpret Wellman's proposal to "export justice" as a way of responding to our obligations to refugees by some of the broader proposals that I will make throughout the book, such as encouraging other countries to resettle refugees, supporting policies around "temporary local integration" rather than refugee camps in countries which host refugees, and ultimately, by working towards a global agreement to set up a just refugee regime.

In short, Wellman's view, that the principle of freedom of association legitimizes a state's right to exclude refugees, cannot hold in a global community where over 65.3 million people are forced to live outside of their homes and some state or states are required to host them on their territory. Further, military intervention as a way of exporting justice may turn out to be more morally problematic than resettling refugees. As such, Wellman's view, like that of Walzer and Miller, does not adequately define our moral obligations to refugees.

§ Benhabib, Carens, and Gibney

In this section I highlight some alternative philosophical perspectives on forced displacement and show the ways in which more robust moral obligations may be grounded. To this end, I discuss the views of Benhabib, Carens, and Gibney, who all argue that we have more robust obligations to the displaced. Their positions show that we need not be constrained in thinking about obligations to refugees in the ways that Walzer, Miller, and Wellman suggest. Yet the views of Carens, Gibney, and Benhabib are limited in several ways. First, all three authors still place the most emphasis on the ethics of admission and working out moral norms around resettlement. As a result, though they all express an awareness of some of the difficulties around the current treatment of the displaced in the refugee regime, no one devotes a sustained analysis to it. Second, they fail to apply the principles they develop to the harms of encampment and containment. There are a number of resources within their positions that help us to think more clearly about what we owe the millions of people who are displaced and will seemingly never find a permanent home.

Seyla Benhabib's work on migration provides rich resources for thinking about our moral obligations to refugees. Benhabib (2004, 2011) takes up the issue of the morality of migration by considering "just membership practices." By just membership practices she means "principles and practices for incorporating aliens and strangers, immigrants and newcomers, refugees and asylum seekers into existing polities" (Benhabib 2004, 1, 2011, 138–139). She aims to lay a moral foundation for democratic states to mediate between the legitimate claims of outsiders who seek entrance into a given state with the will of citizens that, often at least, would prefer to exclude many or all outsiders. Her most important contribution to the debate on our moral obligations to refugees is not, I believe, this normative position, namely that though there is a human right to membership, this right must be balanced with the will of democratic majorities. Though interesting, this position ultimately does not further our moral obligations and lands us close to the current status quo (namely that we have some obligations to refugees but there is a lot of room for discretion). This aspect of her work can be broadly understood to be a contribution to the debate over the ethics of admission, the debate over who we are morally obliged to admit to our countries, and who we can justify excluding.

More significantly, her work shifts our thinking about membership practices per se. Benhabib argues that philosophers need to take seriously the new ways that membership exists around the world and that citizenship can be disaggregated without there being a violation of anyone's rights. In our current philosophical discourse, we have an all or nothing approach—either you are a citizen of a state with the ability to claim rights or you are a displaced person, outside the nation-state system, and at the mercy of host governments and humanitarian organizations which may or may not recognize your rights. What Benhabib points out is that one can imagine other forms of political membership that may be more appropriate for displaced people who live for prolonged periods of time in host states but nonetheless will never be integrated politically, via citizenship, in the country. It is worth looking carefully at her position.

Benhabib starts from the position that we do in fact have moral obligations to non-citizens, including refugees, who want to become members of our polities and goes so far as to claim that there is a "human right to membership," though no right to be admitted to a state.[9] A human right to membership is *not* a right to be admitted to the country of your choosing. The right only becomes relevant once you have been admitted to a state. Benhabib distinguishes five stages of migration—emigration, entry into a foreign country, absorption of short or long duration (visitation, study, business), residency of significant duration, and finally naturalization (i.e., access to citizenship rights). Once an individual has been admitted to a state in the second stage and has fulfilled certain conditions, a right to membership follows.[10] These obligations to non-citizens on the part of states are grounded on (i) our radical interdependence, and (ii) the fact that human migration is not an aberration but a feature of human existence. Let me begin by explaining the latter point.

For Benhabib, not only should migration not be treated as an anomaly that need not be taken seriously in normative theory (as Rawls does[11]), but rather she acknowledges a new contemporary reality where migration is a fact of life and non-citizens occupy various political positions. One of the grounds for Benhabib's argument for a human right to membership is the observation that in our contemporary, globalized world, "new modalities of membership" have emerged as a result of trends in migration and the reality that many non-citizens of various statuses live in a given territory (Benhabib 2004, 1). The result is that it no longer makes sense to think about political membership as it had been thought of before: as a status given only to long-term residents of a given territory, united by a shared national identity and culture, and comprising political citizenship. Rather than fear these new forms of attachments and see them as threats to national stability, Benhabib argues that "subnational as well as supranational spaces for democratic attachments and agency are emerging in the contemporary world, and they ought to be advanced with, rather than in lieu of, existing polities" (Benhabib 2004, 3). Though this view of citizenship challenges conventional understandings of sovereignty, she insists that this challenge need not be feared but ought to be embraced. Benhabib's account is particularly helpful since she acknowledges the importance of the role that transnational political actors—migrants, refugees, stateless people for example—play in contemporary political life and the need to find a place for them in our moral theory.

"Peoples are radically and not merely episodically interdependent" (Benhabib 2004, 93). This acknowledgment of our fundamental interdependence must be understood as the second ground of the right to membership. "The international system of peoples and states is characterized by such extensive interdependencies and the historical crisscrossing of fates and fortunes that the scope of special as well as general moral obligations to our fellow human beings far transcends the perspective of the territorially bounded state-centric system" (Benhabib 2004, 37). Indeed, she argues that recognition of the economic interdependence of peoples in a world society is what is missing from both Kant and Arendt, and renders them of limited use in the contemporary world in which economic interdependence is inescapable (Benhabib 2004, 72).

For Benhabib, the correct way to understand justice and moral obligations is not from the point of view of citizens within states but from the "world society" perspective, a perspective that sees migration as a complex global phenomenon. This perspective holds that the state is one entity on the global stage but certainly not the only or even necessarily the most important one. In the "global civil society," there are a host of other forms of associations that play increasingly important roles—individuals who move between states (migrants, refugees, asylum seekers); global economic institutions like the WTO and IMF; and transnational political institutions like the UN and the European Union. This means that in an important sense, the international political world has different levels of organization, association, and networks of interdependence that have different principles of organization (Benhabib 2004, 112).

It is from this perspective of a world society that we can correctly reason about our obligations across borders (Benhabib 2004, 37). According to this perspective, we ought to acknowledge the Kantian principle that if my actions affect the actions of others, then we have an obligation to regulate our actions under a common law that respects our equality as moral agents. Consequences of actions generate moral obligations, and once we become aware of how our actions influence the well-being of others, we must assume responsibility for the unintended and invisible consequences of our actions (Benhabib 2004, 104). The more we become aware of our interdependencies and the effects of our actions on others, the more responsible we become. This leads her to conclude in agreement with Pogge and Beitz that radical interdependence and *de facto* migration means that we have obligations beyond the Rawlsian "duty to assist" (Rawls 2001). For example, we have become increasingly aware that our patterns of energy consumption have environmental implications for people on the other side of the planet; "there is a dialectic here between the growth of social knowledge and the spread of moral responsibility" (Benhabib 2004, 104). One implication of this interdependence for Benhabib is that national policies and laws around citizenship and refugees should not be seen as unilateral acts of self-determination, where individual states exercise their right to determine the shape of their own communities. Rather, such decisions must be seen as "decisions with multilateral consequences that influence other entities in the world community. Sovereignty is a relational concept" (Benhabib 2004, 21).

Her *moral* argument for this right is as follows. If I am a member of a state in to which you are seeking membership, then I must be able to show you with good grounds, "grounds that would be acceptable to each of us equally," why you can never join (Benhabib 2004, 138). In order for these grounds to be mutually acceptable, they cannot be based on the *kind* of being that you are; that is, they cannot be based on your race, religion, gender, etc. Such grounds would not be permissible because they would reduce your capacity to exercise communicative freedom to the characteristics which were given to you by chance that you did not choose (Benhabib 2004, 139). Criteria that do not deny your communicative freedom—such as qualifications, marketable skills, material resources, length of stay, and language skills—are acceptable.

Benhabib puts forth an argument in favor of a disaggregated model of citizenship, where the practices and institutions of citizenship can be separated into three distinct categories: collective identity, privileges of political membership, and social rights and claims (Benhabib 2004, 145). This can be contrasted with what she refers to as the unitary model, where continuous residence in a territory is combined with a shared national identity, political rights, and common administrative jurisdiction. The existence of such disaggregated citizenship can be seen in the EU, where although the rights of European citizens are separated from those of non-citizens, there are different rights and privileges that are afforded to non-members at local, national, and supranational levels. As a result, a person "can have one set of rights but not another: one can have political rights without being a national, as is the case for EU nationals" (Benhabib 2004, 146). The Dutch model seems to be one exemplary way of distributing rights. The Netherlands grants "city-citizenship" to foreigners after five years of residency and allows them to take part in citywide elections and form political parties. This is a way of granting political voice, agency, and representation to non-citizens who are long-term residents and allows their views and needs to be better represented in national political dialogues. This does not alter their citizenship status as such—they are still not permitted to move freely within the EU as other European citizens are, for example—but it does provide a crucial way to grant some political rights to non-citizen residents. The danger, as Benhabib acknowledges, is that some residents will be permanently alienated from citizenship rights in this model but disaggregation seems to be the way political membership is moving. Because of its political importance, political philosophers ought to take this model more seriously in theorizing about citizenship.

Though Benhabib is at heart a cosmopolitan, she takes seriously the importance of local attachments. At the core of her work is the idea that there must be some mediation and convergence between the will of democratic majorities and international moral and legal norms. This work of mediation is best done, she argues, through "democratic iterations," which are "complex processes of public argument, deliberation, and learning through which universalist right claims are contested and contextualized, invoked and revoked, throughout legal and political institutions as well as in the public sphere of liberal democracies" (Benhabib 2004, 19). Elsewhere she writes that democratic iterations are "moral and political dialogues in which global principles and norms are appropriated and reiterated by constituencies of all sizes, in a series of interlocking conversations and interactions" (Benhabib 2004, 113). The idea of democratic iterations is roughly Benhabib's response to the question "what do we owe refugees?" In short, the answer is not absolute, but open to a degree of variation depending on how individual states mediate between local claims and international norms. Such mediation will not lead to clear and predictable outcomes but has the benefit of avoiding coercive enforcement since states are able to make international principles compatible with their national orientations.

Benhabib is clear that our radical interdependence and the moral responsibilities that this gives rise to must be balanced with the will of democratic states, and this constrains what we are obliged to do for refugees and others. Her belief in a human right to membership and the importance of disaggregated citizenship leads her to oppose practices that prevent people from seeking access to Western countries, especially refugees. For example, as a result of the perceived will of the citizens of Europe, European Union officials have begun to cooperate with leaders of the countries from which many refugees flee ("sender" countries) in order to prevent asylum seekers from arriving on European shores and to facilitate their readmission to their home countries. This of course is terrible for the asylum seekers themselves, who are fleeing these states that they perceive as oppressive. In other words, the simple will of a democracy is not sufficient to justify policies around membership practices; these must also be balanced with the moral obligations that arise out of our deep global interdependence.

Ultimately Benhabib agrees with Hannah Arendt (whom I will discuss in more detail in the next chapter) on the current condition of refugees. She acknowledges that although we have made a lot of progress on our treatment of refugees, Arendt's claim that losing citizenship status is tantamount to losing human rights is not altogether wrong. "Even in one of the most developed rights regimes of our world, refugees and asylum seekers still find themselves in quasi-criminal status. Their human rights are curtailed; they have no civil and political rights of association and representation. The extension of full human rights to these individuals and the decriminalization of their status is one of the most important tasks of cosmopolitan justice in our world" (Benhabib 2004, 168).

Though innovative in many ways, Benhabib's position does not help us to see how to extend our moral obligations to the displaced much beyond the status quo. Because so much of her work is focused on our moral obligations to admit refugees, she does not consider how we ought to treat the millions of people for whom no one acknowledges a right to membership. Further, she thinks that states can deny entrance to people so long as the state does not deny their communicative freedom; a state must be able to give "grounds that would be acceptable to each of us equally" why an individual cannot join (Benhabib 2004, 138). Grounds that do not deny communicative freedom are qualifications, marketable skills, material resources, length of stay, and language skills. This in many ways seems to parallel the justification that states that host large populations of displaced people give for not integrating them, temporarily or permanently. Namely, the justification that the displaced can be denied membership is often precisely that they would be too much of an economic drain on the society since they lack skills and material resources, and may be linguistically, racially, and ethnically different. In Benhabib's view, this would seem to be a sufficient reason to deny membership since it does not deny the communicative freedom of the displaced. Yet this is precisely the thinking that has led to the current status quo around refugee warehousing and long-term encampment.

Nonetheless, there are two essential elements from Benhabib's analysis that are important for a richer understanding of our moral obligations to refugees. First, we must understand the problem of displacement from a global perspective, from the perspective of a "world society" (Benhabib

2004). When we look at the problem of refugees from a state level and focus only on how many refugees we are obliged to admit, it is easy to ignore the question of what happens to the millions of people who are excluded from all states. It is also a perspective that allows us to see—and morally evaluate—non-state actors who play important roles in the refugee regime, such as the UNHCR and other NGOs. From Benhabib's perspective, the complexity of migration and the increasing role of "global civil society" is not a fact to be lamented. Rather, it points to the reality that the older nation-state perspective is not the only one with moral or political significance. It is from this perspective that we can begin to see how our interconnection with others may ground our responsibility. For Benhabib it shows that we ought to take Kantian moral principles seriously and acknowledge that if our actions affect others, we have a moral obligation to regulate our actions so that they treat others as equals. In other words, we have to take seriously the consequences of our actions, intentional and unintentional, and the way they may have a collective impact.

This is why her claim that sovereignty must be understood as a relational concept is useful. Sovereignty, like individual autonomy, is a legitimate moral good and necessary for self-rule, yet it cannot be excised without consideration of all those with whom a state is interconnected and interdependent. This is crucial for seeing the injustices in the refugee regime. Many of the harms of the refugee regime result not from the actions of a single harmful policy, but are often the collective result of many different states and international organizations all serving their own purposes. But since refugees and stateless people bear the brunt of the collective outcome of various states' policies on refugees, they must be considered in seemingly sovereign decisions. National policies around displaced people cannot be understood as unilateral acts of sovereignty. The collective result of these policies is the *de facto* exclusion of millions of people from all states, a consequence that ought to be considered unacceptable even if the outcome is not the result of bad intentions.[12] In order to avoid this outcome, states must take seriously the effect that their policies will have for the millions of displaced people.

The second aspect of Benhabib's work that is important is her model of disaggregated citizenship, one where long-term residents are granted rights, but rights that may be different from citizens' rights. On this view, membership in a state is not an all or nothing proposition but can be separated and the rights and responsibilities divided. This stands in contrast to the unitary model where citizenship is assumed to mean continuous residence on a territory combined with a shared national identity, political rights, and common administrative jurisdiction. There can be subnational as well as supranational spaces for democratic attachments that ought to be encouraged alongside normal political processes.

Concerning the rights of refugees, it is common to still think in terms of the unitary, all or nothing model. Either a displaced person is resettled in a third country or voluntarily returns to their home countries and receives full citizenship; or the displaced person remains in refugee camps or urban spaces without the ability to claim even the most basic of rights, often for prolonged periods of time. A disaggregated model of citizenship would allow us to devise ways that refugees and stateless people could be incorporated into the territories in which they are living, either temporarily or permanently, in ways that our current approach does not. Her example of disaggregated citizenship in the Netherlands provides an example of what disaggregated citizenship in a refugee camp might look like. Long-term residents have "city citizenship," which allows them to vote and form political parties, even though they are not considered citizens of the EU. They are able to take part in the political process, are granted basic rights, and are considered part of the political community though only in a limited way.

The model of disaggregated citizenship would help us to overcome what Aleinikoff calls the "membership bias" on the part of Western states, the assumption that what refugees want most is membership in a new state (Aleinikoff 1992). In his view, refugees themselves do not necessarily share this assumption. "It is at least plausible that refugees might prefer an ambiguity and flexibility that does not compel an immediate consideration of identity questions and that keeps options open for future return or resettlement" (Aleinikoff 1992, 134). Benhabib's model of disaggregated citizenship would be a way of implementing this kind of ambiguity and flexibility and may be an improvement over the current ways that most people live out their lives in refugee camps, without access to political forums, and the ability to participate in their collective outcome or act with political voice and agency. Though, as Benhabib acknowledges, there is always a danger of permanent alienage, this danger is already the reality for the vast majority of long-term displaced people. A disaggregated model of citizenship would at least provide an alternative to this de facto outcome.

Two other philosophers, Joseph Carens and Matthew Gibney, try to reorient the moral approach liberal democratic states take towards refugees. Carens' recent work on immigration and refugees is concerned with reforming the global refugee regime even while he focuses on the moral obligations of liberal democracies in particular. He acknowledges that although important, resettlement is actually "irrelevant to most" refugees because of the high number of refugees compared to the few places available for resettlement (Carens 2013, 197). Further, he acknowledges that many refugees stay in camps for years, and this "clearly represents a terrible failure to meet the moral claims of refugees" (Carens 2013, 206). He derives two claims from this that are important. First, he argues that resettlement ought to be a duty and not merely an act of charity or generosity. If states acknowledged resettlement as a binding duty, like non-refoulement, resettlement may be able to address the needs of the displaced. Second, he argues that we ought to work out a way of distributing resettlement that is just and does not disproportionately burden some states. Gibney similarly argues for both of these duties, as well as the duty to work towards creating a national and international climate that is more favorable for refugee protection.

For Carens, there are three possible grounds that can generate obligations to admit refugees. First, it is widely agreed that if states cause the production of refugees, they have stronger obligations to help them than do states that are not involved. In other words, causal connections generate moral duties. For example, many agree that we had stronger obligations to help Vietnamese refugees during the Vietnam War than refugees fleeing conflicts that we were not involved with. Second, humanitarian considerations can also generate duties to help refugees. Because refugees often have such urgent needs, and because we are in a position to help them, this can give rise to obligations to admit refugees. Third, the normative presuppositions of the modern state system can give rise to obligations to admit refugees. Because the world is divided into sovereign states where each state is responsible for its citizens, obligations arise when this system breaks down, as it does in the case of refugees. States have a collective responsibility to correct the foreseeable failures with this institutional arrangement by admitting people into their states whose government has failed to provide them safety and meet their basic needs. In this case, the duty to admit refugees arises from the claim of states to legitimately exercise power in a world divided into states.

In Carens' view, the obligation of Western democracies to admit refugees arises most strongly from the second ground, the profound need of refugees and our ability to help (also known as Samaritan duties). While it would also be true that we have obligations to refugees that we helped create, this ground cannot account for our moral obligations in general. Further, he argues that while it would be pragmatically useful to be able to appeal to the self-interest of people living in the receiving states—they would be better off in some way—Carens doesn't believe this can be done in a sufficiently robust way. Helping refugees is rarely in our best interest, and in many cases opposes what usually seems good or important for a state.

Our obligations towards refugees are grounded in humanitarian concern for the urgent needs of the displaced. Once we take this seriously, we can begin to see, according to Carens, that refugees have two distinct sets of needs—needs in the long and short terms. What is unique about this approach is his emphasis that both sets of obligations are equally important. For Carens, because the primary consideration for refugees in the immediate aftermath of their displacement is safety, refugee camps may be appropriate as a response to a particular emergency. However, "this is not sufficient as a permanent solution" (Carens 2013, 203). Because all people have a right to membership in a society, refugees must either be allowed to settle in the country they are living in or be resettled in a new country.[13] This is rooted in the moral principle that people cannot be kept in a temporary status indefinitely. "One implication of this idea of a right to membership," he argues, "is that there is a limit to how long refugees can be kept in a temporary status" (Carens 2013, 204). In his view, the fact that time has passed for refugees living in camps does not make our moral obligations to them weaker; on the contrary, the longer refugees are in limbo, the stronger are our obligations to find a home for them. He insists that refugee camps are "a terrible failure to meet the moral claims of refugees" (Carens 2013, 206). Yet unlike David Miller, who also agrees that refugee camps are morally problematic, Carens argues that the unacceptability of refugee camps gives rise to a duty to resettle refugees. For Miller, although camps are morally problematic, the right of self-determination still takes precedence and does not require states to resettle refugees if they do not want to. For Carens, by contrast, the current state of the refugee regime means that we have a "strong and extensive moral duty" to resettle refugees (Carens 2013, 198).

Matthew Gibney too argues that resettlement ought to be a duty, and this duty is rooted in the "humanitarian principle," the principle that states have an obligation to assist refugees when the costs of doing so are low.[14] Gibney grounds his view of the moral obligations of states in the humanitarian principle because he sees it as a way of compromising between the commitments of nationalism or partialism (the belief that the interests of compatriots ought to take precedence over others) and cosmopolitanism or impartialism (the belief that all people, regardless of nationality, ought to be given the same moral consideration). Because the humanitarian principle recognizes that there are duties that arise from our common humanity, as impartialists stress, it takes seriously the values that underlie this moral orientation. But because it only obliges states to do what is "low cost," it leaves room for states to determine their own policies, as partialists stress. For this reason, he argues that the humanitarian principle will be able to gain the widest possible acceptance as the ground for our moral obligations to refugees. Though both Carens and Gibney understand this principle in a similar way to Walzer (who also argued that our obligations to refugees are rooted in a principle of "mutual aid"), they derive very different conclusions from it. For Carens and Gibney, the humanitarian principle entails that states shift the focus away from asylum and towards resettling refugees currently living in camps. They both claim that resettlement should be seen not as a supererogatory act—"burdens that states undertake separately from their duties under international law and less explicitly, common morality" (Gibney 2004, 239)—but as duties or obligations.

For Gibney, this means that resettlement should take priority over non-refoulement as a moral principle.[15] It's not that there is an inherent tension between non-refoulement and resettlement; rather, Gibney is challenging the political choice to take more seriously the moral demands of asylum seekers (and the right of non-refoulement) over refugees in camps. In Gibney's view, ethically speaking, we ought to give priority to resettlement over non-refoulement. The principle of non-refoulement asserts implicitly that we have stronger obligations to those close to us, on our territory than those far away from us, regardless of their need.[16] This link between aid and connection made sense prior to technological communication and globalization. But with current technology, "universal obligations to refugees can now be exercised universally" (Gibney 2004, 240). Further, refugees who are able to reach Western countries and claim asylum are often the ones with contacts and resources and who are young and healthy enough to make the trip. These are not necessarily the refugees who are most in need. Ultimately, as Carens also suggests, though resettlement ought to take priority over non-refoulement, we should not abandon the principle of non-refoulement given its wide moral acceptance. The point for Gibney is simply that much more concern ought to be directed towards resettlement.[17]

For Gibney, in addition to seeing resettlement as a duty, the humanitarian principle demands that Western states respect the principle of non-refoulement, boost efforts around the world to resettle refugees and, in the long term, work towards creating a national and international climate that is more favorable for refugee protection. The extent to which states are willing to uphold these obligations will depend on the way the idea of "cost" is interpreted. This gives rise to one further obligation grounded in the principle of humanity: states ought to try to shape the political climate so that these costs are interpreted in ways favorable to refugees. States, he writes, have "a supplementary duty to do what they can to create a domestic and international environment in which the amount of protection provided for refugees at low cost will be maximized" (Gibney 2004, 244). This could take the form of influencing the public's opinion through public campaigns, supporting programs that try to overcome xenophobia and racism, engendering more bipartisanship, and promoting the value of asylum. When foreigners are misunderstood as legitimate threats, anything goes in terms of how states are permitted to deal with them (expanded detention, new deportation procedures, and indefinite detention are examples). States can do a lot to untangle the fear of refugees based on their character with a more legitimate fear of refugees based on their anonymity (i.e., that we don't have knowledge about their backgrounds or intentions and, even after screening, the fear that ill-intentioned people will infiltrate our countries). This may help to overcome the "unprecedented consensus" among liberal democratic states and their citizens that refugees constitute as much a threat as an asset (Gibney 2004, 255).

Both Gibney and Carens also agree that states recognizing the principle of humanity as a ground for our moral obligations to refugees must also acknowledge they have a strong reason to participate in and promote cooperative burden sharing plans.[18] For Carens, the factors that would determine what a fair allocation of responsibilities would entail are the following: receiving states' absorptive capacity, population density, economic capacity (overall wealth and economic dynamism), cultural similarity, religion and ethnicity, and history of admitting immigrants. This process of allocating refugees wouldn't need an enforcement body; just an international covenant to formalize the process. Gibney argues that to determine fair allocation of responsibilities for resettlement, we must look at the "integrative abilities" of each state. He acknowledges that this is not a straightforward question, since "integrative ability" is politically constructed and will depend on how states see their economy, history, cultural affinity, etc. Consequently, he thinks the best way to determine how many refugees a state is able to integrate is by looking at the judgments that states themselves make about this question by examining their immigration policies and commitments. Carens, like Gibney, acknowledges that how the duty to resettle gets implemented is bound to be contested; he points out, though, that even this would be an improvement. "At this point it would be a tremendous advance for most states even to acknowledge that they have a binding responsibility to resettle refugees" and hence to engage in public debates about how to discharge this duty (Carens 2013, 215). Even the US, the country that resettles the most refugees, does not acknowledge a formal obligation but insists that it is a matter of charity.[19]

Finally, what if a state, like the US or Canada, decides that it has done enough to help refugees, even while there still remain millions of refugees in need of a permanent state? In other words, when can a state say that it has done enough? In Carens' view, the answer is "almost never" (Carens 2013, 219). Given the inability of refugees to meet their basic needs and to have their most basic rights protected, Carens thinks that it is hard for states to argue that their less imperative interests ought to take precedence over this. This view is of course not universally shared. Miller and Walzer argue that ultimately states have the final say on when they have done enough. For Carens, however, "the fact that a state has the moral right to make a decision does not entail the view that its decision is justifiable or that it is immune from criticism. Having the right to make a decision is not the same as having a right to act arbitrarily or with complete discretion" (Carens 2013, 219). The example of the St. Lewis, the ship carrying hundreds of Jewish refugees during the Second World War that was turned away by the US, is the kind of example he has in mind. This case shows that often a state's collective moral judgment can be deeply flawed. In other words, simply because a state believes they have done enough to help refugees is not sufficient to show that they in fact have done so.

Like Benhabib, both Gibney and Carens show how we might develop more robust obligations to the forcibly displaced. They are both helpful in pointing out that the principle of humanitarianism gives rise to a duty to resettle, along with a duty to fairly distribute this burden. Both norms would go a long way towards improving the refugee regime and the lives of millions of people and ought to be included in a just refugee regime. However, though Carens is concerned with how democratic states ought to treat refugees, he does not explicitly discuss the ways that policies and practices of democratic states impact the decisions of other countries. For example, he says that a "rich democratic state cannot create camps where refugees are prevented from having contact with the rest of the population and are provided only with basic levels of food, clothing, and shelter, even if the provision of such basic levels of support would be equal to what the refugees could have expected if their membership rights had been respected in their country of origin" (Carens 2013, 204). However, he doesn't discuss the extent to which we tolerate and even promote such policies on the part of states in other parts of the world, or at the very least, fail to challenge the acceptability of practices like these. Presumably, if it's wrong for us to do it, it should be wrong for us to support it as well.

Carens and Gibney are right about the moral obligations that arise from the principle of humanitarianism—given the current state of the refugee regime, resettlement ought to be greatly expanded and thought of as a duty. However, the duty to resettle needs to be supplemented with an *ethics of the temporary*. That is, we ought to think much more seriously about a morally acceptable way to house refugees and allow them to live with dignity while they are waiting to be resettled or to return to their home countries. In addition to the obligations that Carens and Gibney argue for, we have an obligation to explore other ways that the refugee regime might be structured so that refugees are not kept in camps and maintain their dignity and autonomy. In other words, while resettlement may be the ultimate goal we should support, we have to morally scrutinize the ways in which the global community cares for the displaced while they are waiting for something more permanent, since, as I discussed in Chapter One, this temporary period can last decades, even generations.

The more expansive set of obligations that Benhabib, Gibney, and Carens argue for are helpful in seeing the moral status of the forcibly displaced. But their views still overwhelmingly focus on the ethics of admission and fail to take seriously the role that liberal democracies play in setting up and sustaining many of the injustices associated with the current refugee regime. As a result, though they all express an awareness of some of the difficulties around the current treatment of the displaced, no one devotes a sustained analysis to it. Benhabib, Carens, and Gibney each apply their principles only in a limited way to the issue of the harms of encampment and containment even though there are a number of resources within their positions that help us to think more clearly about what we owe the millions of people who are displaced and will never find a permanent home.

§ Conclusion

In conclusion, I'd like to turn to what I see as one of the primary limitations of the various philosophical views discussed in this chapter. The limitation has to do with how the problem around refugees is framed and an assumption which underlies many of the approaches. What many of the authors in this chapter have been grappling with is how to give a foundation for our moral obligation to admit refugees while simultaneously maintaining an ethical basis for closure. For philosophers like Walzer and Miller, the primary philosophical question is to what extent we are obliged to admit refugees and on what basis we are justified in excluding people with urgent moral claims. This question remains the dominant one whether you agree that we have much stronger obligations to admit refugees than we currently do (as people like Benhabib, Carens, and Gibney do) or that states are justified in closing their doors to "all potential immigrants, even refugees desperately seeking asylum from incompetent or corrupt political regimes" (Wellman 2008, 109). Though not the only concern, justifying including or excluding the displaced from our political communities can be seen as one of the biggest concerns for philosophers of immigration and refugees.

The question that is rarely raised in the debate is: what happens to people who we justifiably exclude? Do we have any moral obligations to people who remain outside of all political communities? Such people remain in a position of statelessness for a prolonged period of time, where they are without political rights, community, or representation. Prolonged encampment and long-term displacement, which are the result of uncoordinated policies of various sovereign states, are never raised as moral issues by normative philosophers, as I argue they ought to be. The reason these questions are never raised, I argue, has to do with how we understand international institutions in the global political system.

If we look at an institutional analysis of human rights put forth by people like Thomas Pogge (2008) and Charles Beitz (2009), we see an idealized picture of how human rights are supposed to function. Though human rights are the rights we have by virtue of being human, they are nonetheless addressed to us as members of particular states. In Beitz's view, human rights ought to be understood on a two-level model, where human rights apply first to the political institutions of states, including their constitutions, laws, and policies; states bear "the primary responsibilities to respect and protect human rights" (Beitz 2009, 108). When states fail to protect and fulfill human rights, international institutions are supposed to step up. The second level only comes into play when states are not able to respect, protect, and fulfill human rights. Under these circumstances, "the international community and those acting as its agents" become responsible for human rights (Beitz 2009, 108).[20] For Beitz, a "government's failure to carry out its first-level responsibilities may be a reason for action for appropriately placed and capable 'second-level' agents outside of the state" (Beitz 2009, 109). In other words, because human rights are "matters of international concern" (Beitz 2009, 109), when individual states fail to uphold and protect human rights, "appropriately placed and capable" international institutions must step in and assume responsibility.

For Beitz, then, if a state fails to protect the human rights of one of its members and she becomes a refugee, and no other state sees it in their interest to take her in, then "the international community and those acting as its agents" become the responsible parties. Refugees remain protected, and thus it makes sense that we have no other obligations to refugees who remain, justifiably or unjustifiably, outside of our states since we are able to assume that international institutions are mandated to protect them. The assumption underlying normative philosophical discussions around refugees, then, is that international agents like the UN High Commissioner for Refugees (UNHCR) or some similar body will bear the responsibility to respect and protect the human rights of those forcibly displaced from their homes.

As discussed in detail in Chapter One, the reason that this assumption is problematic is because of a number of features of the international system. The consensus, for the most part, is that not only does the international community often fail to respect and protect the human rights of refugees, but often the system itself contributes to their systematic dehumanization.[21] For Agier, humanitarian organizations that work with refugees and displaced people ought to be seen not as a systematic form of care for vulnerable populations, but as a mode of sovereign power and control, an entity which has the power of life and death over the displaced (Agier 2011, 65).[22] In his words, international organizations that step up to help refugees in the name of human rights protection are "no more than a euphemistic justification for controlling the undesirables" (Agier 2011, 211). Rather than protecting the interests and rights of the displaced, as I noted in Chapter One, the UNHCR has come to be seen as serving the interests of Western states that, for the most part, entail keeping large portions of stateless people away from their borders.[23] In the words of one scholar, "states funding the UNHCR have managed to cultivate a shift in the organization's ethic from one of facilitating resettlement to one largely concerned with containing refugee flows close to the regions of displacement" (Franke 2009, 317).

This has led to what Verdirame and Harrell-Bond have called the "Janus face" of refugee humanitarianism. Humanitarianism is in part cosmopolitan and caring, and in part, "often callous, sometimes cruel, and—nearly always—ineffectual" (Verdirame and Harrell-Bond 2005, 333). In this way, "power exercised under a humanitarian guise was not so different from power in other guises" (Verdirame and Harrell-Bond 2005, 333). What is unique, however, in this relationship is that the power of humanitarian organizations in refugee camps is not curtailed by law nor limited by external oversight. This is because the laws of host countries often cease to apply in refugee camps; "camps are spaces that are virtually *beyond the rule of law*" (Verdirame and Harrell-Bond 2005, 334). This situation leads Agier to conclude, "the humanitarian world is a totalitarianism that has power over life (to let live or survive) and death (to let die) over the individual that it views as absolute victim" (Agier 2011, 196). In short, the assumption that international organizations can bear the responsibility for refugees if states justifiably exclude them—and ought to be given the power and resources to do so—is extremely problematic.

If we add to this two well-known facts about contemporary refugee experience, we see further why the normative approach is limited. First, the vast majority of refugees will never be resettled in Western resettlement states; currently less than 1% of people deemed refugees by the UNHCR are ever resettled,[24] and there is no reason, given the current political state of affairs and economic crises, to think that this will improve dramatically in the near future. Second, the vast majority of refugees will be stateless for 15 years or more, so the norm is long-term displacement rather than short-term, emergency situations.[25] The vast majority of people in situations of long-term displacement live in refugee camps that are governed by humanitarian organizations.[26] As Loescher puts it, "the majority of the world's refugees are not offered permanent asylum or opportunity to integrate into local communities by most Third World governments. Rather, they are kept separate and dependent on external assistance provided by the international community" (Loescher 1993, 9). In other words, given that the vast majority of displaced people will spend the duration of their lives outside of states, the vast majority of refugees and stateless people will be unaffected by the ethics of admissions.

What I have demonstrated above is that normative philosophical analysis, with its emphasis on the ethics of admissions, provides an insufficient moral analysis of our obligations to refugees. The failure of the international community to step in and assume the responsibilities for the displaced in lieu of states means that we can no longer take for granted that a refusal to admit refugees means that some other solution will be found.

What I suggest is that given this contemporary reality, it is important to ask two questions. First, what, if anything, do we owe to the millions of people who live for decades in refugee camps without the prospect of being resettled in a new state or able to return to their own states? Second, given that the institutional understanding of human rights is insufficient to grapple with the contemporary experience of refugees and encampment, how can we reframe the harm of statelessness in order to better address this reality? In order to address these questions, we need to take seriously that in losing membership in a political community, one loses something fundamental to the human condition. I refer to this as the ontological deprivation of statelessness. Once we take these ideas seriously, we can see that it is urgent to find ways to protect the dignity of the displaced while they are in these in-between situations, between home and a durable solution, between being a citizen of one state and a citizen of another. A phenomenological understanding of the experience of being without a state is missing from these normative analyses. The aim of the following chapter is to develop such an account.

Notes

1 I refer to philosophers who are interested in thinking about our moral obligations to refugees, such as the ones I discuss in this chapter, as normative philosophers to distinguish them from continental philosophers, whom I will discuss in Chapter Three, who are more interested in a phenomenological understanding of refugees. I've chosen to use this term to avoid the sometimes ambiguous

phrase "liberal philosophers," since "liberal" can have different connotations in different contexts, though most normative philosophers are liberal in the most general sense.
2 Not all philosophers believe this can be done. Philip Cole, for example, argues that the question of membership shows that "there is an irresolvable contradiction between liberal theory's apparent universalism and its concealed particularism" (Cole 2000, 2).
3 For example, Singer and Singer (1988), Carens (1992), Barbieri (1998), Cole (2000), Gibney (2004), Nyers (2006), and Wellman (2008), among others, have all written about our moral obligations to refugees. Although there is no consensus on the question of obligations, one important point is agreed upon by all these authors: the question of whether we are obliged to admit refugees to our country is *the* primary moral question.
4 As we will see in the discussion below, both Walzer's and Wellman's views of refugees are rooted in the principle of mutual aid, but they draw very different conclusions. For Walzer, this principle gives rise to the obligation to admit *some* refugees but allows latitude in terms of choosing which refugees and how many to admit. For Wellman, duties to refugees based on the principle of mutual aid do not trump the right to freedom of association and thus do not give rise to any obligations to admit refugees, only to "export justice" to help them.
5 We need only think of any of the measures taken by EU, Australian, or American officials to prevent the thousands of "helpless and desperate people" from reaching their shores (discussed in Chapter One) to realize that these conditions simply do not hold in the contemporary world.
6 It is worth pointing out Joseph Carens' criticism of this point. Cities in the US seem to have very distinct characters—Boston is very different from Miami, LA is very different from South Bend. Yet this has not required that cities close their borders and only permit residents like themselves (Carens 1992). It is not clear then that "communities of character" do require the right to exclude. Also see Scheffler (2007).
7 Though both Miller and Walzer think that military intervention is a way to discharge our duties to refugees, politically speaking it is highly implausible. Western states have been reluctant to intervene to stop even terrible abuses of state power. Indeed, Samantha Power has shown that we have *very rarely* intervened to stop even genocide when death tolls are in the hundreds of thousands and there are effective methods to do so (Bosnia is the one exception) (Power 2013). Given this tremendous reluctance to get involved militarily in genocides or other civil conflicts for *any* reason, it hardly seems like a plausible solution to think that states will intervene militarily on behalf of refugees. In some ways, this is asking even more than to allow refugees to resettle.
8 I am taking this insight from Jeremy Waldron, who made a similar claim for homeless people in the US (Waldron 1991).
9 The other aspect of a right to membership is an injunction against denaturalization.
10 There are a number of other rights entailed in the right to membership. For example, there is a right to know how to become a citizen that obliges the state to make conditions for naturalization clear, transparent, and accessible, rather than subject to bureaucratic will. Further, states cannot criminalize simply being an immigrant or foreigner—such a person must have due process, the right to representation in one's language, and the right to council. These are the civil and political rights that must accompany a human right to membership.
11 Rawls writes, "a democratic society . . . is to be viewed as a . . . closed social system . . . in that entry into it is only by birth and exit from it is only by death" (Rawls, *Political Liberalism* 1993, 41). Further, his methodological starting point for his analysis of global justice in *Law of Peoples* is that the causes

of migration (human rights violations by non-liberal and non-decent regimes) would no longer exist: "the problem of immigration is ... eliminated as a serious problem in a realistic utopia" (Rawls, *Law of Peoples* 2001, 9).

12 Thomas Nagel argues that "radical poverty" is unacceptable primarily because of its outcome, not because of the intentions of the actors who created it. He writes that radical inequality is wrong even if it is not the result of anyone doing anything illegal or morally wrong, and thus any system that permits this outcome is morally objectionable. For Nagel, "the pure workings of market exchange, governed entirely by supply and demand, do not constitute a legitimate institution of property if they permit certain kinds of outcomes" (Nagel 2008, 54).

13 Carens argues that there is a right to membership implicit in the Refugee Convention. "In effect, the Convention says that it is not enough to provide refugees with physical safety. People have a right to membership in a society. If they cannot any longer be members of their country of origin, they must be given access to membership in some other state" (Carens 2013, 203–204).

14 In Gibney's view, the principle of humanitarianism is also rooted in a "duty of charity" found in the natural law tradition. For example, see Locke: "so *Charity* gives every man a Title to so much out of another's Plenty, as will keep him from extreme want, where he has no means to subsist otherwise" (Locke, first treaty, sec 42; quoted in Gibney 2004, 232).

15 For Gibney, there are also practical benefits to this change in perspective: resettlement can be arranged before refugees arrive in a country and thus there is greater predictability, less risk, and greater financial ease.

16 Carens too argues that we ought to "break the link between claim and place" (Carens 2013, 216).

17 This is in line with Carens' view that it would be imprudent to abandon the principle of non-refoulement because it does not prioritize those most in need (as Singer and Singer argue) precisely because it would be imprudent to abandon a principle of aid that is already widely accepted (see Singer and Singer [1988] and Carens [1992]).

18 Ferracioli argues that what must *precede* the establishment of a more just refugee regime is a large increase in resettlement. For her, the international community should move "collectively and progressively" to increase their quotas in order to alleviate some of the motivational constraints to reformulating the refugee regime (Ferracioli 2014, 139).

19 According to the 1980 Refugee Act, the legal framework for the US action on refugees, the official US position denies any duty or obligation to resettle refugees. The Refugee Act explicitly states that "the underlying principle is that refugee admission is an exceptional *ex gratia* act provided by the United States in furthering foreign and humanitarian policies" (quoted in Singer and Singer 1988, 116).

20 He notes that this second level of international concern and action is perhaps the most distinctive feature of contemporary human rights practice (Beitz 2009, 115).

21 "UNHCR is the main authority that exercises power and effective control in camps; combined with its role in the status-determination process, this power means that UNHCR is not simply unable to promote respect for the rights of refugees, but is often responsible for the violation of these rights" (Verdirame and Harrell-Bond 2005, 17).

22 "There is a specific order and *organization of power* in the camp and more generally in the place of humanitarian intervention, which the concept of 'humanitarian government' is designed to express as closely as possible. This power defines its own space as one of exception, a frontier, an out-place in the sense

that individuals are treated and managed as nameless victims devoid of identity" (Agier 2011, 213–214).
23 As noted in Chapter One, the reason the UNHCR is so interested in fulfilling the interests of the West is that they are dependent on them for funding. "Financed by donations and periodic appeals, rather than as a structural part of the United Nations, it has always been constrained by the interests of the rich 'donor nations'" (Stevens 2006, 54). Likewise, keeping the displaced in camps can be seen as an effective funding strategy—in camps, the displaced can be seen and counted, and thus support the UNHCR's claims for funding. This is what allows Verdirame and Harrell-Bond to conclude that "UNHCR continued to support the encampment policy because of its perceived attraction to donors" (Verdirame and Harrell-Bond 2005, 17). In other words, what determined the UNHCR's policy was not protection of refugees, but institutional survival in a competitive funding environment.
24 Specifically, less than 1% of the 10.5 million people that the UNHCR considers refugees are ever recommended by the agency for resettlement (cited on the website for the United Nations High Commissioner for Refugees: http://www.unhcr.org/pages/4a16b1676.html).
25 In the view of the International Federation of Red Cross and Red Crescent Societies, most forced migrants are either in a situation of protracted displacement or are permanently dispossessed. Of the 10.4 million people the UNHCR considers refugees, 70% are in protracted exile (International Federation of Red Cross and Red Crescent Societies 2012, 9 and 17).
26 Arendt was perhaps the first to notice this phenomenon in *The Origins of Totalitarianism*, first published in 1948. She writes that the internment camp, which prior to WWI was the exception rather than the rule, "has become the routine solution for the problem of domicile of the 'displaced persons'" (Arendt 1978, 279).

3 Hannah Arendt and the Ontological Deprivation of Statelessness

I have been arguing throughout this book that we ought to morally scrutinize how the forcibly displaced are treated while they are between homes and the use of refugee camps as a way to deal with large-scale, protracted refugee situations. I have suggested that once we understand the refugee regime and the harms that arise from it, we have a moral obligation to reject the policy of long-term encampment as the de facto solution to the problem of unwanted and superfluous people in the world. In order to do this, we need to expand our approach to thinking about moral obligations. For a number of reasons, the primary moral obligation states and their citizens have considered is the obligation to resettle refugees. Yet I have shown in the previous chapters why this is insufficient: it fails to consider our treatment of refugees while they are awaiting a solution and does not take seriously encampment as a moral harm. I argue throughout the book that we have obligations to ensure that the displaced live dignified lives while they are awaiting a more permanent solution.

In this chapter, I seek to deepen our understanding of the harm of encampment in order to support my claim that we ought to reject encampment as a solution. Using the work of Hannah Arendt, I demonstrate that forced displacement (or statelessness, as she sometimes refers to it) entails two distinct harms that must be analyzed separately. The first harm is legal/political—the loss of a political community and a legal identity in the form of citizenship. Arendt's first critique of statelessness is that it entails the loss of a legal identity and a political community, and it is only within this political community that human rights can be protected. Despite over 50 years of changes in international law and human rights conventions around stateless people and refugees, their rights—both legal and human—remain fundamentally precarious outside the nation-state.

Though this is a crucial point in understanding statelessness, this is not Arendt's most fundamental critique of statelessness. If this were the only harm of statelessness, we might say that the harm could be addressed by simply insisting on more resettlement or quicker repatriation, and refugee camps, since they are necessary in order for these solutions to occur, would be seen as unproblematic. Arendt argued that there is a much more fundamental loss that comes with statelessness, one to which prolonged encampment contributes. I refer to this loss as the *ontological* deprivation, that is, the loss of something fundamental to a person's humanity. I argue that ignoring the agency of refugees for long durations through policies of encampment and containment constitutes a moral harm to refugees. Taking seriously the ontological deprivation of statelessness has important consequences for how we think about our moral obligations.

The ontological deprivation has three different dimensions: the loss of identity and reduction to bare life; the expulsion from common humanity; and finally, the loss of agency understood not as a subjective disposition, but an ability to have your words and actions be recognized as meaningful and politically relevant. I make two points about the nature of the ontological deprivation. First, when stateless people are placed into camps or allowed to disappear into crowded urban centers with no formal recognition, this exclusion itself represents a fundamental harm. Many believe that refugee camps are a matter of practical necessity—there is nowhere else to put large groups of unwanted people. Yet for Arendt, I argue, it is important to see these camps as morally problematic because they effectively exclude people from what she referred to as "the common world." This expulsion from the common world is a fundamental aspect of the ontological deprivation. This point supports my argument that encampment ought to be seen as a moral harm. Second, I argue that we must understand this exclusion as a form of abandonment, in Giorgio Agamben's sense of the term. Abandonment for him does not mean that stateless people are left to themselves, but rather that they remain directly impacted by us through their formal exclusion. Their very identities and modes of existence are defined almost entirely by their exclusion. Agamben terms this form of abandonment the inclusive exclusion. This in turn grounds the connection I use to establish responsibility for forced displacement in Chapter Four.

Importantly, once we take seriously the ontological deprivation as a distinct harm, other moral obligations and ways we ought to help the displaced become more evident. Addressing the ontological deprivation of statelessness may require that we think about ways that stateless people may be able to keep a meaningful political identity, and resist a reduction to bare life, even though they may be formally bereft of citizenship or political membership. Once these two sets of harms are pulled apart, we will see that even though we have had limited success in addressing the political harm of a lack of citizenship (i.e., by resettling stateless people in new political communities or repatriating them to their old ones), there are nonetheless other ways to address the second kind of harm, the ontological deprivation. Refugee policy, supported by Western states, ought to be concerned with addressing the ontological deprivation of statelessness, and not merely the political harm of a loss of citizenship.

§ Arendt on Statelessness—The Legal Dimension

One of the first philosophical analyses of statelessness can be found in 1948 in Arendt's *The Origins of Totalitarianism*. Her analysis begins with the observation that starting shortly after World War I, the nature of forced migration began to change. While there had always been "war refugees," what was unique about people fleeing after WWI is they "were welcomed nowhere and could be assimilated nowhere. Once they had left their homelands they remained homeless, once they had left their state they became stateless; once they had been deprived of their human rights they were rightless, the scum of the earth" (Arendt 1978, 267). For Arendt, there is a direct causal connection between losing your national citizenship, becoming stateless, and becoming, in her words, "rightless."

To clarify her terminology, Arendt distinguished between *de jure stateless* people, people who have lost their citizenship as a matter of recognizable fact and meet the legal definition of statelessness, and *de facto stateless* people, people who are effectively without citizenship though they have retained their legal identity. The *de jure* stateless were relatively small in number, and thus Arendt considered them to be a relatively small problem. Similarly, refugees who met the legal definition of a refugee, as someone fleeing *individual political persecution*, were not the real issue for Arendt. In fact, she claimed that they were not a "genuine political problem," since besides being relatively few in number, the asylum laws that existed at the time did act as a genuine substitute for national laws (Arendt 1978, 295). By contrast, de facto stateless people comprised the "core of statelessness" for Arendt and were in her view identical with "the refugee question" (Arendt 1978, 279). For Arendt, de facto stateless people included all people who were forcibly displaced and without any form of effective citizenship or political belonging, regardless of how they were categorized legally (i.e., as refugees, asylum seekers, forcibly displaced, *sans papiers*, internally displaced persons, war refugees, etc.). People in this situation, whether they are referred to as refugees or stateless people, are, in her words, fundamentally rightless; they belong "to no internationally recognizable community whatever" and are thus outside "of mankind as a whole" (Arendt 2003, 150).[1]

What did it mean to become rightless for Arendt? Rightlessness has both a legal/political dimension and an ontological one. Legally, it meant that once you cease living under the jurisdiction of your domestic law, you are without the protection of any other law (Arendt 1978, 286). In other words, once you are removed from your own national law, there is no effective way to treat you as a legal subject and you remain outside the pale of the law.[2] This is tied to her critique of human rights, which were understood as natural and inalienable and thus without the need for positive law to protect them. For her, "the loss of national rights was identical with the loss of human rights" (Arendt 1978, 292). Thus, for stateless people, as soon as they lost their citizenship and had only their humanity and human rights to protect them, it turned out that there was no institution willing and able to guarantee them. Human rights proved impossible to enforce outside of a political community. If the legal meaning of statelessness is the absence of a meaningful legal identity, the political meaning of statelessness is the absence of a rights ensuring community.[3]

Hannah Arendt and the Ontological Deprivation of Statelessness 85

This point has been somewhat mitigated since Arendt wrote this in 1948, with the advent of numerous human rights treaties and declarations, the 1951 Refugee Convention, and treaties concerning stateless people, which were all designed precisely to deal with people who had lost the protection of their home states. Despite this legal progress, as many scholars have pointed out, the legal protections of refugees and stateless people remain fundamentally precarious.[4] From the point of view of normative philosophy, it is important to highlight that though there is a legal framework in existence for the protection of refugees, many states are still reluctant to acknowledge significant *obligations* to refugees. The most widely accepted obligation, non-refoulement, is often respected in principle though not in practice. Further, few states acknowledge positive obligations to help refugees by admitting them to their states or granting them the right to residence. Most nations feel that they *ought* to help refugees and that it would be wrong simply to let them die of starvation or exposure, but few see it as a moral, political, or legal obligation except in the most minimal sense. Given this, Arendt's fundamental critique of the way stateless people are treated when they are outside of their state remains true: "the prolongation of their lives is due to charity and not to right, for no law exists which could force the nations to feed them" (Arendt 1978, 296).

To summarize, Arendt's first critique of statelessness is that it entails the loss of a particular identity and a political community, and it is only within this political community that human rights can be protected. Despite over 50 years of changes in international law and human rights conventions around stateless people and refugees, their rights—both legal and human—remain fundamentally precarious outside the nation-state. Though this is a crucial point in understanding statelessness, this is not Arendt's most fundamental critique of statelessness. If this were the only harm of statelessness, we might say that the harm could be addressed by simply insisting on more resettlement or quicker repatriation, and refugee camps, since they are necessary in order for these solutions to occur, would be seen as unproblematic. Yet as I argue below, Arendt argued that there is a much more fundamental loss that comes with statelessness, one which prolonged encampment contributes to. It is the loss of certain fundamental features of our humanity. I refer to this loss as the ontological deprivation. This loss, I argue, ought to be taken more seriously in our moral theorizing around refugees.

§ The Ontological Deprivation—Bare Life and Individual Identity

The ontological deprivation has three different dimensions: the loss of identity and reduction to bare life; the expulsion from common humanity; and finally, the loss of agency, understood not as a subjective disposition, but an ability to have your words and actions be recognized as meaningful and politically relevant. Below I explain each aspect in detail.

What concerned Arendt was not merely the way that being forced outside a state transformed a person's legal identity; she was concerned with the way it transformed a person's identity *as such*. In her words, statelessness deprived a person "of all clearly established, officially *recognized* identity" (Arendt 1978, 287; italics added). From a purely legal or institutional point of view, this might not seem like an important matter, but from the perspective of the experience of refugees, it is crucial. Arendt, herself a refugee, argued that one of the hardest things for refugees is being undistinguished from a giant, nameless mass. Indeed, the main complaint of refugees, from all strata of society, in her view is that "nobody here knows who I am" (Arendt 1978, 287).[5] This anonymity is not only existentially difficult; there is a practical side. Individuals who are seen as having a unique identity have a greater chance to survive, to gain resources, and even to access opportunities for resettlement. As she puts it rather bitterly, chances of survival increase with a name, "just as a dog with a name has a better chance to survive than a stray dog who is just a dog in general" (Arendt 1978, 287).

In the transformation of identity that occurs in the process of becoming stateless, one's formerly meaningful identity is replaced with a new one, that of a *human being in general*. This for Arendt is a tragic loss and one of the worst identities a person could have. The loss of human rights suffered by stateless people is paradoxical because when a person became a human being in general, "without a profession, without a citizenship, without an opinion, without a deed by which to identify and specify himself," his private identity, "which, deprived of expression within and action upon a common world, loses all significance" (Arendt 1978, 302). Stateless people appeared to the outside world as "nothing but human beings," entirely innocent and without responsibility (Arendt 1978, 295). Importantly, this human status did not give rise to respect, awe, or humanitarian sentiment, as Enlightenment thinkers thought it would, but quite the opposite: "the world found nothing sacred in the abstract nakedness of being human" (Arendt 1978, 299). According to the traditional view of human rights, if a human being loses her political status, she should be able to fall back on her natural, inalienable human rights. "Actually the opposite is the case," writes Arendt. "It seems that a man who is nothing but a man has lost the very qualities which make it possible for other people to treat him as a fellow-man" (Arendt 1978, 300).

In other words, once a person is stripped of her political persona and citizenship, she appears as an abstract human being who, precisely because of this abstraction, does not appear to be fully human. Though Arendt introduced this observation into political philosophy, it is Giorgio Agamben who has done the most to elaborate and develop it.[6] Through his work, this dimension of political existence has come to be known as *bare life*. For Agamben, bare life refers to the separation of biological life from political existence. Though this separation is a common feature of all political life, it becomes especially important in modernity.

There is a significant political impact to this. Agamben insists that the separation of bare life from political life is not an accidental feature of contemporary politics or the result of misguided policies, and thus, something that can easily be fixed with a new international agreement or more generous domestic policies; rather, for him it is fundamental to the way the modern nation-state is structured such that it is incapable of dealing with stateless people who have become "nothing but human" and must, by definition, keep them in a permanent state of exclusion. As such, on his account, when human beings are separated from their political persona, they by definition cannot be included in common political life.

Let me briefly recap his argument for this.[7] Agamben traces the ambivalent relationship between politics and bare life back to Aristotle. For him, there were two fundamental kinds of life: *zoë*, the biological life that we share in common with animals, and *bios*, the kind of life that is distinctive to human beings, embodied in our political capacities for speech and action. Aristotle argued that *zoë*, biological life, ought to be excluded from the polis since politics was concerned with what was distinctly human. Agamben takes Aristotle's work to be the original foundation of politics, and thus for him, the original foundation of politics is the exclusion of bare life. This relationship is transformed in modernity, where bare life becomes the source of sovereignty. What the French *Declaration of the Rights of Man and Citizen*, for example, demonstrates is that the state receives its justification from its ability to protect the biological life of its citizens. It is important to note the double movement here: though bare life moves to the center of politics—the justification of sovereignty is the state's ability to protect the bare life of its citizens—bare life is immediately understood as the life of citizens.[8] In other words, though bare life becomes important to politics, this life becomes inseparable from a political dimension. Consequently, bare life that is not also the life of a citizen is by definition excluded from the political. This is what Agamben means when he writes, "there is no autonomous space in the political order of the nation-state for something like the pure human itself" (Agamben 1998, 20).

The implications for stateless people on this view are clear. Stateless people, as a form of bare life not mediated through citizenship, are excluded politically not merely as a contingent outcome of political circumstances, but as a *structural feature* of modern political life. If Agamben is right about the structural relationship of bare life to the nation-state, then we must consider stateless people as a relatively permanent feature of the contemporary political landscape. This explains, at least in part, why long-term displacement is the norm and not the exception, and further, why we ought to think about moral norms that may govern people in this relatively permanent state of exclusion.[9]

Taking his cue from Agamben and Arendt, the French anthropologist Michel Agier elaborates on the way that bare life manifests itself in the current refugee regime. As he puts it, the way in which refugees are bare life is that they "are certainly alive, but they no longer 'exist', that is, they no longer have a social or political existence apart from their biological one" (Agier 2008, 49). This is so in his view because of the way that stateless people are seen and treated in refugee camps. In his experience working in refugee camps around the world, refugees are seen by the others as having two fundamental features—they are both victims and undesirable: because they are undesirable, they are excluded from all political communities, yet they are still included in a way because they are seen as victims in need of humanitarian concern.

This view is held in part because of a requirement for humanitarian aid: that the people seeking it ask for it not as individuals, members of a particular nation or group, but only as "human beings." In other words, refugees can *only* make claims for humanitarian aid and protection as *bare life*. This is the rationale for the existence of humanitarian agencies—they are supposed to protect people *qua* human being, not *qua* particular identity, and thus stateless people must assume this standpoint in order to receive aid. With the loss of identity and reduction to victimhood, aid can come from states or regions that may be either friendly or hostile. This requires the "social and political non-existence of the beneficiaries of aid" (Agier 2011, 133). Rather than being political *subjects*, they become *objects* of humanitarian aid, bodies to be cared for and protected.[10] This political non-existence is a requirement of humanitarian aid since aid cannot be given to a person qua a member of a social group or citizenship but simply on the basis of one's humanity. Hence in refugee camps individuals must identify as bare life simply in order to survive. In this sense, humanitarianism acts *against* politics by producing exceptionality and presenting the displaced as victims who are guilty, vulnerable, and undesirable, "all incompatible with those of the subject and the citizen" (Agier 2011, 215). It is the way that this specific identity is constructed, claims Agier, that prevents us from integrating the fate of the displaced with the fate of humanity in general, and permits us to treat them as entirely superfluous (Agier 2008, 30).

Yet this does not mean that refugees do not strive to be more than this.[11] Agier narrates various stories of protests against humanitarian organizations and the UN in camps. In one story, for example, he begins by describing the de facto way that refugees make a life for themselves in camps: by selling their ration cards or crossing over the border to work illegally. When NGO workers learned about this, they became outraged that their help was being taken advantage of and decided to institute stricter measures such as head counts. When refugees discovered that this small amount of freedom was being taken away, there were huge protests (Agier 2011, 55). It is clear that refugees do speak and act in these largely depoliticized spaces, and thus that they do retain at least a partial political dimension.[12] For Agier, when refugees speak out in the name of refugees or the vulnerable, politics is introduced in the camp (Agier 2011, 156).

Yet despite speaking up and acting in various ways, political agency within camps is ultimately limited because refugees are not recognized in their own speech. Their voice or speech has no meaning because it is not recognized as political, only as the claims of an unmediated victim whose well-being and autonomy lie in the hands of humanitarian agents who act on their behalf; their voice has no ability to lead to meaningful results. He writes, "undesirable as well as vulnerable, they can be forced to remain or to leave from one day to the next, they see 'their' camp disappear, according to the unfathomable goodwill of the international organizations that opened it" (Agier 2011, 196). Because refugee voices cannot be heard in camps, they cannot have the full political existence they strive for. For Agier, camps are paradoxical in this way: everything is possible yet nothing really develops; people can act in the gap between the emergency and the resumption of life, yet this action never sustains the meaning that is hoped for.

Didier Fassin provides a clear example of how bare life functions in the contemporary refugee regime. Fassin demonstrates that asylum seekers in France are largely discredited and the stories they tell are assumed to be untrue. Speech is replaced instead by the body, which is thought to better demonstrate the truth. He argues that there is a tension between the low rate of granting refugee status to asylum seekers in France and its claims to uphold human rights. For Fassin, this has been "resolved ideologically by increasingly discrediting the word of asylum seekers so as to justify the progressive reduction in the rate of acceptance of their request" (Fassin 2012, 109). Officials claim to be getting tougher on "bogus refugees," but under these conditions, "the asylum seeker's accounts, long the only evidence testifying to their story and justifying their request were no longer sufficient to confirm the truth of the alleged persecution. The body, which could have retained a trace of it, came to be seen as potentially providing tangible proofs" (Fassin 2012, 110). Words of asylum seekers are no longer seen as truthful; the body—as evidenced by medical experts—is now the only source of truth for asylum seekers. This in his view is the "new regime of truth," where truth is no longer sought in asylum seekers' words but "of which their body stills bears the trace, in the form of the physical consequences of torture that only medical examination is competent to state" (Fassin 2012, 111).

The point of the section above is to argue that Arendt's insight that stateless people are seen as "nothing but a human being," or bare life in Agamben's words, remains important to understanding the experience of statelessness. Having lost the identity that was bound up with their citizenship, they are now seen by the outside world in this abstract formulation, one that is by definition devoid of a political basis. The reduction of stateless people to bare life allows stateless people to be excluded from the common world, as I discuss below. Conversely, if we wish to address the ontological harm of statelessness, we need to think about ways that stateless people may be able to keep a meaningful political identity and resist the reduction to bare life, even though they may be formally bereft of citizenship.

§ Rejection from the Common World and Abandonment

In this section, I make two points about the nature of the ontological deprivation. First, when stateless people are placed into camps or allowed to disappear into crowded urban centers with no formal recognition, this exclusion itself represents a fundamental harm. Many citizens of Western states think that refugee camps are a matter of practical necessity—there is nowhere else to put large groups of unwanted people. Yet for Arendt, I argue, it is important to see these camps as morally problematic because they effectively exclude people from what she referred to as "the common world." This expulsion from the common world is a fundamental aspect of the ontological deprivation. Second, I argue that we must understand this exclusion as a form of abandonment, in Agamben's sense of the term. Abandonment for him does not mean that stateless people are left to themselves, but rather that they remain directly impacted by us through their formal exclusion. Their very identities and modes of existence are defined almost entirely by their exclusion. Agamben terms this form of abandonment the inclusive exclusion. Both of these aspects are important in understanding the ontological harm of statelessness.

Michel Agier draws a clear picture of the way that stateless people are forced outside of the common world. Refugees are often *physically* outside of the geographically recognized world. Refugee camps, for example, are sometimes not even on maps, though they may have existed for a decade or longer.[13] Stateless people are *economically* outside the common world, since the stateless are not permitted to engage in the global economy except through being passive recipients of the world's charity for their minimal biological existence. Finally, they are *socially and politically* outside the common world, since they are denied social integration and political rights or agency in the states where they reside (Agier 2008). Since refugees are not permitted to integrate into the communities where they reside and very few are ever resettled, stateless people spend the duration of their lives outside of any social or political community and thus are effectively excluded from the common realm.

For Arendt, this physical, economic, social, and political exclusion has an extra dimension—taken together, they represent the exclusion of stateless people from the "common world." This is because in her words, we live in "one world" that is completely interconnected, such that being expelled from one place effectively means that you are expelled from all places since there is no uninhabited space that a person could move to. Arendt notes that when one loses citizenship, one also loses "a distinct place in the world," and the possibility of finding a new one is severely reduced (Arendt 1978, 293). Segregated into camps or forgotten in urban spaces, stateless people no longer have a meaningful place in the common world. This is why statelessness, which entails physical, economic, social, and political exclusion, represents an exclusion from the common world as such.

Hannah Arendt and the Ontological Deprivation of Statelessness

For her, the common world "is not identical with the earth or with nature. . . . It is related, rather, to the human artifact, the fabrication of human hands, as well as to affairs which go on among those who inhabit the man-made world together" (Arendt 1998, 52). The common world is (at times) synonymous with the public realm, which "gathers us together and yet prevents our falling over each other" (Arendt 1998, 52). In other words, the common world is both what relates us to each other as beings who must share the same worldly space, and separates us from each other and allows us to maintain our individual identities. In this sense, the common world is the ground of plurality, our uniqueness and difference that is so fundamental to politics.

Having been excluded from this realm of shared meaning, experience, and fabrication, stateless people have a kind of worldlessness, and are uprooted and rendered superfluous. She writes that to be "uprooted means to have no place in the world, recognized and guaranteed by others; to be superfluous means not to belong to the world at all. Uprootedness can be the preliminary condition of superfluousness" (Arendt 1978, 475). To be rendered superfluous means that you cease to matter to the world and cease to be able to affect the world in a meaningful way. Arendt's controversial claim is that individuality without some form of public, political expression lacks meaning. She writes that when a refugee represents "nothing but his own absolutely unique individuality," because it is deprived of "expression within and action upon a common world," it "loses all significance" (Arendt 1978, 302).

To be rendered superfluous and to no longer be able to affect the world in a meaningful way represents a loss of *dignity*. In her words, "respect for human dignity implies the recognition of my fellow-men or our fellow-nations as subjects, as builders of worlds or cobuilders of a common world" (Arendt 1978, 458). Thus being prevented through statelessness from being a "cobuilder" of the common world means that a person in this position has lost something fundamental. This in turn makes it all the more difficult for people to see their fundamental human dignity in their condition of statelessness. In short, for Arendt, to be excluded physically, economically, socially, and politically, as stateless people are, from the common world constitutes part of the ontological deprivation because this means that an individual loses her place in a common public space from which action, speech, and hence identity become meaningful. It is the loss of the *ground* from which one can engage meaningfully with others and with the world that is shared in common.

The exclusion from the common world and the worldlessness of stateless people constitutes the ontological deprivation in a second way, described by Agamben. For Agamben, being excluded from the common realm means that stateless people remain in a state of *abandonment*. Because modern nation states cannot deal politically with bare life, they are forced to keep it outside of politics in what he refers to as a state of abandonment.

To be abandoned for Agamben does not mean that states simply put aside stateless people and no longer have anything to do with them. Rather, in Agamben's analysis, states remain in a relationship with what that they have abandoned in the form of an *inclusive exclusion* (a concept I return to in more detail in Chapter Four). States formally exclude stateless people as non-citizens and even criminals, yet stateless people remain dependent upon a given state both for their material needs (since they are formally excluded from economic activities, they are reliant on the international community and their states of residence for all material goods), as well as their identities. They are defined by their exclusion—as either refugees, asylum seekers, failed asylum seekers, economic migrants, etc.—and this definition has a direct bearing on their chances for survival and future prospects. In this sense, to say that stateless people are abandoned by humanity is not simply to say that they are ignored; rather, they continue to exist in relation to the other entities—countries in the Global North and Global South, the UNHCR, other NGOs—through their vulnerability and dependence on them, both for their material needs and their ontological status and definition. Stateless people are excluded as members of a given state but included in that they receive their identity and status by virtue of this exclusion. Abandonment of course is not a morally neutral state; to be abandoned is to be left in a condition of exposure under the threat of violence (Agamben 1998, 18).

What precisely does it mean to say that stateless people have been "abandoned" by the world? Stateless people are abandoned by states, both in the Global North, where many refugees would like to resettle, and in the Global South, where the vast majority of refugees live, in the sense that no country is willing to resettle or integrate large numbers of refugees. In Chapter One, I discussed in detail the challenge that large-scale refugee populations appear to pose for states, politically and economically. Because refugees also seem to be a challenge to the very basis of state sovereignty and the state's ability to control membership, it is perhaps not surprising that states are anxious to distance themselves from stateless people. However, the assumption is that when this happens, *international institutions* are supposed to be able to step up and protect the rights of people by virtue of their humanity, rather than citizenship. This is precisely the reason that the UNHCR was created by the United Nations in 1950. But the conclusion reached by many who study the refugee regime is that this does not happen.[14] So, despite the scale of the office for the UNHCR, refugees essentially have no one acting on *their* behalf, and no one who can speak for their interests or rights;[15] they have no one to *represent* them.[16] In short, Arendt appears to be right that once a person becomes stateless and is rejected from the common world, phenomenologically, if not legally, the forcibly displaced person remains in a state of abandonment.[17]

§ Meaningful Speech and Action—The Thorny Question of Agency

In this chapter, I have argued that the harm of statelessness occurs on two levels—the legal/political and the ontological. Thus far, we have seen that the ontological deprivation consists in a transformation of identity from individual citizen to human being in general or "bare life," and the effective removal of stateless people from the common realm of humanity and abandonment. There is one more crucial element in the ontological deprivation that arises directly as a result of the first two transformations: because they are no longer part of the common world and no longer have a political persona to speak through, stateless people lose the ability to *act*. The final aspect of the ontological deprivation is that statelessness renders a person unable to speak and act in a meaningful way. In this sense, a stateless person has lost her political *agency*, her ability to act in the specific Arendtian sense of the term, as the freedom to act *with* others and have her actions and speech recognized. There are two important features of action: first, it is only through action that we reveal who we are as individuals and are able to mark our place in the world; and second, action in a given public space is the very essence of freedom.

Agency for Arendt is tantamount to the ability to *act*. To act in the most general sense means to begin, to set something into motion, which can neither be predicted nor controlled. Action thus is "unexpected," and the "fact that man is capable of action means that the unexpected can be expected from him, that he is able to perform what is infinitely improbable" (Arendt 1998, 178). Arendt often speaks as though action and speech were the same thing, because they both "contain the answer to the question asked of every newcomer: 'Who are you?'" (Arendt 1998, 178). In other words, in action and speech, "men show who they are, reveal actively their unique personal identities and thus make their appearance in a human world" (Arendt 1998, 179).

Action's power to disclose human identity is connected with a second fundamental feature of action—to act and to be *free* are the same thing. "Men *are* free," writes Arendt, "as long as they act, neither before nor after; for to *be* free and to act are the same" (Arendt 1993, 153). This aspect of Arendt's thought is often jarring to contemporary readers who understand freedom as an inner disposition or subjective state connected to the will, where I am free when I can do what I will or desire to do. Freedom is not a subjective state or inner disposition for Arendt. For her, freedom is a fundamental human experience that is actualized primarily in political action, where a person discloses her uniqueness in conjunction with other people. "Freedom," writes Arendt, "is actually the reason that men live together in political organization at all. Without it, political life as such would be meaningless" (Arendt 1993, 146). Action is by definition *intersubjective*, not subjective, in that it requires the presence and recognition of others in a common, public realm. "Without a politically guaranteed public realm, freedom lacks the worldly space to make its appearance" (Arendt 1993, 149).

Given Arendt's understanding of action, and its connection to freedom and identity, it is not surprising that the fundamental harm of statelessness is that a person loses the ability to speak and act in a meaningful way. How are stateless people deprived of the capacity for action and hence agency? First, because they are outside of the common world and public realm, they lack a space in which their actions can be seen and words understood. This is why Arendt insists that stateless people are in a fundamental condition of rightlessness even though they have certain rights in principle, such as freedom of expression or opinion. Without a political community, regardless of whether one is able to say what they think and believe, opinions and actions cease to matter. So fundamental is speaking and acting in a human life that Arendt defines the most fundamental right, the right to have rights, as the right "to live in a framework where one is judged by one's actions and opinions" (Arendt 1978, 296). Conversely, the deprivation of human rights "is manifested first and above all in the deprivation of a place in the world which makes opinions significant and actions effective" (Arendt 1978, 296). To be sure, it's not that stateless people are no longer capable of these things but rather, in the condition that they are in, their words and actions can no longer be seen and recognized as being meaningful.[18] In Hayden's words, the problem with statelessness is that stateless people are at risk of "becoming irrelevant to the world in that their actions and opinions no longer matter to anyone; it's as if they cease to exist" (Hayden 2009, 65).

This aspect of the ontological deprivation is connected to the exclusion of stateless people from the common world and reduction to bare life. For Arendt, our participation in the common world allows us to disclose ourselves meaningfully through speech and action. Our humanity—hence our dignity—is fundamentally bound up with being able to reveal ourselves in speech and action in the common realm. Thus the harm of being excluded from the common realm is that one cannot *act*, in Arendt's sense, and hence reveal one's unique identity and individuality. One no longer has a common public realm to give one's actions and identity meaning. Dramatically, Arendt claims that "a life without speech and without action . . . is literally dead to the world" (Arendt 1998, 176).

I want to stress that for Arendt, the loss of the ability to act is such a fundamental loss not because it means that a person *can* no longer speak or act, but rather, they are no longer *judged* according to this but instead according to what is "merely given" about their existence—the fact that they are human beings in general. This highlights that for Arendt speech and action are intersubjective—they require the presence and *recognition* of others. Without a meaningful public persona and public stage on which

Hannah Arendt and the Ontological Deprivation of Statelessness 95

to appear, stateless people are judged not according to their actions and opinions—according to "who" they are—but according to how they are seen by others—according to "what" they are. This is why stateless people can be treated as bare life, as bodies without a meaningful identity that are indistinguishable from other suffering bodies. The stateless person has lost "his place in community, his political status in the struggle of his time and the legal personality which makes his actions and part of his destiny a consistent whole" (Arendt 1978, 301).

To summarize, the ontological deprivation contains three separated but interdependent elements that together show that statelessness deprives people of certain essential features of their humanity. This deprivation, if taken more seriously when theorizing about our moral obligations to refugees, gives rise to a different set of moral obligations. Or so I will argue. Before I turn to that, I would like to address a common objection to Arendt's and Agamben's critique of statelessness. The objection is that Arendt and Agamben fail to adequately represent the *agency* of refugees and stateless people, and thus their position is too extreme a criticism of statelessness. What I show below is that while this criticism leveled at their positions is true to an extent, their fundamental insight about statelessness nonetheless remains relevant. I seek to clarify and defend Arendt and argue that the ontological deprivation should still play a role in our understanding of statelessness, and in our thinking of how to rectify the harm of statelessness.

The criticism that Arendt and Agamben exaggerate the loss of agency of refugees and stateless people is made in at least three different ways. A first criticism is based on what many people know about refugee camps: namely, that in many cases, they are breeding grounds for various forms of political violence. Hamas in the Palestinian territory and the Interahamwe in Rwanda are all examples of political agency exercised by refugees. Given this, it appears that Arendt and Agamben are overstating the extent to which refugees become bare life and cease to be political agents.

A second criticism comes from Dunn and Conns (2012), who focus on Agamben's analysis of bare life and argue that his analysis of refugees as bare life is inaccurate. They argue that for Agamben, refugees are socially dead and without any capacity for political action. They are thus objects of bureaucratic action but not subjects who have the power to influence their own lives.[19] Yet this is contrary to their observations through their work in refugee camps. Refugees, in their experience, do shape the way they are governed in important ways. They are able to rebuild normal lives—not in the sense that they are able to attain their pre-conflict "normal," but they are able to have social and economic lives that are more than just mere biological survival. "It's a life that, however makeshift, unpleasant, or uncomfortable is stable and relatively predictable, and which makes sense" (Dunn and Conns 2012). Thus rather than being seen as devoid of agency, they must be understood as exercising a "burdened agency" (Meyers 2011) in that though they have to work within enormous constraints, they are still able to reassemble a regular existence.

Finally, a similar but more philosophically grounded criticism can be found in Jacques Rancière's reading of Arendt. Rancière is critical of Arendt's interpretation of human rights as ending in "either a void or a tautology" (Rancière 2004, 302). If human rights are the rights of citizens, then they are simply the rights of people who already have rights, and thus a tautology. If they are the rights of the unpoliticized person, the person who is "nothing but a human being" and thus without rights, then they amount to nothing and are simply void. What he argues instead is that politics is precisely about staging a *dissensus* (a dispute about what is given) over this exact question. In Rancière's well-known phrase, the Rights of Man are the rights of those who have not the rights that they have and have the rights that they have not (Rancière 2004, 302). Politics is about the back and forth between the first inscription of rights and the dissensus where they are put to the test—and this is why they can be invoked even in refugee camps (Rancière 2004, 305). "These [rights] are theirs when they can do something with them to construct a dissensus against the denial of rights they suffer. And there are always people among them who do it" (Rancière 2004, 305–306). In Schaap's interpretation of Rancière, politics is the staging of a dissensus in which those who are deemed to lack speech make themselves heard as political animals (Schaap 2011). In other words, Arendt and, by consequence, Agamben, are wrong to think that stateless people lack agency. For Rancière, stateless people are able to stage a dissensus to demand their rights and challenge the status quo, and thus can speak and act in a very meaningful way.

The critiques above add something important to our understanding of statelessness. It is important to point out that becoming stateless and "nothing but a human being" does not mean that this is how people see themselves or that they are not capable of doing anything meaningful in their lives. It also does not mean that they never have the capacity for speech and action. The authors above are quite right to point out that many stateless people contest this status, engage meaningfully and creatively with each other and the communities that they find themselves in, and maintain agency in important ways. The critique is correct in that Arendt and Agamben do not take this aspect of agency seriously enough.

Yet, I argue below that this criticism does not render the importance of the ontological deprivation void. To understand why not, we must employ Arendt's contested categories of the public and the private. I argue below that *politically* and *publicly*, stateless people are still treated as bare life or "nothing but human." Politically speaking, their words, opinions, and actions still do not "matter," in the sense that they are not acknowledged or valued by others—neither by the humanitarian organizations that care for and control them, nor by states where they reside or hope to reside. This is evident in the ways that their interests are taken or fail to be taken into consideration; the way that their claims are assessed in asylum hearings; and the more general way that stateless people are represented in our political landscape. Though there are exceptions to this—people who are able to make themselves seen and heard—the vast majority of stateless people remain a "what'—a body to be cared for, a life to be preserved—rather than a political subject. For the outside world, especially for the political agents who make important decisions about their lives, they are still fundamentally seen as bare life, bodies devoid of a political existence. Speech and action for Arendt must be recognized by others in order to be meaningful and genuine. This is particularly important when it comes to making *political* demands and claims—they make their claims to material necessities and human rights as bodies in need, not as political subjects. While it is true that stateless people have much more agency privately and socially than Arendt and Agamben give them credit for, this public, political deprivation of status remains fundamental and, as I argue in the Conclusion, needs to be philosophically addressed.

Let me address each critique in turn. The first critique held that because refugee camps often produce military and violent forces, they must be understood as being political spaces and the people in them, political agents. However, though this is a common way of understanding armed groups, Arendt would not have agreed with this. For her, violence is not politics; in fact, it's the very opposite. Violence in Arendt's view is instrumental in nature—it is a means to achieve a given end. Regardless of what the end is and whether or not it is morally justifiable, the means of violence is not the same as action. This is because violence has to do with "making" and is thus connected to the activity of fabrication. Action, by contrast, is not a means to a given end but about beginning, starting something which is unpredictable and through which "something new comes into the world" (Arendt 1993, 166). Action is precisely about spontaneity, self-disclosure, and collaboration. This is why action, for Arendt, is tantamount to freedom, while violence is connected to necessity and lack of freedom. If the primary examples of refugee actors are Hamas and the Interahamwe—two groups known for the use of violence to achieve particular political ends—then Arendt would deny that they are indeed political actors. Violence becomes necessary where genuine political power is absent.

Second, to respond to Dunn and Cons (2012), while it is correct to say that refugees in camps exercise a "burdened agency" rather than a lack of agency, it remains true that there is something lacking for them as public, political actors. They have no political *persona*, no mask to speak through, and ultimately often fail to be seen as political actors making claims to their rights. In other words, stateless people are still treated as "bare life" and make their claims as such (for material goods to preserve this life), even if they are able to manipulate NGOs, reappropriate resources and materials, and exercise agency within this identity. This remains a fundamental loss for stateless people, even though they can survive and make a relatively "normal" life without it.

For Arendt, what the ontological deprivation entails is that speech and action are no longer meaningful, not to ourselves and those close to us, but to those who are different from us and to those in front of whom we try to distinguish ourselves. In other words, without the political, personal speech lacks meaning; it is a "fool's freedom" because it gains no recognition either from local NGOs, the UN, host states, or Western states that may resettle them. What they have lost is action in the Arendtian sense as self-disclosive and world-building. On the contrary, because stateless people are seen merely as "what" they are—bodies to be cared for or people who threaten the state—they are often considered to be liars who will say anything to get into "our" country or take more resources. Their speech is thus disvalued, dismissed, and certainly not seen as meaningful. Without a meaningful political identity within the context of the common world, a fundamental dimension of speaking and acting is lost.

In other words, Arendt may agree with Dunn and Cons that stateless people are agents in the sense that they can follow their wills and desires on occasion, even though they face obstacles, and so life in refugee camps may be similar to life at home. Yet they still lack agency in the Arendtian sense, understood as the freedom to act in concert with others in a way that discloses a self and gives it a worldly reality. Agency, then, for Arendt is more than just a subjective experience of how an individual feels about herself or perceives her ability to get things done. She still lacks the intersubjective recognition that would allow her identity to be meaningful and thus give a foundation to her speech and action. Despite how she may feel about herself, the public, political aspect of her existence remains lost.

Let me draw on an example discussed by Didier Fassin to make this point clearer. He tells the story of Marie, a Haitian woman who sought asylum in France in 2000. The reason she sought asylum was that she was gang raped in Haiti in the context of generalized political violence. She was denied asylum in France because the gang rape was not thought to be politically motivated and too ordinary to amount to persecution to justify asylum (only 3.3% of Haitian applicants received asylum during that period in France) (Fassin 2012, 142). Like the 80% of asylum seekers whose applications are turned down, she became an illegal immigrant. After two years of living in isolation and becoming increasingly sicker, malnourished, and depressed, she finally saw a doctor. They learned that she was HIV positive and suffering from advanced AIDS, the result of the gang rape experienced in Haiti. She sought and won residence on medical grounds, granted under the so-called humanitarian rationale. "Her words about the violence she had suffered were doubted, but ultimately her body spoke for her" (Fassin 2012, 142). I use this example to show that for Marie, her words and actions were meaningless to the authorities who had the power to define her either as a legitimate person entitled to asylum and citizenship, or as illegitimate, a liar, and illegal. It was only when her body, her bare life, made her suffering and trauma clear that she could be believed. This, I think, is what Arendt has in mind when she argues that statelessness makes speech and action impossible—there was simply nobody who found her words meaningful.

Finally, to respond to Rancière's criticism of Arendt, it is important to note that in a fundamental way, Arendt would agree with him. For Arendt, human beings always have the capacity to begin, to start something new, since this is rooted in the fundamental human condition of natality. I quoted Arendt earlier as saying that the "fact that man is capable of action means that the unexpected can be expected from him, that he is able to perform what is infinitely improbable" (Arendt 1998, 178). The fundamental human condition of natality means that all people have the capacity to begin, and action is "the actualization of the human condition of natality" (Arendt 1998, 178). But under the condition of epistemic injustice (Fricker 2007)[20]—where stateless people are not recognized as agents who speak (despite the fact that they might) but as objects to be cared for or protected from—this capacity is precisely what is erased (though never entirely eliminated). This is why the deprivation of statelessness is an *ontological* deprivation—it deprives people precisely of this human capacity in a fundamental way.

For Arendt, even in the worst of times, such as in the concentration camps of World War II, people were able to begin. For her, politics is precisely these completely unexpected and improbable beginnings. Indeed, she ends her reflections on totalitarianism with a quote from St. Augustine to this end: "that a beginning be made man was created" (Arendt 1978, 479). Thus Arendt would fundamentally be in agreement with Rancière that people—whether in concentration camps or refugee camps—retain this capacity to act since it is the very core of our human condition. But there are forms of political life that contribute more and less to our humanity. Refugee camps systematically deny refugees this opportunity and make it as difficult as possible. Again, it is not to say that it is impossible to act—something Arendt explicitly denied—but refugee camps create the conditions where such action is unlikely and difficult, and so not a form of political life that is conducive to fulfilling our humanity. In short, Rancière is right to point out the importance of the capacity for acting and speaking, and contesting the status quo that stateless people retain even in the worst condition. Yet this does not invalidate Arendt's fundamental point.

§ Conclusion

I have argued above that we ought to take seriously the ontological deprivation of statelessness, theorized by Arendt and Agamben, in our analysis of our moral obligations to refugees and stateless people. I have suggested that refugee camps and other spaces of containment may provide for their biological life, but deprives stateless people of a place in the common realm of humanity and the ability to be recognized as speaking and acting agents. Statelessness deprives people of certain essential features of their humanity, and this deprivation, if taken more seriously when theorizing about our moral obligations to refugees, gives rise to a different set of moral obligations. Given that the vast majority of stateless people are never resettled and remain displaced for prolonged periods of time, we ought to be concerned with ethical norms that will help stateless people mitigate, if not entirely overcome, the ontological deprivation and remain part of the common realm of humanity, even while they are formally excluded from political membership. I conclude this chapter by discussing some suggestions for ways to overcome the ontological deprivation and return refugees to the common world, even though they may remain refugees.

First, if we recognize the ontological deprivation as a legitimate and serious harm, we must reconsider the use of refugee camps as a way to contain and confine refugee populations over the long term. Indeed, as I have suggested in other chapters, we must reject refugee camps as the de facto way of containing large-scale refugee flows. Refugee camps—not for the sake of emergency aid but as a long-term solution—deprive refugees of a place in the common realm of humanity, contribute to their reduction to bare life, and impair the ability of refugees for agency, their ability to be recognized as speaking and acting agents. In this way, framing one of the harms of forced displacement as the ontological deprivation helps us to see that encampment constitutes a serious moral harm in and of itself.

Second, the *average* length of time a person will live as a refugee without formal political belonging or protection is close to 20 years. Given the fact that displacement is neither exceptional nor short-term, we must consider ways of remedying the ontological deprivation even while people remain displaced. In other words, while the current political climate means that it is virtually impossible that all displaced people will find a permanent home in a political community (either through resettlement in a Western state, since less than 1% will ever be resettled, or through repatriation to their home states), and thus have the political harm of statelessness rectified, this does not mean that the ontological deprivation of statelessness can't be remedied.

How might this occur? One obligation, then, is to think of ways that the long-term displaced can be reintegrated back into the common world, even though they may remain without citizenship. Such a reintegration may take many different forms. An example discussed in Chapter One is the "temporary local integration" of refugees while a permanent durable solution is negotiated, as advocated by the US Committee for Refugees and Immigrants (USCRI). Here the UNHCR would fund programs that allow stateless people to integrate locally, such as by funding educational programs, primary schooling for children, and co-op and other work programs. Rather than funding camps that segregate people from the common world, the UNHCR would fund education, employment, and social services within states that host refugees that would both allow stateless people to be integrated into a political community (temporarily, until a more permanent solution is found) and would be materially beneficial to host states (Smith 2004). Importantly, in such a scenario, refugees would have the ability to participate in governance and be able to hold others accountable for their failure to uphold human rights.

Second, given the influence (financially and politically) that Western states exercise at the UNHCR, members of these states ought to advocate for a more ethical aid policy concerning refugees one that respects them as members of the common realm and political agents. This may entail, for example, insisting that when refugee camps are necessary as the only way to provide aid, they respect human rights. Currently, though the Refugee Convention lists rights that all refugees have even while displaced—including the right to earn wages, the right to education, the right to public assistance at the same level as nationals, the right to courts and travel documents, and, perhaps most importantly, the right to freedom of movement—they are routinely denied to stateless people, and this is seen as morally unproblematic. An ethical policy ought to take the denial of the humanity of stateless people more seriously in our policies concerning them.

To be sure, I do not mean to claim that the above suggestions would provide a comprehensive solution to the global refugee crisis. Rather, they are meant simply to point in the direction that our ethical thinking might take. My aim in arguing for the ontological deprivation is that when the harm of statelessness is reframed in this way, we see that many other obligations become at least conceivable. If the harm is partly that stateless people are excluded from the common realm and cannot be recognized as political agents, then philosophers ought to be concerned with thinking about ways that this harm can be mitigated if not entirely eliminated in the current global political context. We must be concerned with our ethical obligations to the millions of people who will never be resettled in the West and will spend decades living in refugee camps that are supported, at least in part, by the policies of our states. Yet as many have pointed out, it is not easy to see who bears the responsibility for discharging this duty. I turn to this challenging question in the next chapter.

Notes

1 More precisely, because refugees and stateless people belong to no recognizable community, they cannot be held politically responsible for anything and are "the absolutely innocent ones." In Arendt's view, it is this innocence that condemns them to a position outside of humanity (Arendt 2003, 150).
2 It is worth remembering Arendt's idiosyncratic test for this. "The best criterion," she writes, "by which to decide whether someone has been forced outside the pale of the law is to ask if he would benefit by committing a crime. If a small burglary is likely to improve his legal position, at least temporarily, one may be sure he has been deprived of human rights" (Arendt 1978, 286). The stateless person benefits by committing a crime and being prosecuted for it because as a criminal, the stateless person has a status and is treated like a normal, national citizen, with rights and protections. As a criminal, she is practically a citizen, since she will be treated according to the law. She is judged by her actions, not merely her status, and has thus regained a form of equality.

3 For Patrick Hayden, this shows that human rights for Arendt are both contingent and historical—they can be neither exercised nor protected outside a political community, and can only be guaranteed "by those actual others of cosmopolitanized historical humanity with whom we must necessarily share a world" (Hayden 2009, 65).
4 The general consensus seems to be that human rights of people who lack the protection of a national identity and effective citizenship are at best precarious and at worst, non-existent. The title of a recent book on the subject, *Are Human Rights For Migrants?*, is telling (Dembour and Kelly 2011). For a more Arendtian analysis, see Gündoğdu (2012, 2015).
5 This is a sentiment that Arendt reported in her own biographical account of life as a refugee in "We Refugees" (Arendt 2008).
6 That Agamben's concept of bare life is the necessary consequence of Arendt's view of statelessness is a position also held by Jacques Rancière. For him, "the radical suspension of politics in the exception of bare life is the ultimate consequence of Arendt's archipolitical position" (Rancière 2004, 301).
7 To be clear, I do not mean to suggest that we follow Agamben's analysis concerning refugees to its conclusion. I agree with many of the critiques of Agamben that he is too extreme in the conclusions that he reaches. I do, however, want to argue that his development of the concept of bare life and the relation of abandonment remain important concepts in helping us develop a fuller understanding of statelessness in the contemporary world.
8 We see this in the first three articles. In the first article, natural life is equated with the possession of rights ("Men are born and remain free and equal in rights," Article 1). In the second article, we learn that the legitimacy of a state rests on its ability to preserve these natural rights ("The aim of every political association is the preservation of the natural and inalienable rights of man," Article 2). But in the very next article, it becomes clear that the natural rights that the state is supposed to protect are the rights of citizens, not human beings as such. It is the protection of the natural life of citizens that is the basis of sovereignty ("The source of all sovereignty resides essentially in the nation," Article 3). By Article 6, the *Declaration* refers to the rights of "all citizens" rather than "men" as it had in the first Article ("All citizens have the right to participate . . ." "All citizens, being equal before [the law] . . .").
9 That refugees and stateless people are exemplars of bare life has been much discussed in recent years. For examples of scholars using Agamben to discuss the problem of refugees and statelessness, see Jenkins (2004), Doty (2007), Basaran (2008), Haddad (2008), Coleman and Grove (2009), Owens (2009), Jennings (2011), Hagmann and Korf (2012).
10 Though this reduction to victimhood might have its origins in a practical necessity—the functioning of humanitarian organizations—because this identity gets solidified, it has much deeper consequences. In Agier's view, it prevents us from integrating the fate of the displaced with the fate of humanity in general, and permits us to treat them as superfluous (Agier 2008, 30). In other words, their status as victims and bare life justifies their exclusion from the common world and renders it morally unproblematic.
11 This reflects a limitation in Agamben's analysis of refugees. In the view of Agier, Agamben's critique of refugee camps goes too far by denying the possibility for anything other than dehumanization and social and political death. He fails to take seriously the ways individuals are still able to resist, speak, and act, though in limited ways, within refugee camps.
12 Agier at times has an overly simplistic view of politics as simply making speeches or acting against what you are told. He does not take seriously enough that

speech and action can only be political if there is someone to recognize it as such, someone to take it seriously as disclosing something worth considering.
13 See Bauman (2007, 38) for examples of this. Though of course the internet and digital technology have made refugee camps much more visible in recent years, they still remain spaces that are physically hard to access, even for journalists and scholars.
14 This is the consensus of a number of scholars who study this issue (Hyndman 2000, Verdirame and Harrell-Bond 2005, Franke 2009).
15 Other international refugee organizations and local NGOs are similarly unable to help stateless people. Because other humanitarian organizations and refugee NGOs work closely with the UNHCR, they are often reluctant to go against them and to advocate for refugees in ways that would have been challenging to the UNHCR. Local NGOs in developing countries often do not include refugees in their work, since their focus is on local problems.
16 Lack of political representation thus remains a problem since Arendt first noticed it in *The Origins of Totalitarianism*. One of the main problems for stateless people was that they "had no government to *represent* and protect them" (Arendt 1978, 269, italics added).
17 Agier describes this condition existentially as "no-longer-being-in-the-world" (Agier 2008, 15).
18 Rancière takes up this point and argues that politics is precisely about deciding what counts as genuine political speech and what is mere noise (Rancière 2004).
19 There are others who argue that refugees demonstrate significant agency in refugee camps. See, for example, Nyers (2006) and Krause (2008). Even Agier, despite his sympathy with Arendt's and Agamben's interpretations of the refugee experience, also notes many ways that refugees exercise agency in camps (Agier 2011).
20 Specifically, this kind of injustice is akin to Fricker's description of a testimonial injustice, where a speaker's credibility as a knower is downgraded due to her identity. This constitutes a harm to the individual as a knower and undermines her "very humanity" (Fricker 2007, 44).

4 Responsibility for the Forcibly Displaced

I have been suggesting throughout this book that our moral obligations to refugees and the forcibly displaced include the rejection of long-term encampment and the mitigation of the ontological deprivation. Thus far I have tried to motivate this argument by explaining the nature of these harms and trying to account for why they have not received the moral attention that they deserve. I have argued that whatever obligations we have to refugees, they must include an ethics of the temporary. Yet I have also claimed that it is important to take seriously the fact that most states deny *responsibility* for refugees. Most states hold that because the suffering of refugees is great, they ought to help them out of a humanitarian impulse or a Good Samaritan principle. Though they may recognize the duty of non-refoulement and perhaps even a duty to resettle some refugees, most states do not believe that the principle of mutual aid generates other more robust obligations, such as large-scale resettlement or even the sufficient funding of organizations that aid refugees. Most states are clear that helping refugees is a matter of benevolence, not responsibility. This denial of responsibility has led to the situation of encampment and long-term statelessness, and their concomitant violations of human rights and dignity.

This is not a problem unique to refugees and forced migrants. Theorists of global justice who focus on other complex, multi-institutional, global problems such as poverty and climate change face similar hurdles in establishing responsibility. When a problem, however serious, is not caused by the actions of one particular state nor can be traced causally to any given entity, traditional accounts of responsibility cannot provide a sufficient ground for responsibility. How do we determine who is responsible for addressing the problem? An inability to answer this question in a way that is satisfying, morally as well as politically, is without a doubt one of the big stumbling blocks that prevent a more robust response to global displacement.

In this chapter I review at length three non-traditional models of global responsibility that are important for developing a plausible account of responsibility for global displacement. I go into the details of each account to show their validity and intuitive plausibility, despite being different from our traditional ways of thinking about responsibility. I suggest that Iris

Young, David Miller, and Thomas Pogge, supplemented with the work of Elizabeth Ashford and Gillian Brock, provide us with tools to develop an account of responsibility for displacement that does not require that an individual or state be causally connected to the given harm and is not rooted in a traditional phenomenology of agency, where we are responsible for only what we experience ourselves as having caused (Scheffler 2003). I develop each account at length in order to show why their views of responsibility ought to be taken seriously.

There are three key elements that I take from their accounts that, I argue, are useful in establishing responsibility for forced displacement. First, we ought to understand some of the injustices in the global refugee regime as forms of structural injustice, that is, as moral wrongs that are not intentional or deliberate but the result of independent agents acting according to their own interests. To be sure, not all of the harms and injustices of the contemporary treatment of refugees can be understood in this way; many are simply straightforward moral harms in the sense that they violate clearly accepted moral duties or legal principles. Yet I nonetheless argue that seeing some dimensions of the current refugee regime, long-term warehousing in particular, as structural injustices is both accurate and helpful in grounding responsibility. Second, we ought to shift the focus of responsibility from *outcome* to *remedial* responsibility, focusing on who ought to remedy the harm rather than who caused it. Finally, in order to determine remedial responsibility we ought to expand the way we think about our connection to global displacement and the refugee regime. All three authors I examine have much to say about how we ought to think about our connections to global structures and they urge us to interrogate more deeply the ways we are connected to both the causes of global displacement and the outcomes, namely prolonged encampment and the violations of human rights and dignity discussed in Chapter One. The ground for our remedial responsibility is our co-participation in a global system from which Western states derive significant benefits.

While these authors give us the tools to begin the task of rethinking our connections to forced displacement, I suggest that we turn to Giorgio Agamben, who saw the relationship between refugees and the state differently than many currently do. Though Agamben's writing on refugees has been much criticized,[1] I argue that we ought to take seriously the connection he refers to as the "inclusive exclusion." For him, the international order is constituted through a relationship between inside and outside, between excluded and included. Sovereign states are not merely connected to those forced outside of them through historically contingent political circumstances, but are co-dependent at their very foundation. I argue that politically speaking we ought to take this ontological connection much more seriously than we do.

Ultimately what I hope to establish in this chapter is a reframing of how we think about the ways in which Western countries are connected to the problem of global displacement and consequently, the way that we see our responsibility for this problem. Seeing the ground of responsibility in the ways I suggest in this chapter is important, since it grounds our obligations to reject encampment and take seriously the ethical treatment of the displaced while they are displaced.

§ Three Alternative Models of Global Responsibility—Global Order

Moral responsibility is usually grounded in one of two ways. In the clearest cases, we are causally connected to what we are morally responsible for. Indeed, most people believe that they are only morally responsible for their voluntary actions and the foreseeable effects of these actions. One of the reasons many think that we have relatively weak obligations to forced migrants, especially those not already on our territory claiming asylum, is that receiving states often bear little or no responsibility for causing their plight. In our ordinary use of the term, we see ourselves as responsible for remedying a problem only when our voluntary actions caused the problem, and we knew, at least in part, what the outcome would be. It is hard to ground a country like Finland's obligations to accept refugees from the Syrian civil war on the ground that they in some way caused the situation that led to the mass displacement, since their direct voluntary actions did not contribute to the civil war that is causing people to flee the country. Even in cases where a country is causally responsible for the conditions that cause displacement—such as America's interventions in Iraq and Afghanistan—responsibility is often denied since mass displacement was not the intended outcome. Grounding responsibility for refugees in a causal connection is thus unlikely to yield an acceptance of robust obligations to refugees.[2] As we have seen over and over, states are anxious to avoid responsibility. It is clear that traditional modes of responsibility do not get us very far when it comes to accepting responsibility for refugees.

One way to ground moral responsibility to those we do not already have a connection to is through the Good Samaritan principle, also known as the principle of mutual aid. This principle holds that if someone's need is great and we are in a position to help at a low cost, we ought to do so, regardless of whether or not they are a fellow citizen or share affiliation with us in some other way. As we saw in Chapter Two, Carens, Walzer, Miller, and Gibney all refer to this principle. For these authors, this is the ground of our obligation to needy non-citizens like refugees and asylum seekers that generates the obligation to resettle at least some refugees. Yet this too has yielded weak normative obligations for involuntary migrants, especially the kind that I've suggested have been neglected. At best, it engenders the sort of attitude that underlies the current status quo: refugees and displaced people are not *our* responsibility or problem, but out of beneficence and generosity we will help to the extent that we deem sufficient. With conventional models of responsibility in place, it has been fairly easy to avoid any robust attribution of responsibility for the crisis of global displacement. Below, I examine the work by three theorists who challenge this dominant paradigm of responsibility in relation to global problems and develop more robust accounts of responsibility that are applicable to the problem of responsibility for forced displacement.

One of the earliest and most influential reconsiderations of responsibility comes from Thomas Pogge. Pogge himself does not see his work as providing a new account of global responsibility; he sees his project in a more limited way as merely showing why we have a negative duty to refrain from harming the global poor, rather than a positive duty to aid (as Peter Singer and others have claimed) (Singer 1972). Even if this is the case, the *ground* of his claim that we have a negative duty to the global poor is instructive for building a viable account of responsibility for global problems. His view of global justice is premised on the claim that the causes of severe poverty and inequality must be understood as resulting from the structure of the global economic order, and not solely the result of poor decision making or bad luck on the part of poor states. Nor can the global economic order be understood as a neutral set of economic rules immune from critiques of justice. Members of Western states and their governments are responsible for global poverty insofar as we contribute to and benefit from the global economic order (Pogge 2008, 2004).

Many deny that Western countries are responsible for global poverty since we do not see ourselves as having *caused* the poverty. On this view, the primary causes of global poverty come from the poor states themselves in the form of corrupt leadership or other kinds of mismanagement of resources, aid, and loans. Pogge acknowledges that though it may appear at first glance that poor states are responsible for their own poverty, Western states have fundamentally created the conditions that allow for this in a number of ways. First, Western states and the international community in general treat the corrupt governments of poor states as entitled to represent their people, and thus, these governments gain their legitimacy, at least in part, by this international recognition. Even more directly, our governments have helped put in place many repressive governments and sold them weapons that helped them stay in power. Additionally, Western states confer resources and borrowing privileges on countries that fail to represent the interests of their people. That is, we recognize corrupt regimes as entitled to sell natural resources and to borrow money in the name of their country and people, privileges that facilitate oppressive rule and encourage coup attempts and civil wars (Pogge 2004).

Pogge makes a compelling case for the fact that we ought to think of our connection to, and hence responsibility for, global poverty in a very different way. For him, not only are we responsible because we in a sense help to sustain global poverty, but we are responsible because we directly benefit from it. Take three examples. First, when we purchase natural resources from poor or corrupt states, we are able to purchase them at much lower rates than if we were purchasing them from states who were not so desperately in need of revenue. Second, World Trade Organization rules, as a further example, permit "affluent countries to protect their markets against cheap imports (agricultural products, textiles and apparel, steel, and much else) through tariffs, anti-dumping duties, quotas, export credits, and huge subsidies to domestic producers" (Pogge 2010, 20). Such measures make it less profitable for poor countries to export their goods so much so that according to some estimates, developing countries would realize a gain of $100 billion dollars annually if these measures were not in place (Pogge 2010, 20). The benefits developing countries receive are directly at the expense of the global poor. Third, Western states largely benefit from the globalization of intellectual property rights, through agreements like TRIPS, Trade-Related Aspects of Intellectual Property Rights. TRIPS requires participants to grant 20-year monopoly patents on many innovations, including seeds and medicines, and has resulted in huge profits for Western pharmaceutical companies while limiting access to medicines and seeds of many of the poorest in the world. This structure also discourages research in diseases that affect the global poor more than those in developing countries, and benefits those in the developing world by focusing on ailments that are important to them. In short, Western states can be said to be responsible for the global economic structure that harms the poor because of the disproportionate benefits received by Western states.

This leads to Pogge's conclusion that our responsibility is not merely to help the global poor by providing aid to help relieve the suffering imposed by their own states or through natural disasters. Rather, our responsibility is to stop harming the global poor—a strictly negative duty—by reforming the global institutional order in a way that is just. "We should not think of individual donations as helping the poor but as protecting them from the effects of global rules whose injustice benefits us" (Pogge 2008, 23). In other words, we are responsible for reforming a global order we impose that contributes to severe poverty around the world. The question of responsibility for global injustice has to do with reforming the global order so that aid becomes less necessary.

What Pogge's arguments show is that global poverty emerges out of a kind of global interdependence that Western states have been reluctant to recognize. Responsibility is rooted in this previously unseen interconnection that has played a role in the prosperity of some countries and impoverishment of others. Addressing global poverty then must not be understood as a kind of benevolence but rather a way of redressing a harm that Western states both caused and benefit from. Pogge sets the foundation for thinking of global responsibility as rooted in global interdependence, a crucial step for understanding responsibility for global displacement, as I argue below. But equally important, Pogge demonstrates the importance of connecting responsibility to those who *benefit* from injustice.

Elizabeth Ashford takes up Pogge's framework but argues that a different understanding of responsibility ought to emerge from it. She argues for an account of responsibility of *individuals* in Western states to the global poor. Ashford begins by noting that for most people the West's failure to eliminate global poverty either through institutional reform or aid is not seen as problematic or something that individuals or institutions should be held accountable for. By contrast, Ashford argues that this ought to be understood as a human rights violation and a failure of responsibility. Unlike Pogge, who thinks that human rights are claims against social institutions and only indirectly against the individuals who participate in them, Ashford thinks that responsibility for human rights violations lies directly with individual agents. She argues that this responsibility is shared by many people but grounded in our co-participation in unjust social institutions and through our conformity with unjust social norms. She attributes much responsibility for global poverty to individual agents in relatively wealthy Western countries. Given the contemporary social context, individuals are implicated in responsibility for human rights violations such as global poverty because of their participation in global and domestic social institutions. For Ashford, this shows that direct responsibility for violating human rights cannot be limited to official agents, but extends to others based on their participation in informal social mores and cultural norms.

Ashford's account of responsibility is rooted, like Young's account, as we will see below, in the everyday acceptable behavior of millions of people that, for her, is structured by their participation in domestic and global social institutions, as well as their conformity with standard social norms. The harms of global poverty are not the result of direct intentional harms, but the "ongoing effects that systemically result from certain aspects of the normal behavior of millions of agents" (Ashford 2014, 103). Ashford uses Parfit's harmless torturers scenario to illustrate this point. In this scenario, a group of a thousand torturers administer agonizing electric shocks through a central system that randomly distributes them among prisoners. Though no particular agent's actions can be said to be responsible for a given prisoner's pain, they nonetheless clearly constitute a grave moral harm. Yet this harm cannot be seen by focusing solely on the particular actions of individual agents. As Ashford insists, "in order for the violation to be seen, each agent's action must be evaluated in the context of what other agents are doing" (Ashford 2014, 103).

Her claim is that ultimately direct responsibility for severe poverty as a human rights violation is shared by agents of affluent countries who participate in the operation of the global economic order. But further, members of affluent states share responsibility because they uphold social norms and practices that contribute to a given harm like poverty. In Ashford's examples, the pursuit of profit at any cost, the imperative to maximize growth, and the insistence by consumers on purchasing the cheapest products all contribute to extreme poverty. For these two reasons, individuals are implicated in the infliction of severe poverty. Take sweatshop labor for example. While it is clear that a particular employer may be directly harming a particular victim, the employee, what is less clear is the role that members of affluent states play in this harm. Ashford argues that moral responsibility accrues to all those who participate in a global economic order that creates the background conditions that make it rational for people to choose employment in sweatshops over the status quo (abject poverty). Responsibility is shared by a vast number of agents to varying degrees.

§ Global Poverty as Structural

A second influential account of responsibility for global justice comes from Iris Young, who argues that we ought to treat certain global harms as kinds of structural injustice, which she understands as the unintended but unjust outcome of the actions of millions of differently positioned individuals acting according to normally accepted rules. While Pogge's stress is on the set of global rules and policies that ultimately benefit Western states, Young's focus is on the way that the practices that most people regard as morally acceptable can still yield unjust results such as sweatshops in the global South, in which many of the most vulnerable people in the world labor in terrible conditions for our benefit (Young 2011, 95). For her, when global injustice is understood in this way, a new account of responsibility is required.

According to Young, injustice must be viewed from two irreducible different points of view: the interactional and the institutional. The interactional model asks us to look at the ways in which our actions and the actions of others contributed to an injustice. Did I lie, cheat, or steal, and did these actions result in the given injustice? On the other hand, we must also ask how we contributed "by our actions to structural processes that produce vulnerabilities to deprivation and domination for some people who find themselves in certain positions with limited options compared to others" (Young 2011, 73). The institutional perspective asks us to look at how we contribute to unjust institutions and structures that result in a particular harm or injustice. It is from the institutional point of view that we can see how our actions contribute to structural injustice. What I suggest below is that though we have taken seriously the interactional point of view—the ways in which states help or fail to help refugees through resettlement policies—we have given insufficient attention to the latter, institutional perspective, the ways in which our policies contribute to structural injustice. It's not that the first perspective is incorrect; merely that it is not the whole story. By viewing encampment as a kind of structural injustice, we are better able to see the ways that we contribute to the domination and deprivation of long-term encamped refugees through our policies of containment.

Young's account of structural injustice provides a novel framework with which to understand global injustice. Structural injustice refers to an unjust set of background conditions and the distinct harms that arise as a result of these conditions. They are distinct from harms that arise through individual interaction and state policies and institutions. The term refers to situations in which something is *morally* wrong, but there is no clear causal explanation, that is, they are not the result of a victim's bad choices, bad luck, the wrongful actions of some persons, or overtly discriminatory laws and policies, or other powerful institutions. Young defines structural injustice as arising "when social processes put large groups of persons under systematic threat of domination or deprivation at the same time that these processes enable others to dominate or to have a wide range of opportunities for developing and exercising capacities available to them" (Young 2011, 52). It occurs as a *consequence* of many individuals and institutions acting to pursue their particular goals and interests within the limits of accepted rules and norms. For example, global poverty may be understood as a structural injustice, and sweatshop labor is a harm that results from it. The injustice that many people must perform labor under terrible conditions is not the result of malicious intentions on the part of factory owners or managers, nor bad choices of the workers; rather, the choice to work in sweatshop conditions is a reasonable one, given the background of extreme poverty and inequality.

Put another way, global poverty makes particular individuals vulnerable to the harms of sweatshop labor because of their position vis-a-vis certain global social structures. Global poverty constrains the range of options available to certain people and makes certain outcomes possible, though not necessary (whether a person will end up employed as a sweatshop worker will depend on other factors such as their own choices, brute luck, and the actions of others). As Iris Young puts it, people who are in a social structural position affected by structural injustice are vulnerable to harm, and their situation differs from people not in this situation in terms of the range of options available to them and the kinds of constraints on their actions. Whether a person in this position actually experiences harm, or experiences specific kinds of harm, will depend on a number of factors (their own choices and actions, luck, the choices and actions of others), but the injustice is that some are made vulnerable to these harms because of the social structural position they are in, while others are not and may even benefit. The key point, though, is that a harm results not from an injustice, deliberate or otherwise, done by a particular person, policy, or law (we cannot attribute sweatshops to the choices of greedy owners, corrupt governments, cruel bosses, etc.). The source of the harm, as I discuss below, is the actions of large numbers of people acting according to accepted rules and practices.

One crucial difference between structural injustice and other more well understood forms of injustice, such as wrongful actions by individual or discriminatory laws and policies, is how it comes about. Iris Young explains that structural injustice arises from the actions of many people (thousands on a domestic level; millions on a global level) acting according to normal rules and morally neutral or even morally positive practices (Young 2007, 48).[3] In other words, structural injustice emerges from people living their everyday lives and pursuing their own interests. The results, however, are social-structural processes that create channels for action, channels which guide people to act in certain ways and constrain them in others. People are not restricted in any obvious and direct way, but nonetheless the ways choices are made and actions taken are directly affected. This is true for how all social structures are created. What makes some unjust and others neutral or positive are the results that they have on individuals.

There are two features of Young's analysis that are crucial for thinking about responsibility for the current problem of mass displacement and encampment. The first is that thinking about harms as structural forces us to pay attention to *outcomes*, rather than *intentions*. For example, Young makes clear that poor people's vulnerability to homelessness can, at least in many cases, be understood as the result of structural features of society, and not necessarily the result of unjust policies, bad luck, or ill will on the part of landlords. The lack of affordable housing in many cities is a structural feature. Indeed, she insists that a lack of affordable housing will be "predictable and explainable" in areas where developers target high-income renters and large-scale nonprofit housing is absent.[4] The lack of affordable housing and the vulnerability to homelessness that many poor and working class people experience is also not the result of repressive state policies, but the outcome of people pursuing their own interests within ordinary legal channels. Similarly, we can say that mass displacement and encampment are predictable features of a system of sovereign states where people are forced to leave for various reasons but have no right to entrance in any other country. Though there may be many problematic policies around refugees and displacement, the problem is not primarily the result of malicious policy or cruel intentions on the part of any one state or the UNHCR. Rather, we can see it as the *outcome* of many different states acting in accordance with their own specific goals around immigration and economic development. States see it as being in their interest to prevent the displaced from entering or integrating into their societies, and this is grounded in the morally defensible right of self-determination. The problem is that the outcome is long-term encampment and mass exclusion from political communities. What Young shows so clearly is the need to take seriously this outcome, even if the intentions behind it are not morally problematic.[5] Unless we move beyond examining the morality of individual decisions (such as whether or not it is morally permissible for a particular state to exclude refugees and stateless people), we cannot address the structural features of global injustice.

Second, Young makes a distinction between guilt and political responsibility that is important for our analysis. Following Arendt's use of the terms, Young argues that guilt applies only to deeds and can be applied only where an individual can be singled out for what she has done. By contrast, political responsibility can be attributed to those who support governments, institutions, and practices that commit harms. It is a way of connecting individuals to certain kinds of moral harms, but without conflating this connection to moral culpability. Duties are strict moral rules that tell us exactly what is required of us. Responsibility, on the other hand, is more open to interpretation as to what actions are called for. The difference between responsibility and duty maps onto Kant's distinction between perfect and imperfect duties. Responsibility arises when actions are taken in our name. So though we—as citizens of Western states, as members of the international community, etc.—may not be guilty for causing mass displacement, or intentionally placing thousands of people for years on end in camps, we are nonetheless responsible for this outcome and have a political responsibility to redress it. To have a political responsibility, as opposed to a duty, for Young means we have an obligation to address whatever harm we are connected to. We have a responsibility to remedy structural injustice, and though this is no less stringent than a duty, it involves more discretion for agents to determine what actions to do to discharge it. It is up to the agents who have responsibility to decide what to do.[6]

One of the challenges that comes with seeing global injustices as structural is that assigning responsibility is daunting. That we acknowledge it as an injustice means that someone ought to be held responsible, yet because it is structural and reproduced through the morally acceptable actions of different actors, pinpointing responsibility is not obvious. The usual methods of assigning responsibility rely on tracing a causal chain and assigning responsibility to the most proximate cause. Because of these constraints, Young develops her own model of responsibility she deems more appropriate to this kind of injustice. She calls this the social connection model of political responsibility.

Grounded in her social connection model, Young argues that individuals bear responsibility for structural injustice because they contribute by their actions to the processes that produce unjust outcomes. "Responsibility in relation to injustice thus derives not from living under a common constitution, but rather from participating in the diverse institutional processes that produce structural injustice" (Young 2011, 105). More specifically, for Young we can determine the way we are connected to a structural injustice by thinking through some *parameters of reasoning* that individuals can reference to think about the ways they are implicated in structural injustice and the responsibility they have to remedy it. There are four "parameters": power, privilege, interest, and collective agency.

The first parameter in determining responsibility is power. Young suggests that the more actual power or influence over a process that produces unjust outcomes, the more responsibility ensues. The anti-sweatshop movement seemed to adopt this principle by focusing on those with the most power to change conditions for the workers producing their garments, namely multinational designers and retailers. Pragmatically speaking, since we cannot respond to all the injustices we are connected to, it makes sense to focus on those that we have the greatest capacity to address. Second, one is responsible to the extent that one has relative privilege in relation to the unjust structure or is the beneficiary of the processes that produce structural injustice. For example, middle class clothing consumers, while not necessarily powerful in regards to the injustice of sweatshops, are nonetheless privileged vis-à-vis the sweatshop workers. Privilege is relevant for Young because it means that those individuals are better able to change their practices without suffering deprivation. Third, responsibility maps onto the extent of our interest in the structural injustice. For example, victims of structural injustice have a unique interest in remedying it, and thus share responsibility for changing the structures (along with others, to be sure).[7] Those with the most interest in a particular injustice are often in a privileged position to know what needs to be done and how things ought to change. Refugees, for example, often have a lot to say about how they would prefer to be treated, under what conditions they would like to return home, and how the global refugee regime might be changed in order to genuinely benefit them, though they are rarely consulted about this. Finally, we are responsible to the extent that we have a "collective ability," that is, we are in positions where we can draw on the resources of organized entities and use them in new ways to promote change (Young 2013, 147). In this sense, unions, churches, student groups, etc., have a particular kind and degree of responsibility because they can help to coordinate action.

Her account can be understood as situated between a cosmopolitan conception of responsibility and a nationalist one. From a cosmopolitan perspective, membership in a state is not relevant in assigning responsibility; rather, we have obligations to all of humanity to relieve suffering, though membership in a state may be the most efficient way to discharge this duty. A nationalist perspective says that our primary obligations are towards fellow citizens. Though we have some obligations that transcend borders (such as mutual aid), these obligations are not as strong or deep as the obligations of justice we have by virtue of sharing membership in a political state. Our responsibilities are always first and foremost to fellow members. Young thinks that both of these positions are limited. Against the cosmopolitan perspective, she argues that it's far too demanding and doesn't take seriously enough the value that people put in their place of membership. Against nationalists, she insists that nationality is arbitrary from a moral point of view and it discounts the relationships we have with people outside of our states. Her view, she argues, mediates between these two positions. It takes seriously the cosmopolitan intuition that we have obligations that extend beyond those to whom we are explicitly connected. But rather than all of humanity, Young finds a way to delineate those to whom we are responsible—namely, those with whom we participate in institutional processes that produce structural injustice. Her position allows us to take seriously our situatedness within a given state but not to artificially limit our responsibilities to this ground.

One of the most important features of Young's account is that determining responsibility for structural global injustice requires that we judge background conditions. On the usual liability model, a particular harm is considered a deviation from an acceptable norm; there is an assumption that background conditions are just and morally acceptable, even if not perfect. The harm then is considered a discrete, bounded event that breaks from the normal state of affairs. Seeing harm as resulting from structural injustice, however, requires that we interrogate the background that it emerged from and prevents us from assuming that the background conditions are just and morally acceptable.

Two other features of the social connection model are important as well. First, Young insists that responsibility in this sense ought to be primarily forward and not backward looking. The goal is not to look backwards to determine the cause of the harm in order to find an individual to blame. Rather, because the injustices she is concerned with are ongoing, it becomes important to think about how to transform the processes that cause injustice so that they are better in the future. The only reason to look backwards is to try to understand how the injustice has come about so that it can be rectified in the future. Second, the social connection model of responsibility is always a shared responsibility in the sense that while an individual or individual state bears responsibility, they do not bear it alone. The ground of my responsibility is my participation in structural processes that have unjust outcomes, and so we must take seriously that there are others who share responsibility in this sense. Because responsibility is shared, it must be discharged through collective action. While Young has in mind the collective action of individual citizens as opposed to the state, it's not hard to imagine that on the international level collective action would entail collective action on the part of states. That is, it would require states working together to reform international structures that lead to long-term displacement and encampment.

Finally, Young acknowledges that perhaps the biggest obstacle to addressing structural global injustice is that powerful agents often have an interest in perpetuating them. Again, it's not that they intend the outcome, but they may have an interest in the predictable, foreseeable consequences of an action. Especially if they believe that the purpose behind the action is legitimate, powerful agents may be even more reluctant to change them. Given the analysis in Chapter One, it's not hard to see how this obstacle will arise concerning global displacement. Powerful Western states benefit from policies that lead to encampment by having large numbers of people unable to make asylum claims and exercise their legal right to seek asylum. The motivation behind many of these policies can be understood as neutral or even morally positive; recall that the moral basis for containment is that it is best for refugees to be returned to their home countries once conflict has ended, and thus it is better that they be housed "temporarily" in camps in neighboring countries rather than being integrated or moved to a third country further away. Pointing out this limitation is often one of the first things that needs to be accomplished.

§ Causal versus Remedial Responsibility

A third major contribution to theories of responsibility for global justice comes from David Miller, whose view is importantly different from that of both Pogge and Young.[8] One of Miller's most fundamental distinctions is crucial for an account of responsibility for global displacement—outcome and remedial responsibility. Outcome responsibility is the responsibility that arises from the consequences of our actions. In terms of refugees, we would be *outcome* responsible for refugees if we created the situation that made people refugees, for example by persecuting a particular ethnic minority or potentially by supporting a regime that did so. As previously discussed, most accounts of responsibility for refugees hinge on outcome responsibility and as a result, artificially limit the responsibility that Western states take for this issue. On the other hand, remedial responsibility is the responsibility we have to remediate or fix a situation. This kind of responsibility can be linked to outcome responsibility but can also be established in other ways. Remedial responsibility must be assigned in some way and may be justified or unjustified, but unlike outcome responsibility, cannot be correct or incorrect.

Under what conditions can someone or some group be held remedially responsible? For Miller, we start with something that is in need of a remedy—in our case, the millions of stateless people living in camps—and ask whether there is anyone who can correct this situation. In doing so, he brackets the question of the source of the harm and focuses on the moral unacceptability of the harm in question. The worry in this approach is that the duty to aid the situation will remain undistributed—if we cannot pinpoint a causal agent, there will be no specific agent able to discharge the duty. The challenge, then, is to find a way of identifying an agent who is responsible since there is no obvious agent causally tied to the situation.

For Miller, we can say that someone is remedially responsible for a certain situation if they are *connected* in one of the following six ways; this is Miller's connection theory of remedial responsibility. First, we may be remedially responsible if we are also *morally* responsible for the situation. To be morally responsible for Miller means you are outcome responsible and act in a way that displays moral fault. In his examples, an artist is outcome responsible for a beautiful work of art she has created, but not morally responsible since she is not the author of her talent; an untalented gardener is outcome responsible for the lawn not being green, but, assuming he tried his best, is not morally blameworthy since it is not the kind of error that is subject to moral blame or praise (Miller 2007). Second, you may be *outcome* responsible for a situation, though not morally responsible. In Miller's example, you may engage fairly in business and cause someone else to go out of business. In this case you are outcome responsible for your competitor going out of business but not morally responsible. Third, you can be remedially responsible if you are *causally* responsible. Miller uses this category to distinguish acts that had an effect that was not intentionally caused nor was the effect reasonably foreseeable. For example, if I fall and knock someone off a ladder, I caused the person to fall and thus am causally responsible, but am not outcome responsible since I could not have anticipated the effects of my action.

Beyond those three somewhat standard ways of drawing connections between individuals and certain outcomes, Miller goes on to develop grounds for three less conventional ones. For Miller, we may be remedially responsible if we receive a *benefit* from the harm, though not responsible in any of the three ways discussed above. Though this *may* be a way of establishing remedial responsibility, it is not a particularly strong one in Miller's view. In common sense morality we do not often think that people have obligations because they have gained some benefit from a situation that has resulted in someone else's harm. Being linked through community is another way that Miller thinks we may be remedially responsible. Community—family, nation, religion—picks people out as bearers of responsibility, and thus may make us remedially responsible though not causally so.

Finally, and perhaps most importantly for questions of global justice, Miller argues that we may be remedially responsible if we have the *capacity* to help or ability to supply a remedy. In Miller's example, if I am the only person walking along a riverbank and a child falls in, I am responsible for saving him. Capacity as a way of justifying remedial responsibility blends two elements—effectiveness and cost. In other words, the person who has the capacity to fix a situation may be the person who can do this the most effectively (the best swimmer, in the above example, if there is more than one person who sees the child fall in) or the person who would bear the smallest cost (of two possible rescuers, perhaps the person least afraid of strong currents). Evaluating not only who is capable of helping but also who can do so most effectively and at the lowest cost must be part of the calculation.

Miller is careful to note that often more than one connection can be made between a particular state of affairs and various individuals. While it would be tempting to rank the kinds of connections that can be made, this is not totally plausible, especially for the last three modes of connection. Rather, we must bear in mind that in reality "assigning remedial responsibility involves applying multiple criteria which are opaque" (Miller 2007, 107). There is no formula that can resolve disputes, only better and worse arguments that can be made to justify various intuitions.[9]

Miller is ultimately interested in defending an account of *collective national responsibility* in which, under appropriate circumstances, members of a national community ought to be held responsible for the gains and losses they create for themselves and others (and these can be inherited across generations). This is a form of outcome responsibility that he argues is the first way one should track responsibility. Contra Pogge,[10] he argues that it is often the case that individual states can be held outcome responsible for their impoverishment because of historical decisions or culture; at the very least, he argues, there is a shared responsibility between the global order and specific countries in terms of outcome responsibility. Western states, he argues, cannot for the most part be held outcome responsible for global poverty.

Yet Miller is aware that many poor states cannot or will not discharge their responsibility for their country's poverty. In this case, citizens of Western states have a remedial responsibility to the world's poor. There are some circumstances in which this is particularly clear. First, Western states have remedial responsibilities towards the world's poor when the poverty is the result of a past injustice and we can establish a causal link between the past injustice and the contemporary harm. This responsibility is grounded in the fact that states in this case are also outcome responsible. Second, we have responsibility to the global poor when there is a failure to implement fair terms of cooperation, that is, economic rules of interaction that are fair to both sides. This, he claims, is clearly the case at present. In his view, fair rules would allow poor countries reasonable opportunities to develop and allow them to choose between different policies for achieving this. He writes, "a fair international order cannot simply mean a free market in which nations and corporations pursue their interests without regard to the consequences for vulnerable poor people. The responsibility of citizens of rich countries is to ensure fairness in this sense" (Miller 2007, 253). In this way, his conclusion is not far from Pogge's and Ashford's, though Miller stresses that Western states are remedially but not outcome responsible for global poverty. Importantly, when people are so poor that they fall below a minimum threshold and rich countries are able to aid them, the responsibility to address poverty should be considered a duty of justice, not merely beneficence. In sum, Miller claims that his view is superior to Pogge's because Pogge encourages us to think that poverty will disappear if we fix the resource and borrowing privileges. For Miller, this clearly would not make local sources of poverty disappear, and this is why it's important to ask where responsibility for world poverty really lies and not assume that it lies with those agents able to discharge remedial responsibilities (in this case, wealthy Western states).

Gillian Brock combines elements of both Miller's and Young's analysis of responsibility. Recall that for Young, structural injustice implies that the background conditions of our experiences are themselves morally problematic. Brock takes up this idea and focuses our attention on responsibility for the baseline conditions that allow an injustice like global poverty to emerge. When there is "systematic injustice in the background conditions," our responsibility is to remedy this (Brock 2014, 122). Brock sees global poverty as a systematic injustice, one that "involves people having to endure a situation where their basic entitlements are routinely ignored, remain unconsidered or insufficiently considered by those who have responsibilities to respect such basic entitlements" (Brock 2014, 141). In the case of global poverty, what Brock has in mind is this. Poverty reduction requires a number of conditions in poor states—economic growth, an effective state, active and engaged citizens. Western states can play either a positive or negative role in these conditions, and for the most part, we have played a negative one by supporting institutions in the global economy that undermine the capacity for poorer states to develop effectively.

She draws on two examples. Because of the way Western states invest in developing ones, there is pressure to create favorable tax environments by creating tax havens. This leads to illegal activity such as bribery, organized crime, and tax evasion, all of which ultimately destabilize the international economy. Though there are ways around this—such as the creation of unitary taxation for multinationals and participation in the Extractive Industries Transparency Initiative, which make it more likely that poor citizens would benefit from natural resources—most Western states have failed to do this. Second, developing countries support the "brain drain"—allowing skilled health workers (i.e., doctors and nurses) to immigrate to the developing world without any kind of compensation.

Brock argues that because practices like the ones listed above and others prevent people from living decent lives, we help to sustain poverty and harm the poor. Because we are morally culpable for global poverty, we are responsible for changing the global order and our patterns of behavior. Yet she acknowledges that it's a big claim to say that citizens of Western states have a moral responsibility to bring about an international order that undermines rather than sustains global poverty. To support this claim, Brock draws on David Miller's distinction between outcome and remedial responsibilities. Based on Miller's account, we may hold citizens of Western states remedially responsible for harmful actions performed on their behalf. Remedial responsibility for Brock is rooted in the ways we are connected to the global poor. First, we benefit from the structure of the global economy. The average citizen of Western states, she writes, benefits from unjust tax and migration policies that keep prices on consumer objects low. As a result of low prices for consumer goods, we have more disposable income to spend and the state has more income to tax in order to improve roads, schools, and other public goods. She writes, "the benefits of unjust enrichment spread to all citizens, even the morally scrupulous" (Brock 2014, 138). Even if I buy only fair trade goods, and refuse anything made in sweatshops, the benefits of having the kind of economy we do mean that I, and individuals who make similar spending choices, still benefit. Further, having a large supply of health care workers means that I'm likely to have more access to doctors, nurses, and other health care providers.

For Brock, we are also connected to the global poor *causally* insofar as we are implicated in practices that encourage deprivation. For example, tax evasion originates in and is sustained by actors in Western states. We are also remedially responsible because of our capacity—we can assist the global poor at a lower cost and through effective institutions. Finally, we are remedially responsible because we have the capacity to help. Capacity combines two components: cost and effectiveness. Western countries are able to help at a lower cost and in a more effective way than most states. Because of all these levels of connection, Brock concludes that we can assign remedial responsibility to citizens of affluent states and their governments who act on their behalf. The responsibility is to reform policies that create the background conditions of poverty and contribute to deprivation, through "reasonable modifications" to taxation, migration policy, and other international rules (Brock 2014, 141).

§ Elements of a New Ground of Responsibility

The previous discussion of responsibility for global poverty established a number of crucial features of a more robust account of responsibility for global justice, which, I argue below, can be applied to other global problems such as mass displacement and the global refugee regime. Global poverty shares a number of features in common with the problems of global displacement—neither can be attributed solely to discrete wrongs or omissions by specific agents but involve causal chains of numerous people around the globe; no specific agent can be singled out as fully responsible; both take place within complex systems that have little central structure; both result in grave moral harms; both seem changeable with sufficient political will, but such will would require a serious change in public attitudes on the issue; both injustices are sustained because they support important economic and political interests. There are also important differences. Many more people are affected by severe poverty than by displacement (even though numbers of the displaced are growing); the public tends to be more fearful of migrants and more likely to see them as threats than the global poor.

Despite these differences, I want to suggest that we can use tools from Young, Miller, and Pogge to develop an account of responsibility for displacement that does not require that an individual or state be causally connected to the given harm. What I have tried to demonstrate in the previous section is that Pogge, Young, and Miller provide three alternative groundings for responsibility that are not rooted in a traditional phenomenology of agency (where we are responsible for only what we experience ourselves as having caused) (Scheffler 2003). I have tried to draw out the merits of each view and make a case for why their views of responsibility ought to be taken seriously. Having established the intuitive plausibility of their views, I now turn back to the question of responsibility for global displacement.

How can their views supplement and improve our ways of thinking about responsibility, both for the causes of refugees and for the way we respond to mass displacement via the global refugee regime? There are three crucial elements. First, we ought to understand some of the injustices in the global refugee regime, such as encampment, as forms of structural injustice, that is, as moral wrongs that are not intentional or deliberate but the result of independent agents acting according to their own interests. Second, we ought to understand our responsibility for global displacement as remedial, that is, we are responsible for fixing the problem in front of us because of the various ways we are connected to the situation, even though we did not cause it. Finally, in order to determine remedial responsibility, we ought to expand the way we think about our connection to global displacement and the refugee regime. The ground for our remedial responsibility is our co-participation in a global system from which Western states derive significant benefits. All three models require us to interrogate much more deeply the ways in which we (Western states, citizens of these states, members of the international community, funders of the UNHCR, etc.) are *connected* to both the causes of global displacement and the outcome, namely, the prolonged encampment and violations of rights.

§ Refugee Regime as Structural Injustice

Many of the harms associated with the refugee regime ought to be understood as forms of structural injustice. Recall that for Young, structural injustice is the unintended outcome of the actions of many different individuals and collectives acting on accepted norms and for morally positive or neutral purposes. It refers to situations in which something is *morally* wrong, but there is no clear causal explanation or clear intention on someone's behalf to cause harm. It occurs as a *consequence* of many individuals and institutions acting to pursue their particular goals and interests within the limits of accepted rules and norms.

Some of the worst harms associated with displacement arise in this manner. Prolonged encampment, for example, and the violations of dignity and rights that go along with it, is clearly morally wrong, yet it is not the result of deliberate or explicit policy. As I showed in Chapter One, it arises as a consequence of various sovereign states acting according to their interests and encouraging international organizations like the UNHCR to do what seems best for the displaced, namely keeping them in camps close to their countries of origin, for their own safety and for the sake of facilitating repatriation. No state is acting on an immoral principle, since they are acting to protect their citizens and the well-being of their states, and, in principle at least, acting in the interest of the displaced themselves. States are acting according to a widely accepted moral norm, namely that states have a sovereign right to control admission to their state. Nonetheless these processes create structural barriers that prevent the displaced from accessing resources, such as security, education, and health care, and ultimately a permanent solution, and contribute to one of the worst harms of displacement, encampment.

The reason it's helpful to use Young's conception of structural injustice to talk about some of the injustices surrounding the refugee regime is precisely because it helps us to avoid unhelpful talk of causality and ill-intentions. While the sources of displacement—civil war, genocide, political repression—can be understood as straightforward injustices, and the individuals responsible for these are certainly morally culpable, the injustices around the refugee regime are better understood as forms of structural injustice. The current crisis around displacement is not the result of Western countries actively trying to harm refugees by keeping them in camps; nor is it the result of corrupt officials from international organizations trying to do the bidding of powerful countries to maintain access to funds. In most cases, the actors in the global refugee regime are acting according to their interests and pursuing what they think is the good. Yet Young's account allows us to say that even in the absence of culpable wrong-doing or cruel intentions, an injustice is being committed. Because it is an injustice, regardless of how it arose, we are called on to fix it. This, I think, is a helpful supplement to the traditional way of understanding the injustice around the global refugee regime and the requirement of responsibility. It leaves room for moral culpability, but permits us to foreground structural harms.

If we understand the harms involved in the global refugee regime in this way, it becomes easier to see why a new account of responsibility is called for. At the same time, it complicates the question of responsibility in a particular way. Because warehousing and other injustices in the global refugee regime are structural, it is particularly difficult to assign responsibility. That we acknowledge it as an injustice means that someone ought to be held responsible, yet because it is structural and reproduced through the morally acceptable actions of different actors, pinpointing responsibility is not obvious. On what grounds can we say that some entity, such as Western states, is responsible for rectifying this structural injustice?

§ Remedial Responsibility

In order to answer that question, we must move away from a traditional understanding of responsibility and shift towards thinking about responsibility as *remedial*, in David Miller's sense of the term. The usual mode of understanding responsibility maps onto Miller's concept of *outcome* responsibility, where we are responsible only for what we knowingly and intentionally caused. Remedial responsibility, on the other hand, is not necessarily linked to causality (though it may be) but starts by addressing the question of who is going to fix a situation or rectify an injustice. To use Miller's example, if a teacher comes back to her kindergarten class and finds a mess on the floor, her question, "who is responsible for this?", might mean two things. It could mean, "who made the mess?", that is, who *caused* it. Or, it could mean, "who is responsible for fixing it?" This may refer to the person who was supposed to be in charge, or perhaps the group of students whose turn it was to clean up messes. What Miller is so helpful in doing is showing that this distinction is rooted in our everyday sense of responsibility, where we acknowledge both kinds of responsibility. In many discussions of global issues such as poverty and displacement, we artificially restrict responsibility to outcome responsibility and ignore remedial responsibility. Miller shows how important it is that this kind of responsibility be discharged, especially when outcome responsibility either cannot be determined or the person who is outcome responsible is unable or unwilling to discharge it.

One of the reasons we are apt to focus on outcome responsibility is that it is much easier to assign a party to it. Who did the action that resulted in the harm that needs to be addressed? If this straightforward question can be reasonably answered, assigning outcome responsibility is possible. However, assigning remedial responsibility is not so straightforward. Unlike outcome responsibility, it cannot be causally traced back to a particular source. The only thing we can do is to consider arguments that may *justify* remedial responsibility. Remedial responsibility, because it simply must be assigned rather than discovered, may be justified or unjustified; unlike outcome responsibility, it cannot be correct or incorrect. Justifying who might be remedially responsible for "fixing" the global refugee regime, rather than who is causally responsible for the situation, shifts how we think about the way Western states may be connected to the refugee regime.

§ How to Justify Remedial Responsibility?

Miller, Young, and Pogge have much to say about how we might think about remedial responsibility that can be applied to the injustices around the refugee regime. For all three thinkers, what is required is that we shift the way we think about our connection to global harms like poverty or displacement.

For Miller we become remedially responsible because of our *connection* to an injustice. Recall that for Miller, we start with something that is in need of a remedy—in our case, the millions of stateless people living in camps—and ask whether there is anyone who can correct this situation, bracketing the question of the source of the harm. Once we do that, we must look to see who, if anyone, is connected to the situation in one of the six ways he thinks can generate remedial responsibility: moral, outcome, causal, benefit, privilege, and capacity. While Western states may or may not be morally, outcome, or causally connected to a given refugee crises, they are certainly connected to the global refugee regime through capacity, privilege, and benefit.

Miller argues that we may be remedially responsible if we have the *capacity* to help or ability to supply a remedy. In Miller's example, if I am the only person walking along a riverbank and a child falls in, I am responsible for saving her since I have the capacity to do so at a low cost to myself. Additionally, for Miller, we may be remedially responsible if we receive a *benefit* from the harm, though in his view this is not a particularly strong way to ground responsibility. Receiving a benefit from a particular harm—for example, being able to buy cheaply made clothes because laborers work under "sweatshop" conditions—binds and connects otherwise unconnected entities in morally significant ways.

It is not difficult to see how Miller's argument can be applied to the relationship between Western states and the global refugee regime. Western states have both the capacity to help and receive benefits as a result of the situation. That Western states have the capacity to help solve global issues is rarely disputed. However, it is not as obvious how Western states benefit from the current refugee regime. For one, by denying political *obligations* to aid refugees and displaced people not on their shores, the legal framework for the refugee regime allows most countries to treat refugees and displaced people as a matter of discretion—they may choose to help or not, but they violate no moral or political norm if they choose not to. Further, though funding the refugee regime is costly, Western states are able to avoid the more politically weighty costs of hosting large numbers of ethnically and religiously diverse people within their territories, spending state revenue on social programs for a large group of non-nationals, and dealing with the environmental damage and disease burdens that come with large population increases. These certainly constitute benefits that Western states receive because of the current structure of the refugee regime that connects Western states directly to the problems associated with the refugee regime. That we have a remedial responsibility based on our capacity—effectiveness and cost—is the same as with global poverty; we have the capacity to aid effectively and at a relatively low cost. Once we move away from outcome responsibility for refugee situations, we can attend to the subtler ways that we are connected to the phenomenon of global displacement and the injustices around warehousing and human rights violations, and see the ways in which these connections ground our responsibility.

§ Responsibility as Grounded in Participation

Young argues that individuals bear responsibility for structural injustice because they contribute by their actions to the processes that produce unjust outcomes (Young 2011, 105). Responsibility here derives from our interdependence in global processes of cooperation and competition in which we seek benefits and realize our own aims and projects. So though we are not guilty or liable in a legal sense for an unjust action or moral harm, our co-imbrication means that we must take responsibility for remedying the injustices that arise as outcomes of our actions. "Responsibility in relation to injustice thus derives not from living under a common constitution, but rather from participating in the diverse institutional processes that produce structural injustice" (Young 2011, 105).

It is worthwhile to recall Young's distinction between *responsibility* on the one hand, and *guilt* on the other. Young argues that guilt applies only to deeds and can be applied only where an individual can be singled out for what she has done. In other words, someone is responsible in virtue of their guilt only if we can trace the harmful outcome back to their specific actions, similar to the way we ascribe outcome responsibility for Miller. By contrast, political responsibility can be attributed to those who support governments, institutions, and practices that commit harms or whose actions contribute to structural harms. It is a way of connecting individuals to certain kinds of moral harms, but without conflating this connection with moral culpability. Political responsibility may arise when actions are taken in our name, when we contribute through financial or political support, or when we engage in practices that uphold a particular injustice. So though Western states may not be guilty for causing mass displacement, or intentionally placing thousands of people for years on end in camps, we are nonetheless responsible for this outcome and have a political responsibility to redress it because of our participation in this global system.

For Young, thinking through the ways we are connected to structural injustice is a challenge, both for individuals and for collective entities that we support, such as states and international organizations. Her "parameters of reasoning" are an attempt to breakdown this large task into more meaningful pieces. For her, we can see our connection to structural injustice via power, privilege, interest, and collective agency. Young insists that the more real power or influence over a process that produces unjust outcomes, the more responsibility ensues. In terms of power, it is hard to deny the fact that Western states have a great deal of power and influence in how crises around global displacement are dealt with. As we saw in Chapter One, international refugee aid agencies like the UNHCR are largely funded by Western states and can feel pressure to act in ways that support their agendas. This is what Young means by power. For her, simply having power is a deep way of connecting individuals and collective agents to structural injustice.

Further, we can see how privilege and collective agency apply to Western states as well. For Young, one is responsible to the extent that one has relative privilege in relation to the unjust structure or is the beneficiary of the processes that produce structural injustice. Western privilege comes through its influence over policies and practices around the refugee regime, as well as through benefitting from processes that keep millions of needy people far from our shores. When this privilege is truncated—such as when the thousands of child migrants entered the US in the summer of 2014 or when thousands of migrants entered southern Europe in 2015—political crises ensue. So while the benefit of encampment isn't always realized, these examples show why Western states are so insistent that the displaced be kept far away and benefit from this at least in the majority of cases. Because of the role that Western states play in leading or influencing large global institutions such as the World Bank, IMF, and UNHCR, that it has the collective ability to change policies and practices is without question.

For Young, political responsibility is always a *shared* responsibility in the sense that while an individual or individual state bears responsibility, they do not bear it alone. Because responsibility is shared, it can only be discharged through collective action. In terms of global displacement, collective action must take place at the international level. Given Western states' ability to engage in collective action, at least some of the time, we can see why they are well suited to discharging political responsibility. This would require states working together to reform international structures that lead to long-term displacement and encampment. Young's parameters of reasoning give us a clear picture as to how Western states are connected to structural injustice and hence bear responsibility for it.

Young acknowledges that perhaps the biggest obstacle to addressing structural global injustice is that often powerful agents have an interest in perpetuating it, not changing it. This is particularly true if people believe that the purpose behind their interests is morally legitimate (such as the protection of state sovereignty). Powerful Western states benefit from policies that lead to encampment by having large numbers of people unable to exercise their legal right to seek asylum and thus have an interest in maintaining them. The motivation behind many of these policies can be understood as neutral or even morally positive; recall that the moral basis for containment is that it is best for refugees to be returned to their home countries once conflict has ended, and thus it is better that they be housed "temporarily" in camps in neighboring countries rather than being integrated or moved to a third country further away.

For Young, our political responsibility gives rise to certain obligations. One that is particularly relevant for our topic is that responsibility for structural global injustice requires that we judge *background conditions*. On the usual model of responsibility, a particular harm is considered a deviation from an acceptable standard or status quo that is considered morally acceptable and ordinary. We judge the harm, and rarely the background that gives rise to it. For example, if a person is mugged on the street of a poor neighborhood, we are interested in the crime and the criminal, not the conditions that may have led to the poverty or the lack of state security that would give rise to such a crime. The crime is considered a discrete, bounded event that breaks from the normal state of affairs. Yet if we are talking about structural injustice, we are required to interrogate the background itself, since structural injustice is precisely the set of unjust structural conditions that constrain some and benefit others.

With Young's account, it is important to interrogate not only our policies around refugee admission but also the background that allows us to hold such positions and exclude millions of people, even when this means that these people will live for extended periods outside a political community. In other words, while our policies around immigration may themselves be just, the structural injustice comes from the very structure of the international system that permits countries sovereign control of borders on the one hand, and puts millions of people outside of the nation-state system on the other. Young's account of political responsibility asks us to question *this* phenomenon, and not merely particular policies around resettlement.

Brock further develops the idea of responsibility for the baseline conditions that allow an injustice such as encampment to emerge. Recall that for Brock, when there is "systematic injustice in the background conditions," our responsibility is to remedy this (Brock 2014, 122). Brock sees global poverty as a systematic injustice, one that "involves people having to endure a situation where their basic entitlements are routinely ignored, remain unconsidered or insufficiently considered by those who have responsibilities to respect such basic entitlements" (Brock 2014, 141). For Brock, while Western states may not single-handedly create global poverty, they can play a role—either for better or worse—by supporting institutions in the global economy that undermine the capacity for poorer states to develop effectively (such as by promoting just taxation and migration policies). Once we turn our attention to baseline, background conditions as Young and Brock insist that we do, we can attend to the ways in which our policies and practices help to shape an unjust global refugee regime.

Pogge also argues that the ground of our responsibility is our contribution to a larger global system that benefits us. Recall that for both Pogge and Ashford, the global economic order is set up and sustained by Western states in their interests. For them, participation in a global economic order that systematically harms the global poor makes Western states, and the individuals in them, responsible for global poverty. For Pogge this responsibility gives rise to purely negative duties—we must simply stop harming the global poor, and we can do this through institutional reform. For Ashford, this responsibility also gives rise to duties on behalf of individuals to change the attitudes and norms that allow extreme global poverty to go unchallenged.

As Pogge shows, global poverty is not caused by bad decisions made within poor states, but is better understood as the result of policies around trade, immigration, and resource allocation that are made at an international level. Global interdependence grounds responsibility, particularly the responsibility to refrain from harming through this global structure. Ashford shows how this responsibility extends to individual citizens within states who uphold social norms and practices that contribute to the harm. Because of global interdependence, problems that seem domestic in nature—such as poverty or displacement—must be interrogated to see the ways in which they are connected to larger global structures and policy decisions by other states in order to determine responsibility. This is something that has not been done for global displacement for the most part.

How do members of Western states *contribute* to the unjust outcome of mass encampment? The most direct way is through benefiting from policies and practices that guard our sovereign right to control membership and that keep displaced peoples far from our territory. Further, as discussed extensively in Chapter One, Western states play a formative role in the global refugee regime, not by causing displacement but by creating the norms and conditions around which the international community responds to the situation. This response has, not surprisingly, put Western interests ahead of the interests of the displaced in many ways. The West, fearful of mass migration, has sought to contain the displaced close to the sites of displacement and as far as possible from Western shores. Even though this was done in the service of a *moral* principle—it's best for people to live in their own states and thus repatriation, not resettlement, ought to be the preferred solution—it has the effect of protecting Western states from large influxes of migrants and more or less ensuring the encampment of millions of people for prolonged periods of time as they wait for a permanent solution. As the primary funders of the global refugee regime and the UNHCR, Western states have played a crucial role in shaping this global regime and ensuring that it benefits Western states as much as possible. As Pogge points out, there would be nothing wrong with acting in our own interests if not for the fact that doing so also causes severe moral harm to others, in this case for the displaced. In this way, our participation in and support of the global refugee regime, which in many ways not only fails to help as much as it can but harms the displaced, creates the ground of our responsibility to reform this global institution to bring it more in line with moral norms.

There is one final way that we can ground a connection to refugees and the displaced that has not yet been discussed. According to Agamben, refugees are connected to sovereign states because they mutually define and constitute each other. If this is right, then our connection to the displaced is deeper than even the connections mentioned above. Below, I turn to Agamben's analysis of the "inclusive exclusion" and show why it is fundamental that we understand our connection to refugees in this way.

§ Inclusive Exclusion

For Agamben, far from being an anomaly or political aberration, refugees constitute a fundamental part of modern political life. The reason why refugees are a constitutive feature of modern political life has to do with the state's relationship to *bare life*. As discussed in Chapter Three, bare life is life that is stripped of all those particular qualities that make us individuals (they lack what Agamben would call a "form of life"). What remains of their life is only their bodily, biological existence, devoid from a social or political one. As Agier puts it, "refugees are certainly alive, but they no longer 'exist', that is, they no longer have a social or political existence apart from their biological one" (Agier 2008, 49). Refugees are not the only example of bare life in modernity, but they are emblematic of it.

Politics has always had an ambivalent relationship to bare life. On the one hand, politics was originally founded on the exclusion of bare life from the polis. Agamben sees this as originating in the work of Aristotle, who made a distinction between *zoë* (bare or biological life; the kind of life we have in common with animals) and *bios* (the form of life particular to human beings). Aristotle argued that *zoë* ought to be excluded from the polis since politics was concerned with what was distinctly human—using language to decide what is just and what is unjust. Politics, based on the exclusion of *zoë*, defined itself as being opposed to bare life. Hence for Agamben, the original foundation of politics is the exclusion of bare life.

On the other hand, in modernity, bare life was reintroduced into the polis but immediately transformed into something else. In Agamben's view, the modern human rights movement, beginning with the French *Declaration* of 1789, made natural or bare life the source of sovereignty. We see in the first three articles of the *Declaration* that natural life is equated with the possession of rights ("men are born free . . . and equal in rights"), but that this natural life is immediately subsumed into the life of the citizen ("the aim of every political association is the preservation of the . . . rights of man"). In the third article we learn that the protection of the natural life of citizens is the basis of sovereignty. What this shows for Agamben is that in modernity bare life moves to the center of politics—the justification of sovereignty is the state's ability to protect the bare life of its citizens—but this bare life is immediately understood as the life of citizens. In other words, though bare life becomes important to politics, bare life without this political façade becomes invisible. The life of the refugee as a form of bare life not mediated through citizenship must remain excluded. There is no autonomous space in the nation-state for the purely human or bare life. It thus remains a *structural feature* of modern political life that bare life must be excluded from politics. This is why Agamben claims that we cannot confront refugees through political means but only humanitarian ones. In modernity, bare life is always seen as embodied in political life, and anyone who breaks this fiction—such as the refugee—cannot be treated as a political *subject*, but can only be treated, at best, as an *object* of aid and protection.

This point by Agamben is intuitive enough—since politics defines itself by the exclusion of bare life, it makes sense that the permanent exclusion of this category of people is a part of our political landscape. However, Agamben complicates this story by claiming that we should not understand this original exclusion of bare life as putting bare life off limits in a way that no longer affects politics. Rather, in his view, biological life remains *included* within the polis by virtue of being excluded.[11] This is a fundamental point in much of Agamben's work: what is excluded remains in a relationship with the included. "Western politics first constitutes itself through an exclusion (which is simultaneously an inclusion) of bare life" (Agamben 1998, 7). Politics for Agamben is fundamentally the act of separating and opposing ourselves to our bare life and at the same time maintaining a relationship to this bare life in the form of an inclusive exclusion (Agamben 1998, 8).

That political life continues to include bare life even as it tries to distinguish and separate itself from it occurs at an ontological, not a practical level. As Andrew Norris has pointed out, the idea that something can remain included by virtue of its exclusion is similar to Hegel's analysis of the law of identity (Norris 2000, 42). For Hegel the law of identity is self-contradictory in the sense that it necessarily contains difference within itself. Hegel writes that those who assert the principle "A=A . . . do not see that in this very assertion they are themselves saying that *identity is different*; for they are saying that *identity is different* from difference; since this must at the same time be admitted to be the nature of identity, their assertion implies that identity, not externally, but in its own self, in its very nature, is this, to be different" (Hegel 1976, 413). In other words, identity includes difference within itself even as it tries to separate or distinguish itself from it. Similarly, political life continues to include bare life even as it tries to separate itself from it. Politics is a constant attempt to shed bare life, to move past it; but because this is something that it cannot fully succeed in doing, politics remains defined by this struggle. This is how bare life remains included within politics by virtue of its exclusion. Politics for Agamben, as identity was for Hegel, contains its opposite even as it tries to distinguish itself from it.

"Bare life," writes Agamben, "remains included in politics in the form of the exception, that is, as something that is included solely through an exclusion" (Agamben 1998, 11). For him, the implications of a reduction to bare life can be seen most dramatically in the figure of *homo sacer*. *Homo sacer* is a figure from ancient Rome who, having committed a grave crime, is exiled from the city. From the moment of his exile, however, he can be killed by anyone without penalty (that is, it is not considered a homicide) but cannot be a ritualistic sacrifice. This is the original meaning of the term *sacred*, and it is this sacredness that is the original form of the inclusion of bare life in the political community.[12] *Homo sacer* is like an animal which can be killed without anyone seeing it as wrong, but which is too impure to be killed as a sacrifice. Though his biological life remains intact, he has lost all those qualities that make a distinctly human life, so much so that taking this life is not considered murder. The only law that applies to him is the law that exiled him from his community. His life is at the mercy of others.[13] *Homo sacer* is both excluded from political life and remains included within it, insofar as his whole being is determined by his being an exception to the law. As Catherine Mills reminds us, the excluded are not just set outside the law and made indifferent or irrelevant to it, but rather abandoned by it, i.e., "subjected to the unremitting force of the law while the law simultaneously withdraws from its subject" (Mills 2008, 62).

What is excluded from the state and its law remains in a relationship to it as an exception in the sense that it is placed outside of or excluded from the law. More specifically, "what is excluded in the exception maintains itself in relation to the rule in the form of the rule's suspension. *The rule applies to the exception in no longer applying, in withdrawing from it*" (Agamben 1998, 17–18). What the state excludes as an exception remains included within the state in the form of *abandonment*—this is the "relation of exception" by which something is included only through its exclusion (Agamben 1998, 18). This is the potentiality of the law "to maintain itself in its own privation, to apply in no longer applying. The relation of exception is a relation of ban" (Agamben 1998, 28). To be banned means to be in a relation of inclusive exclusion, where the force of the law is felt in the withdrawing of the law. Further, what is banned is not just put aside or made illicit, but is *abandoned* by the law, which is to say that it is left in a condition of exposure and threat of violence. Law, then, maintains a relation to life through abandonment; life is at the mercy of law. Put another way, the ban means that the law is *in force but without significance* (Agamben 1998, 51). Thus, "law is all the more pervasive for its total lack of content" (Agamben 1998, 52).

What would it mean to say that refugees are abandoned by the law? What it means is that refugees remain caught up in our system of sovereignty through their exclusion from it in a number of ways. First, refugees and the forcibly displaced receive their *identity* through their exclusion from, and attempt to enter into, the system of sovereign nation-states. They are defined by their relationship to the law—as people who are not citizens of any country, who fall into or fail to fall into certain legal categories (i.e., refugee, asylum seeker, economic migrant, etc.). This legal status determines the way in which their bare life will be sustained—that is, whether they have the right to work, to food rations, to housing, etc. When sovereign countries refuse entry to asylum seekers or when refugees are warehoused for years in camps, it is as if the world is saying, "our law does not apply to you," yet their whole being is defined by their being outside of the law, being unable to participate in any political system (including the state in which they are residing).

In this sense, *our* law defines them as being outside of the common world. As Michel Agier puts it, they are characterized by no-longer-being-in-the-world.[14] They are not part of the common world in the following sense: they are physically outside of the common world (refugee camps, for example, are often not even on maps through they may have existed for a decade or longer[15]); they are socially and politically outside the common world (since they are denied social integration and political rights or agency); and they are economically outside the common world (since they are not permitted to engage in the global economy except through being passive recipients of the world's "generosity"). Consequently, having been reduced to bare life, they are defined by their exclusion and lack of belonging, and are entirely dependent on the global community for their minimal biological existence.

The reason why this is generally not noticed or considered a problem is because refugees are usually considered to be in a temporary, emergency situation. People in such a situation, it is believed, can best be handled by treating individuals as lacking all identity except for their biological existence and their victimhood. The temporary and emergency nature of their situation seems to justify focusing on the protection of their biological life at the expense of ignoring their social and political existence. The problem of course is that the situation of the forcibly displaced often solidifies into something permanent, yet the de facto permanence of their situation is ignored. Thus there is no way to challenge the definition that is given to them by the global community. This is another way in which refugees remain caught up in our system of sovereignty through their exclusion from it.

Second, Agamben argued that to be abandoned to the law means that the rule of law applies in no longer applying to you. This is apparent in the lives of all but a small portion of the world's refugees (that is, the small percentage who are able to find permanent homes). There is a rule: if you are forced to flee your home, you have the right to claim asylum in our country. But because it is the state which *decides* who is subject to this rule, the state is justified in excluding those it does not want—those who are too poor, from the wrong country, are too numerous, too injured or diseased, etc. In other words, the state decides to whom the rule should apply and to whom it does not. Those in the latter group—who may genuinely lack a political community—thus remain at the mercy of the state or the global community. These people become the exception to the rule—'we will take in all refugee except *you*'—but people to whom the rule still applies in a failed way. The state refuses to apply the rule to them, yet they remain defined by precisely this failure to have the rule applied to them.

Finally, there is an important way that we remain in a relationship with those we have excluded. As Agier explains, we see refugees as being both victims and undesirables. They are not the "good victims" that evoke our desire to help and the feeling that our charity can make things better. They are victims that threaten us—threaten to take our resources, to enter our countries and weaken them. Yet we do acknowledge them as victims and not just criminals and as such, they require some reaction from us. We acknowledge that they are distinct from economic migrants, and like Walzer, generally believe that we have *some* moral obligation to them. There is a tension here that is generated from realizing that this group needs our help and is morally deserving of it, but finding them undesirable and threatening. Because they are threatening, they are excluded from our political communities as a matter of fact, yet remain part of them because we know that, in some way, we are responsible. We need to perpetually justify our exclusion of them while we at the same time acknowledge our moral obligation to them. They remain included in our system by their very exclusion.

To summarize, the situation of the forcibly displaced and their relationship to us is much more complex than is usually acknowledged. Agamben's work is helpful in illuminating the nature of this relationship. In particular, his work complicates the way in which the forcibly displaced are excluded from our political communities—they are de facto excluded but remain in an inclusive relationship by virtue of being abandoned by the law. Far from being a phenomenon that can be ignored or a situation that is easily justifiable, Agamben forces us to rethink the way we conceptualize those who are permanently excluded from our political communities and fundamentally lack political belonging. Agamben's analysis helps to see our deepest connection to refugees and thus grounds our remedial responsibility to them. Rather than being distant objects of charity, Agamben's analysis encourages us to see them as individuals that we remain in a relationship with. They are tied and connected to us in a fundamental way.

§ Conclusion

This chapter has been an attempt to reimagine responsibility for complex, structural injustices such as global displacement and the refugee regime. I have suggested that we rethink not only the model of responsibility we use and the way we frame the injustice, but also that we rethink the way we are connected to the displaced through the inclusive exclusion. These theoretical resources, I suggest, help to move us away from a focus on causal responsibility, which has limited the ability of states and the international community to take seriously our responsibility not only to aid the displaced, but to create a just refugee regime with a fair system of burden sharing. What I have suggested in this chapter is that this is the direction that our thinking about responsibility ought to move; it is not to say that such a change will be easy to achieve.

This conception of responsibility is vulnerable to Samuel Scheffler's critique of all expansive notions of responsibility. He argues that non-restrictive conceptions of responsibility could never become *internalized* by individuals and able to give action-guiding principles. This is because they contradict our experience of ourselves as agents. He argues that we experience ourselves as agents with causal power, where acts have primacy over omissions, near effects have primacy over remote effects, and individual effects have primacy over group effects. What this means is that remedial responsibility for structural injustice, where individuals must take seriously the effects of actions that they did not intend and that we are responsible for effects we did not directly cause, fundamentally contradicts this sense of agency. Further, though there is wide spread agreement that the lives of individuals around the globe are interconnected, we do not yet have a clear picture of what this means for how we should live our lives. We have difficulty in conceptualizing our place in the global chain, and consequently, situating our responsibility, and this is an obstacle that Scheffler thinks will be very difficult to overcome. He doubts that a conception of responsibility for structural injustice could be taken seriously by individuals and used to orient their conduct in a globalized world.

Is there a way to overcome Scheffler's worry? In many ways he is right. The account of responsibility proposed in this chapter is demanding and calls for a reorientation of our thinking that goes against the way most people think about and understand responsibility. Yet as Scheffler also points out, our everyday sense of moral responsibility is a specific cultural product, with its deepest roots in those affluent societies "that have the most to gain from the widespread internalization of a doctrine that limits their responsibility to assist the members of less fortunate societies" (Scheffler 2003, 41). If he's right about this, then it is at least possible to imagine that as global problems develop and intensify, interests may shift; it may become more in the interest of affluent societies to create a just system of burden sharing once migrants start reaching Western shores in larger numbers. Yet even if he is right about the difficulty of changing our thinking, it doesn't change the fact that traditional conceptions of responsibility no longer serve us when thinking about global issues. This chapter is a step towards developing a more meaningful theory of responsibility for forcibly displaced people.

Notes

1. For example, see Darling 2009, Hagmann and Korf 2012, Jenkins 2004, and Owens 2009.
2. Though it is possible, under some circumstances. As Carens pointed out, many Americans believed that the United States had a special responsibility to refugees from Vietnam in the 1960s and 1970s, whose situation was a result of the unpopular war there at the time. Many agreed that because we were responsible for the war, we were responsible for the refugees that resulted from it, especially those who were acting on our behalf.
3. To be sure, within "these structural processes some people often do illegal or immoral things," but these are "not the only perpetrators of the injustice" (Young 2011, 95). In other words, we must still take seriously blatantly immoral or illegal acts. Her point is that we cannot stop our moral analysis with these more obvious forms of harm.
4. See Kusisto (2015).
5. This approach can be distinguished from that of someone like Nozick, for whom transactions are just as long as the background of those transactions are fair, namely that there is no deceit or coercion. Young distinguishes her view from precisely this approach. Unless we focus on the outcome of political decisions, it is impossible to understand and eradicate the most complex forms of injustice.
6. Young makes this distinction in response to the objection that her view of responsibility puts too many demands on individuals. Her response is to say that this is not the case because political responsibility does not specify particular duties, only the requirement that individuals do something to collectively address the harm in question.
7. Young is clear that to say that victims of structural injustice are responsible to change conditions is not at all "victim blaming." For her, this is a way of exercising agency and bringing the unique epistemic privilege of victims to helping find solutions. For example, without the input of sweatshop workers in the anti-sweatshop movement, the solutions proposed (for example, boycotting factories that use sweatshop labor) may end up hurting the people the policies are intended to aid (such as by forcing them into worse forms of labor if their factories close). To be sure, other non-victims may have self-interests that align with those of the workers. For example, one could imagine a competing factory that does not have poor working conditions. Such a factory may not want to give up a competitive advantage to sweatshops and as such, would also have an interest in undermining structural injustice.
8. This is not to say that Miller's theory of responsibility has not been criticized. For some examples, see Lippert-Rasmussen (2009), Brooks (2011, 2014), Amighetti and Nuti (2015).
9. Brooks points out that Miller's argument would be much stronger if there were a two tier procedure in place, first asking who has the capacity and then looking at other connections (Brooks 2011).

10 Miller is highly critical of Pogge's interpretation of responsibility for global poverty because, in his view, it contains an inaccurate understanding of outcome responsibility. In Miller's reading, Pogge focuses on outcome responsibility by wealthy Western states; for Pogge, rich states have a remedial responsibility for their plight because they are responsible for creating it. This creates two forward-looking responsibilities: to redesign the international order so it is not harmful to the poor and to compensate the poor for what we have done until now. Miller argues that for Pogge, Western *capacity* links us to remedial responsibility: because we and only we could reform the global system, we bear primary remedial responsibility for global poverty. But for Miller, Pogge errs in failing to take seriously the role that a country's history and culture play in poverty. Even if it is not the sole factor, it at least shares responsibility with the rules of the global economic order.

11 Agamben interprets Aristotle's claim that we are "born with regard to life, but existing essentially with regard to the good life" as an example of the way that life is included in politics by virtue of its exclusion. It implies, in his view, that politics is "the place in which life had to transform itself into good life and in which what had to be politicized was always already bare life. In Western politics, bare life has the peculiar privilege of being that whose exclusion founds the city of men" (Agamben 1998, 7).

12 This is one reason why for Agamben just emphasizing the sacredness of bare life, such as through the discourse on human rights, is not sufficient to ensure inclusion in political life.

13 As De La Durantaye has pointed out, the reason why Agamben saw *homo sacer* as a paradigmatic figure of our time, despite its small historical significance, is that this exceptional figure is becoming increasingly the rule. States of exception, in which *homo sacer* lives after his exile, are no longer exceptional but an increasing part of our political landscape (De La Durantaye 2009, 238).

14 Agier (2008, 15). Rather than by "being-in-the-world," which Heidegger took to be a constitutive feature of human beings.

15 Bauman (2007, 38).

Conclusion

Home
By Warsan Shire

no one leaves home unless
home is the mouth of a shark
you only run for the border
when you see the whole city running as well

you have to understand,
that no one puts their children in a boat
unless the water is safer than the land
no one burns their palms
under trains
beneath carriages
no one spends days and nights in the stomach of a truck
feeding on newspaper unless the miles travelled
means something more than journey.
no one crawls under fences
no one wants to be beaten
pitied

the
go home blacks
refugees
dirty immigrants
asylum seekers
sucking our country dry
niggers with their hands out
they smell strange
savage
messed up their country and now they want
to mess ours up
how do the words
the dirty looks
roll off your backs
maybe because the blow is softer
than a limb torn off

or the words are more tender
than fourteen men between
your legs
or the insults are easier
to swallow
than rubble
than bone
than your child body
in pieces.[1]

As I write this book, scarcely a day goes by without the global refugee crisis making the front page. The numbers around the Syrian refugee crisis are well known—as of May 2016, more than 50% of the population of Syria has been displaced, 5 million people have left Syria, and an astounding 11.5% of its population have been killed or seriously wounded. These numbers of course do not capture the sorrow and agony of people who have seen their young children killed or starved, men brutally tortured, and women experiencing the violence of war that is known all too well. As Shire makes clear in the poem above, "no one puts their children in a boat unless the water is safer than the land." Nor do the numbers capture the experiences of the millions of others around the world who have been displaced from their homes and eagerly await some kind of durable solution. Yet for most of the forcibly displaced in Syria and elsewhere around the world, solutions do not come quickly, and very often, they do not come at all.

This is the experience that is at the forefront of this book. The focus of this book has been the moral dimension of how the displaced are treated between the time of their exile and when they are finally able to find a permanent durable solution. I have been arguing for a number of moral obligations that we have to all forcibly displaced people, people who cannot find a state to recognize them as a member. The primary moral obligation that we have is to reject long-term encampment as a "solution" for displacement, or to reform it so that it is in line with moral principles and protects the rights and dignity of the displaced. What follows from this is that we have an obligation to work towards a just refugee regime, one that takes seriously the full human rights of the displaced and not merely the desire of states to protect their sovereignty. Discussions about moral obligations to admit asylum seekers or resettle refugees must be supplemented with an *ethics of the temporary*, a morally acceptable way to house refugees and allow them to live with dignity while they are waiting to be resettled or return to their home countries. Whatever else we owe to refugees, we must take seriously the problem of large-scale, protracted refugee situations and the use of refugee camps to deny the displaced basic rights and political participation for prolonged periods of time.

This is not to say that we should ignore the importance of long-term solutions such as resettlement, far from it. But even if one believes that resettlement is an important moral obligation, we still ought to see encampment as a distinct moral issue. The goal of this book was neither to provide solutions to the global refugee crisis nor to put forth policy prescriptions for how an individual state ought to handle refugee issues, but instead to show the importance of focusing on how the forcibly displaced are treated while they are between homes and to demonstrate the moral imperative to reform the current refugee regime.

Further, I sought to challenge how refugee camps are understood. Though generally believed to be not very nice places, the extent to which they violate human rights and undermine human dignity is less well known. As Ben Rawlence has recently put it, the Dadaab refugee camp in Kenya "was, according to Oxfam, 'a public health emergency', and had been for several years. It was a groaning, filthy, disease-ridden slum heaving with traumatized people without enough to eat. Crime was sky high and rape was routine" (Rawlence 2016, 36). Many scholars question whether human rights can be protected even in principle in refugee camps since one of the most foundational human rights, the right to freedom of movement, is denied in these spaces.

Yet the treatment of the displaced is either downplayed or ignored in part because refugee camps are seen as *exceptional* and *temporary*. Yet as I have made clear in this book, this is far from the case. Far from being exceptional, encampment in some form is now the standard way of dealing with large-scale refugee movements; far from being temporary, the average length of time for displacement is close to 20 years. Yet it is hard for many to acknowledge that this is the status quo. "The status quo," writes Rawlence, "is dependent upon not recognizing the refugees as humans. Because to do so would be to acknowledge that they have rights. And to recognize those rights would be to occasion a reckoning with history that would be too traumatic, and it would make the conditions under which they live a crime" (Rawlence 2016, 184–185). It is much easier to believe that refugees are a problem than to acknowledge the extent of the harm that is done to them. Yet as Shire makes clear in the poem, even this demonization and dehumanization is better than what many refugees are fleeing from; "the words are more tender than fourteen men between your legs . . . than rubble, than bone, than your child body in pieces."

An important facet of my argument is that we must take seriously not only the current state of forced displacement, but also the current political consensus regarding our moral and legal obligations to refugees. In the view of many in the West, states have no legal obligation to resettle refugees or other forcibly displaced people, they recognize no moral obligation to resettle refugees, and are unlikely to resettle large numbers of refugees. The exclusion of refugees is a justifiable act of state sovereignty, whether or not it is motivated by the kind of xenophobia described in the poem with which this chapter began. Though I think this view is morally objectionable in a number of ways, we must nonetheless take it seriously as a starting point in order to ask what moral obligations flow from these circumstances. Given what Western states and their populations regard as their interests and as the limits of their duties, large-scale mandated resettlement is not likely to be a realistic solution to the current and growing phenomenon of forced displacement. This is in part why it becomes so crucial to take this in between period seriously. To conclude, let me briefly summarize how I argued for this conclusion and then look at some alternative arrangements for ethically treating refugees while they are displaced.

I began with a detailed examination of the refugee protection regime and the different normative obligations that states have to refugees. By looking at how solutions to the problem of refugees have evolved, from resettlement to repatriation to containment, it became evident that there was a moral ideal that underlies our reliance on the practice of containment: containment is tacitly justified as an unfortunate but necessary step to achieve what is ultimately best for refugees, repatriation. Though this interpretation of containment sees it as motivated by a moral ideal, it is nonetheless a political choice that is highly questionable. Refugee camps have come to function as the de facto "fourth" durable solution even though they often systemically violate basic human rights and undermine human dignity. Yet despite this, containment is a practice that Western states continue to support.

Next, I provided an overview of the ways that our moral obligations to refugees have been understood philosophically, through examining the work of six contemporary philosophers (Walzer, Miller, Wellman, Benhabib, Carens, and Gibney). These theorists, though concerned with the broad question of what justice requires with respect to the treatment of refugees, focus predominantly on the obligations raised by refugees for Western states in terms of resettlement. Though they all agree that the fact that people are forcibly displaced from their states is an injustice that creates moral obligations for other states, they differ as to what moral obligations we, as relatively wealthy Western states, have to the displaced. There was no consensus on this issue. Walzer, Miller, and Wellman all set strong limits on our obligations to resettle refugees. Though I disagreed with their views for a number of reasons, my primary criticism was that they have little or nothing to say about what happens to those whom states refuse to resettle and who are unable to be repatriated within a reasonable amount of time. Though Benhabib, Carens, and Gibney argue for much more extensive obligations to refugees, I suggested that they too do not say enough about how refugees should be treated in the period between their initial displacement and their repatriation or resettlement. As I argued, the duty to resettle needs to be supplemented with an *ethics of the temporary*, a morally acceptable way to house refugees and allow them to live with dignity while they are waiting to be resettled or to return to their home countries.

In Chapter Three, I showed the importance of analyzing the problem of forced displacement from the perspective of continental theorists like Arendt, Agamben, and Agier, and the importance of attending to the ontological as well as political harms of forced displacement. Using the work of Hannah Arendt, I established that forced displacement entails two distinct harms that must be analyzed separately. The first harm is the legal or political harm, namely the loss of a political community and a legal identity in the form of citizenship. This was an important loss in Arendt's view because it is only within a political community that human rights can be protected. Her view remains true, I argued, because despite over 50 years of changes in international law and human rights conventions around stateless people and refugees, the rights of refugees remain fundamentally precarious outside the nation-state.

Yet for Arendt, herself a refugee, this was not the most important loss for refugees. For her, forced displacement entails an *ontological* deprivation, a loss which is deepened by the practices around prolonged encampment. It is a reduction to bare life, an expulsion from the common realm of humanity, and a denial of meaningful agency. The ontological deprivation, I suggest, constitutes a distinct moral harm to refugees. I show that taking seriously the ontological deprivation of statelessness has important consequences for how we think about our moral obligations. My explication of the ontological deprivation serves to support my argument that we have a moral obligation to reject encampment as a solution to the problem of forced displacement. Further, once we take seriously the ontological deprivation as a distinct harm, other ways we ought to help the displaced become more evident. We ought to think about ways that refugees may be able to keep a meaningful political identity and resist a reduction to bare life, even though they may be formally bereft of citizenship or political membership. Though we have had limited success in addressing the political harm of forced displacement, namely a lack of citizenship (i.e., through resettling or repatriation), there are nonetheless other ways to address the ontological deprivation (some of which I discuss in the next section). Refugee policy, supported by Western states, ought to be concerned with addressing the ontological deprivation of statelessness, through affirming the agency of refugees, and not merely the political harm of a loss of citizenship.

In Chapter Four I dealt with perhaps the most challenging problem of global justice, responsibility. Who is or ought to be responsible for implementing the moral obligations I have argued for throughout this book? I looked at three models of global responsibility (developed by Young, Miller, and Pogge) that are alternatives to traditional models of responsibility. Drawing from these alternatives, I suggested that we think about many of the harms associated with the treatment of the forcibly displaced as *structural injustices* that give rise to political responsibility. The way that Iris Young describes it, structural injustices are not the result of deliberate harm or explicitly unjust policies, but the unintentional outcome of the actions of different agents, each working for her own morally acceptable ends. It refers to situations in which something is *morally* wrong, but there is no clear causal explanation or clear intention on someone's behalf to cause the harm.

Conclusion   141

That the displaced are often forced to live in squalid camps for decades is clearly a moral injustice; yet this injustice is neither the result of the deliberate policies of a given state intended to harm the displaced nor the result of ill intentions on the part of international agencies or others. It arises as a consequence of various sovereign states acting according to their interests and encouraging international organizations like the UNHCR to do what seems best for the displaced, namely keeping them in camps close to their countries of origin, for their own safety and for the sake of facilitating repatriation. No state is doing anything illegal, or, for the most part, even immoral, since they are acting to protect their citizens and the interests of their states; in principle at least, they are even acting in the interest of the displaced themselves. Nonetheless these processes create structural barriers that prevent the displaced from seeking asylum and accessing resources, such as security, education, and health care and ultimately a permanent solution. Seeing the injustices around the refugee regime, especially encampment, as structural allows us to avoid the question of moral culpability and focus instead on remedying the injustice.

To be clear, there are also many straightforward harms associated with the refugee regime: repatriating legitimate asylum seekers, preventing refugees from accessing territory to claim asylum, sexual violence perpetrated by NGO workers, police in host states, and UN officials, for example. Further, the failure to resettle large numbers of refugees who cannot be repatriated in a reasonable amount of time represents a moral failure of an international system that was designed to find solutions for displaced people. Yet I think it is still helpful to think of encampment as a structural injustice, since it helps us to get at a more robust account of responsibility. Unless we move beyond examining the morality of individual decisions (such as whether or not it is morally permissible for a particular state to exclude refugees), we cannot address the structural features of global injustice.

Further, I argued that we ought to understand our responsibility for global displacement as a *remedial* responsibility. We are responsible for fixing the problem in front of us because of the various ways we are connected to the situation, even though we did not cause it. In order to determine remedial responsibility we ought to expand the way we think about our connection to global displacement and the refugee regime. The ground for our remedial responsibility is our co-participation in a global system from which Western states derive significant benefits. All three models require us to interrogate much more deeply the ways in which we (as representatives of Western states, citizens of these states, members of the international community, funders of the UNHCR, etc.) are *connected* to both the causes of global displacement and the outcome, namely, prolonged encampment and violations of rights.

While this book is not about solutions, I hope it will help us to find better ways to deal with the growing phenomenon of forced displacement and give a stronger ground for our ethical obligations to the forcibly displaced. While the goal of this book is not to provide an alternative to the status quo—there are many other scholars[2] and NGOs working on this problem—it is intended to provide the moral basis for why it is urgent to consider and support alternatives. Once we see the current refugee regime as a moral injustice, what policies and practices should we support? Below, I examine a few of the policies that are promising.

Two policies that ought to go hand in hand are supporting resettlement as a *duty* of states and policies of local integration while refugees await resettlement or repatriation. As Carens has argued, we have duties to refugees both in the long and short term (Carens 2013). There has been much philosophical analysis about what we owe refugees in the long term in terms of resettlement and asylum. Since I discussed this debate at length in Chapter Two, suffice it to say here that I am sympathetic to the view that we ought to consider resettlement not merely an act of charity, but a duty. Once we take long-term displacement as a norm in our globalized world, it is imperative that states resettle refugees in a much more robust and fair way than they currently do. As Carens argued, states ought to take in an appropriate number based on their causal responsibility, absorptive capacity, ability to assimilate, and what refugees themselves want. This would be an essential feature of any ideal refugee regime, one that we certainly ought to work towards.

What about the short term? What policies should we support for refugees while they are waiting to be resettled or repatriated, given that this may be years or even decades and that many of them will never be resettled or able to return to their homes? It is here where there is the greatest need for creative solutions. One possibility that I see as particularly promising is temporary local integration, where refugees live as part of the communities that they find themselves in until a more permanent solution (resettlement or repatriation) becomes possible. Smith, for example, argues that temporary local integration can be used as an *interim* measure where refugees can enjoy the rights set forth in the Refugee Convention while states work towards a permanent solution (Smith 2004, 52).

Rather than funding camps as separate from the host state, the UNHCR and Western states would fund development projects within host states that would benefit the state, its population, as well as refugees who live there. Aid would go to improving all public facilities (schools, hospitals, job training programs, etc.) and developing the skills and talents of refugees that could be put to use in a host country. The goal is that refugees would become increasingly self-reliant and not dependent on international aid. In Uganda, for example, refugees are allowed a significant amount of economic integration, including the right to work and support in the pursuit of other economic opportunities, pending repatriation. In one study of this, researchers found that not only do refugees themselves benefit, but they positively contribute to local and national economies as well (Betts et al. 2014). This would go a long way in remediating the ontological deprivation of forced displacement.

The International Committee of the Red Cross and Red Crescent also views local integration as an important measure, one that is to a certain degree inevitable:

> More incremental approaches to local integration may help to overcome states' resistance to mass naturalization. In all protracted displacement crises, local integration becomes a reality over time, even where such contact is officially proscribed. Marriages, education and employment can all help to build informal links between displaced and host communities, but a lack of official status means these gains are precarious.... States should accept the inevitability of a degree of local integration and consider what forms of formal status might be granted to some displaced groups. Permanent residency, for instance, might be granted to refugees who own businesses, hold a high school diploma or can fill recognized labour shortages. (ICRC 2012)

One problem with this that many philosophers are aware of is that refugees may end up remaining a permanent sub-class of citizens, living in a country but never achieving full rights or citizenship. Michael Walzer articulated the moral concern around permanent alienage as follows. For him, every immigrant and long-term resident must have at least the potential to become a citizen. This is rooted in the idea that polities ought to be composed of equals, and without the possibility of naturalization you would have a "little tyranny"; the state would be like a family with live-in servants (Walzer 1983). The principle of political justice holds that the process of self-determination through which a state defines its political life must be open to all residents who work in the economy and are subject to its laws. Naturalization can have constraints such as time or qualifications, but it can never in principle be completely out of the question.

David Miller (2007) makes a similar point. For him, the worry about permanent alienage is particularly problematic for liberal states committed to the ideal of equal citizenship. On this view, all members of a political community must have equal rights and responsibilities, and as such, "second class citizens" are morally problematic. What follows from this for Miller is that states have the obligation to make immigrants into full citizens and grant them the same rights as other permanent members.

I would like to suggest that while we take these concerns seriously, we also acknowledge that our current system has implicitly permitted the permanent alienage of millions of refugees who live for decades either in refugee camps or urban areas without political status. It is already a moral harm that is part of the current status quo. Though the dangers associated with permanent alienage are real and important, they are no worse than the current dangers refugees are more or less assured of. As such, this worry doesn't reduce the importance of temporary local integration as one method of ethically treating the displaced while they are awaiting a permanent solution.

144   *Conclusion*

But perhaps being aware of it will encourage states to find permanent solutions so that, as Walzer hoped, every long-term resident has at least the potential to become a citizen.

While reformulating the policies that states rely on to treat the displaced during their displacement is crucial, we ought to also support a reformulation of the UNHCR to make it both more effective and more accountable. The current funding structure of the UNHCR makes it dependent on donor states, and this limits its potential to help the displaced and advocate for political solutions. As noted in Chapter One, the UNHCR's entire budget comes from a handful of countries, with the US, Japan, and the EU accounting for 94% of all state contributions (Loescher 2012, 6). The problems with this funding structure are clear. Because it is dependent on so few states, the ability of the UNHCR to operate independently is compromised. This is especially true when it might go against the perceived interests of these states. The UNHCR, writes Loescher, "is in no position to challenge the policies of its funders and host governments" (Loescher 2012, 6). Greater financial independence is justifiable on the grounds that the global refugee regime ought to work in the interests of the displaced, and it cannot do that if it is beholden to donors. While Western states might not want to lose control of this organization for fear that the UNHCR will challenge their policies on refugees, understandable though it is, this is not a strong moral argument for keeping the status quo in place. In order to make it more effective, we ought to support the mandatory funding of the UNHCR.

Though improving the independence and effectiveness of the UNHCR is crucial, it is equally important to make it and other institutions that serve the displaced more accountable to the displaced themselves. It is widely noted that one of the main disadvantages to the way the UNHCR is currently structured is that it is largely unaccountable to anyone for violations of its mandate. There is no independent monitoring mechanism for the 1951 Convention as there is for other UN human rights conventions, no procedures for overseeing the work of the UNHCR, and no way to make independent reports to the UN about its successes and failures. Nor is there even minimally an ombudsperson who could hear complaints from refugees and report them to the UN or attempt to resolve them. In order to make the UNHCR more accountable, a number of scholars (Verdirame and Harrell-Bond 2005, Loescher 2012) have suggested that there be an independent monitoring mechanism or ombudsman to provide oversight of states' activities around refugee protection. This is to help remedy not only the problems refugees face, but also their *powerlessness* to challenge decisions or find remedies. This seems like a minimal way that the refugee regime could be repaired that would be beneficial to the displaced without directly threatening the sovereignty of member states.

I would like to stress that whatever policies we support, they must treat refugees as agents and respect their voices. One of the problems identified

Conclusion 145

in Chapter Three is the loss of voice and agency that is part and parcel of becoming a refugee. Even though the UNHCR and other agencies are aware of this problem and have introduced new methodologies to address it, the lack of voice and agency remain problems. As I've stressed throughout this book, Western states think that the problem for refugees is primarily a loss of citizenship, whereas for refugees, at least on a day-to-day basis, the problem is the degradation and lack of rights associated with encampment. Aleinikoff, for example, suggests that all refugee issues must be considered from the bottom up, with refugees participating in both the definition of the problem and in finding acceptable solutions. In this sense, international assistance should be thought of as facilitative (focused on aiding refugees in effectuating their choices) rather than control-based (helping asylum countries contain refugee flows) (Aleinikoff 1992, 69).

One perspective that follows from this is that we should reject what Aleinikoff has called the "membership bias" shared by states, theorists and lawyers (Aleinikoff 1992). This bias holds that what refugees want most is membership in a new state. Is this unexamined preference for membership really justified? Aleinikoff does not think so. "It is at least plausible that refugees might prefer an ambiguity and flexibility that does not compel an immediate consideration of identity questions and that keeps options open for future return or resettlement" (Aleinikoff 1992, 134). This requires us to consider other forms of belonging that are not tied to citizenship yet are able to protect human rights, both civil and political, as well as social, economic, and cultural. Further, solutions must include participation by refugees in the definition both of the problem and the solution. How we should prioritize solutions should be *left open* and determined in consultation with the displaced themselves. In the view of the International Committee of the Red Cross and Red Crescent, the "international community therefore needs to consider developing creative alternatives to the traditional solutions and new ways of viewing citizenship" (ICRC 2012).

Finally, it's important to keep in mind that the primary problem around encampment and forced displacement is not that there is a lack of solutions; the problem is a lack of moral determination to change the status quo. As the International Committee of the Red Cross and Red Crescent put it, "there is no shortage of innovative approaches that could help to alleviate the trauma of extended exile. However, the difficulty lies not in the new ideas, but in escaping the old ones. Solving protracted displacement is not impossible, but it requires political will. The misery of prolonged displacement has become 'normal', because many states have effectively decided that the misery of excluded forced migrants is an unfortunate price worth paying to avoid having to confront the difficult political questions raised by the injustices and inequalities of a bordered world" (ICRC 2012, 228). It is my hope that this book has contributed to making clear that the current status quo for refugees ought to be intolerable for those of us in the

West concerned with justice and human rights and that our indifference to this problem is not acceptable. This would be a first step towards challenging protracted encampment and the harms associated with it, and working towards a more just refugee regime.

Notes

1 Abridged. See the full poem, http://seekershub.org/blog/2015/09/home-warsan-shire/
2 See for example Schuck (1997), who offers four proposals for improving refugee protection and advocates for a regionally structured, rather than global, system of refugee protection. Also see Burton (1988), Hathaway (1991), Arulanantham (2000), and more recently, Amnesty International (2015), UNHCR (2016).

Bibliography

Africa Watch Women's Rights Projects; Division of Human Rights Watch. "Seeking Refuge, Finding Terror: The Widespread Rape of Somali Women Refugees in North Eastern Kenya." Vol. 5, No. 13 (October 4, 1993), pp. 3–24.
Agamben, Giorgio. *Homo Sacer: Sovereign Power and Bare Life*. Trans. Daniel Heller Roazen. Stanford: Stanford University Press, 1998.
——. *Means without Ends: Notes on Politics*. Minnesota: University of Minnesota Press, 2000.
Agier, Michel. *On the Margins of the World: The Refugee Experience Today*. Malden, MA: Polity Press, 2008.
——. *Managing the Undesirables: Refugee Camps and Humanitarian Government*. Trans. David Fernbach. Malden, MA: Polity Press, 2011.
Aleinikoff, Alexander T. "State-Centered Refugee Law: From Resettlement to Containment." *Michigan Journal of International Law*, Vol. 14, No. 120 (Fall 1992), pp. 120–138.
Amighetti, Sara and Alasia Nuti. "David Miller's Theory of Redress and the Complexity of Colonial Injustice." *Ethics and Global Politics*, Vol. 8 (2015). http://dx.doi.org/10.3402/egp.v8.26333
Amnesty International. "8 Ways to Solve the World Refugee Crisis." 2015. https://www.amnesty.org/en/latest/campaigns/2015/10/eight-solutions-worldrefugee-crisis
Arendt, Hannah. *The Origins of Totalitarianism*. New York: Meridian Books, 1978.
——. *Essays in Understanding 1930–1954*. Ed. Jerome Kohn. New York: Harcourt Brace, 1993.
——. *The Human Condition*. Chicago: University of Chicago Press, 1998.
——. *Responsibility and Judgment*. Ed. Jerome Kohn. New York: Schocken Books, 2003.
——. *The Jewish Writings*. New York: Schocken Books, 2008.
Aristotle. *Politics*. Trans. Carnes Lord. Chicago: University of Chicago Press, 1984.
Arulanantham, Ahilan T. "Restructured Safe Havens: A Proposal for Reform of the Refugee Protection System." *Human Rights Quarterly*, Vol. 22, No. 1 (February 2000), pp. 1–56.
Ashford, Elizabeth. "Responsibility for Violations of the Human Right to Subsistence." In Meyers, Diana ed. *Poverty, Agency, and Human Rights*. Oxford: Oxford University Press, 2014.
Barbieri, William. *Ethics of Citizenship: Immigration and Group Rights in Germany*. Durham: Duke University Press, 1998.

Bibliography

Barbour, Charles. "Between Politics and Law: Hannah Arendt and the Subject of Rights." In Goldoni, Marco and McCorkindale, Christopher eds. *Hannah Arendt and the Law*. Portland: Hart Publishing, 2012.

Barnett, Michael. "Humanitarianism, Paternalism, and the UNHCR." In Betts, Alexander and Loescher, Gill eds. *Refugees in International Relations*. Oxford: Oxford University Press, 2011.

Barnett, Michael and Martha Finnemore. *Rules for the World: International Organizations in Global Politics*. Ithaca: Cornell University Press, 2004.

Basaran, T. "Security, Law, Borders: Spaces of Exclusion." *International Political Sociology*, No. 2 (2008), pp. 339–354.

Bauman, Zygmunt. *Liquid Times: Living in an Age of Uncertainty*. Malden, MA: Polity Press, 2007.

Bayefsky, Anne F., and Joan Fitzpatrick. *Human Rights and Forced Displacement*. The Hague: Martinus Nijhoff Publishers, 2000.

Beitz, Charles. *The Idea of Human Rights*. Oxford: Oxford University Press, 2009.

Belton, Kristy. "The Neglected Non-Citizen: Statelessness and Liberal Political Theory." *Journal of Global Ethics*, Vol. 7, No. 1 (April 2011), pp. 59–71.

Benhabib, Seyla. *The Rights of Others: Aliens, Residents and Citizens*. Cambridge: Cambridge University Press, 2004.

———. *Dignity in Adversity: Human Rights in Troubled Times*. Malden, MA: Polity Press, 2011.

Betts, Alexander. *Protection by Persuasion*. Ithaca: Cornell University Press, 2009.

———. "International Cooperation in the Refugee Regime." In Betts, Alexander and Loescher, Gill eds. *Refugees in International Relations*. Oxford: Oxford University Press, 2011.

Betts, Alexander and Gill Loescher. "Refugees in International Relations." In *Refugees in International Relations*. Oxford: Oxford University Press, 2011.

Betts, Alexander, Louise Bloom, Josiah Kaplan and Naohiko Omata. *Refugee Economies: Rethinking Popular Assumptions*. Oxford University: Humanitarian Innovation Project, Refugees Studies Centre, 2014.

Bhabha, Jacqueline. "International Gatekeepers? Tension between Asylum Advocacy and Human Rights." *Harvard Human Rights Journal*, Vol. 15 (Spring 2002), pp. 155–181.

Boswell, Christina. *The Ethics of Refugee Policy*. Aldershot: Ashgate, 2005.

Bradley, Megan. *Refugee Repatriation: Justice, Responsibility and Redress*. Cambridge: Cambridge University Press, 2013.

Brookings-LSE. *Under the Radar: Internally Displaced Persons in Non-Camp Settings*. October 2013. http://www.brookings.edu/~/media/research/files/reports/2013/10/noncamp-displaced-persons/under-the-radaridps-outside-of-camps-oct-2013.pdf

Brooks, Thom. "Rethinking Remedial Responsibilities." *Ethics and Global Politics*, Vol. 4, No. 3 (2011), pp. 195–202.

———. "Remedial Responsibilities beyond Nations." *Journal of Global Ethics*, Vol. 10, No. 2 (2014), pp. 156–166.

Brown, Chris. "The Only Thinkable Figure? Ethical and Normative Approaches to Refugees in International Relations." In Betts, Alexander and Loescher, Gill eds. *Refugees in International Relations*. Oxford: Oxford University Press, 2011, pp. 151–168.

Brown, Wendy. "The Most We Can Hope for: Human Rights and the Politics of Fatalism." *The South Atlantic Quarterly*, Vol. 103, No. 2/3 (Spring/Summer 2004), pp. 451–463.

Burton, Eve B. "Leasing Rights: A New International Instrument for Protecting Refugees and Compensating Host Countries." *Columbia Human Rights Law Review*, Vol. 19, No. 2 (1988), pp. 307–332.

Butler, Judith. *Precarious Lives: The Powers of Mourning and Violence*. Brooklyn: Verso, 2006.

Carens, Joseph. "Aliens and Citizens: The Case for Open Borders." *The Review of Politics*, Vol. 49, No. 2 (Spring 1987), pp. 251–273.

———. "Refugees and the Limits of Obligation." *Public Affairs Quarterly*, Vol. 6, No. 1 (January 1992), pp. 31–44.

———. *The Ethics of Immigration*. Oxford: Oxford University Press, 2013.

Chalk, P. "The International Ethics of Refugees: A Case of Internal or External Political Obligations." *Australian Journal of International Affairs*, Vol. 52, No. 2 (1998), pp. 149–163.

Cohen, Roberta. "'What's So Terrible about Rape?' and Other Attitudes at the United Nations." *SAID Review*, Vol. 20, No. 2 (2000), pp. 73–80.

Cole, Phillip. *Philosophies of Exclusion: Liberal Political Theory and Immigration*. Edinburgh: Edinburgh University Press, 2000.

Coleman, M., and K. Grove. "Biopolitics, Biopower, and the Return of Sovereignty." *Environment and Planning D: Society and Space*, Vol. 27 (2009), pp. 489–507.

Crisp, Jeff. "A State of Insecurity: The Political Economy of Violence in Kenya's Refugee Camps." *African Affairs*, Vol. 99 (2000), pp. 601–632.

Crisp, Jeff and Amy Slaughter. "A Surrogate State? The Role of the UNHCR in Protracted Refugee Situations." *New Issues in Refugee Research*, Research Paper No. 168, January 2009.

Darling, Jonathan. "Becoming Bare Life: Asylum, Hospitality, and the Politics of Encampment." *Environment and Planning D: Society and Space*, Vol. 27 (2009), pp. 649–665.

De Genova, Nicholas and Nathalie Peutz. *The Deportation Regime: Sovereignty, Space, and the Freedom of Movement*. Durham: Duke University Press, 2010.

De La Durantaye, Leland. *Giorgio Agamben: A Critical Introduction*. Stanford: Stanford University Press, 2009.

Dembour, Marie-Benedicte and Tobias Kelly. *Are Human Rights for Migrants? Critical Reflections on the Status of Irregular Migrants in Europe and the United States*. New York: Routledge, 2011.

Department of State (United States), Bureau of Population, Refugees, and Migration, Office of Admissions. *Access to the U.S. Refugee Admissions Program*. September 2006. http://www.rcusa.org/uploads/pdfs/Access%20to%20the%20 U.S.%20Refugee%20Admissions%20Program.pdf (accessed July 28, 2015).

Doty, Roxanne. "States of Exception on the Mexico-U.S. Border: Security, 'Decisions' and Civilian Border Patrols." *International Political Sociology*, Vol. 1 (2007), pp. 113–137.

Douglas, Bob, Clare Higgins, Arja Keski-Nummi, Jane McAdam and Travers McLeod. *Beyond the Boats: Building an Asylum and Refugee Policy for the Long Term*. Australia21 in collaboration with the Center for Policy Development and the Andrew and Renata Kaldor Center for International Refugee Law at the

University of New South Wales, November 2014. https://cpd.org.au/wp-content/uploads/2014/11/Beyond-the-boats_LoRes.pdf (accessed July 27, 2015).

Dunn, Jason and Elizabeth Conns. "Aleatory Sovereignty and the Rule of Sensitive Spaces." Unpublished presentation given at Northeastern University, September, 2012, *Workshop on Applied Philosophy: Global Justice and the Ethics of Exclusion*.

Esri, Marina Koren. "Where Are the 50 Most Populous Refugee Camps?" *Smithsonian.com* (June 19, 2013). http://www.smithsonianmag.com/innovation/where-are-50-most-populous-refugee-camps-180947916/?no-ist (accessed July 27, 2015).

Fassin, Didier. "Compassion and Repression: The Moral Economy of Immigration Policies in France." *Cultural Anthropology*, Vol. 20, No. 3 (August 2005), pp. 362–387.

———. *Humanitarian Reason: A Moral History of the Present*. LA: University of California Press, 2012.

Fassin, Didier and M. Pandolfi (Eds.). *Contemporary States of Emergency: The Politics of Military and Humanitarian Intervention*. New York: Zone Books, 2010.

Ferracioli, Laura. "The Appeal and Danger of a New Refugee Convention." *Social Theory and Practice*, Vol. 40, No. 1 (January 2014), pp. 123–144.

Franke, Mark F. N. "Political Exclusion of Refugees in the Ethics of International Relations." In Hayden, Patrick ed. *Ashgate Research Companion to Ethics and International Relations*. Surrey: Ashgate Publishing, 2009, pp. 309–328.

Fricker, Miranda. *Epistemic Injustice: Power and the Ethics of Knowing*. Oxford: Oxford University Press, 2007.

Gibney, Matthew. *The Ethics and Politics of Asylum: Liberal Democracy and the Response to Refugees*. Cambridge: Cambridge University Press, 2004.

Gorlick, Brian. "Refugee Protection in Troubled Times: Reflections on Institutional and Legal Developments at the Crossroads." In Steiner, Niklaus, Gibney, Mark and Loescher, Gill eds. *Problems of Protection: The UNHCR and Human Rights*. New York: Routledge, 2012, pp. 79–100.

Gündoğdu, Ayten. "'Perplexities of the Rights of Man': Arendt on the Aporias of Human Rights." *European Journal of Political Theory*, Vol. 11, No. 1 (2012), pp. 4–24.

———. *Rightlessness in an Age of Rights: Hannah Arendt and the Contemporary Struggles of Migrants*. Oxford: Oxford University Press, 2015.

Haddad, Emma. *The Refugee in International Society: Between Sovereigns*. Cambridge: Cambridge University Press, 2008.

Hagmann, Tobias, and Benedict Korf. "Agamben in the Ogaden: Violence and Sovereignty in the Ethiopian-Somali Frontier." *Political Geography*, Vol. 31 (2012), pp. 205–214.

Hammerstad, Anne. "UNHCR and the Securitization of Forced Migration." In Betts, Alexander and Loescher, Gill eds. *Refugees in International Relations*. Oxford: Oxford University Press, 2011.

Harvey, Colin. "Dissident Voices: Refugees, Human Rights and Asylum in Europe." *Social and Legal Studies*, Vol. 9, No. 3 (2000), pp. 367–396.

Hathaway, James C. "Reconceiving Refugee Law as Human Rights Protection." *Journal of Refugee Studies*, Vol. 4, No. 113 (1991), pp. 126–128.

Hayden, Patrick. *Political Evil in a Global Age: Hannah Arendt and International Theory*. New York: Routledge, 2009.

Hegel, G.W. *The Science of Logic*. Trans. A. V. Miller. New York: Humanities, 1976.

Bibliography 151

Helton, Arthur. "What Is Refugee Protection? A Question Revisited." In Steiner, Niklaus, Gibney, Mark and Loescher, Gill eds. *Problems of Protection: The UNHCR and Human Rights.* New York: Routledge, 2012, pp. 19–37.

Holzer, Elizabeth. "A Case Study of Political Failure in a Refugee Camp." *Journal of Refugee Studies*, Vol. 25, No. 2 (2012), pp. 257–281.

Hovil, Lucy. "With Camps Limiting Many Refugees, the UNHCR's Policy Change Is Welcome." *The Guardian*, October 2, 2014.

Human Rights Watch. *Seeking Protection: Addressing Sexual Violence and Domestic Violence in Tanzania's Refugee Camps.* 2000. http://www.hrw.org/reports/2000/tanzania

Hyndman, Jennifer. *Managing Displacement: Refugees and the Politics of Humanitarianism.* Minneapolis: University of Minnesota Press, 2000.

Hyndman, Jennifer and Alison Mountz. "Another Brick in the Wall? Non-Refoulement and the Externalization of Asylum by Australia and Europe." *Government and Opposition*, Vol. 43, No. 2 (Spring 2008), pp. 249–269.

International Federation of Red Cross and Red Crescent Societies (ICRC). *World Disasters Report 2012: Focus on Forced Migration and Displacement.* http://www.ifrc.org/en/publications-and-reports/world-disasters-report/world-disasters-report-2012---focus-on-forced-migration-and-displacement/

Jackson, Ivor C. *The Refugee Concept in Group Situations.* Cambridge: Cambridge University Press, 1999.

Jenkins, Fiona. "Bare Life: Asylum-Seekers, Australian Politics and Agamben's Critique of Violence." *Australian Journal of Human Rights*, Vol. 10, No. 2 (2004), p. 18.

Jennings, R. "Sovereignty and Political Modernity: A Genealogy of Agamben's Critique of Sovereignty." *Anthropological Theory*, Vol. 11, No. 1 (2011), pp. 23–61.

Kagan, Michael. "Why Do We Still Have Refugee Camps?" *Urban Refugees.Org: Moving the Debate Forward.* October 8, 2013. http://urban-refugees.org/debate/why-do-we-still-have-refugee-camps/

Kingsley, Patrick. "The Journey: Syrian Refugee Hashem Alsouki Risks His Life Crossing the Mediterranean, His Sights Set on Sweden—and Freedom for His Family." *The Guardian*, June 9, 2015. http://www.theguardian.com/world/ng-interactive/2015/jun/09/a-migrants-journey-from-syria-to-sweden-interactive

Klabbers, Jan. "Hannah Arendt and the Language of Global Governance." In Goldoni, Marco and McCorkindale, Christopher eds. *Hannah Arendt and the Law.* Portland: Hart Publishing, 2012.

Krause, Monika. "Undocumented Migrants: An Arendtian Perspective." *European Journal of Political Theory*, Vol. 7, No. 3 (2008), pp. 331–348.

Kuosmanen, Jaakko. "Perfecting Imperfect Duties: The Institutionalisation of a Universal Right to Asylum." *Journal of Political Philosophy*, Vol. 21, No. 1 (2013), pp. 24–43.

Kusisto, Laura. "Minimum Wage in U.S. Cities Not Enough to Afford Rent, Report Says." *Wall Street Journal*, May 22, 2015. http://blogs.wsj.com/economics/2015/05/19/report-minimum-wage-in-u-s-cities-not-enough-to-afford-rent/ (accessed May 22, 2015).

Lippert-Rasmussen, Kasper. "Responsible Nations: Miller on National Responsibility." *Ethics and Global Politics*, Vol. 2, No. 2 (2009), pp. 109–130.

Loescher, Gil. *Beyond Charity: International Cooperation and the Global Refugee Crisis.* Oxford: Oxford University Press, 1993.

Bibliography

———. "UNHCR at Fifty: Refugee Protection and World Politics." In Steiner, Niklaus, Gibney, Mark and Loescher, Gill eds. *Problems of Protection: The UNHCR and Human Rights*. New York: Routledge, 2012, pp. 3–18.

Loescher, Gil and James Milner. "Understanding the Challenge." *Forced Migration Review*, No. 33 (September 2009), pp. 9–11.

Loescher, Gil, et al. *Protracted Refugee Situations*. New York: United Nations University Press, 2008a.

Loescher, Gil, et al. *The United Nations High Commissioner for Refugees (UNHCR)*. New York: Routledge, 2008b.

Long, Katy. *The Point of No Return: Refugees, Rights and Repatriation*. Oxford: Oxford University Press, 2013.

Malkki, Liisa H. "Speechless Emissaries: Refugees, Humanitarianism, and Dehistoricization." *Cultural Anthropology*, Vol. 11, No. 3 (August 1996), pp. 377–404.

Meyers, Diana. "Two Victim Paradigms and the Problem of 'Impure' Victims." *Humanity*, Vol. 2, No. 2 (2011), pp. 255–275.

Millbank, Adrienne, Social Policy Group. *The Problem with the 1951 Refugee Convention*. Parliament of Australia, Research Paper 5, September 2000.

Miller, David. *National Responsibility and Global Justice*. Oxford: Oxford University Press, 2007.

Mills, Catherine. *The Philosophy of Agamben*. Montreal and Kingston: McGill-Queen's University Press, 2008.

Nagel, Thomas. "Poverty and Food: Why Charity is Not Enough." In Pogge and Mollendorf eds. *Global Justice: Seminal Essays*. St Paul: Paragone House, 2008

Neubauer, Ian Lloyd. "Australia Will Keep Detaining Refugees Indefinitely, Whatever the World Thinks." *Time.com*, March 6, 2014. http://time.com/13682/australia-asylum-seeker-policy-compared-to-guantanamo/ (accessed July 27, 2015).

Norris, Andrew. "Giorgio Agamben and the Politics of the Living Dead." *Diacritics*, Vol. 30, No. 4 (Winter 2000), pp. 38–58.

———. "The Exemplary Exception: Philosophical and Political Decisions in Giorgio Agamben's *Homo Sacer*." In Andrew Norris, ed. *Politics, Metaphysics, and Death*. Durham: Duke University Press, 2005, pp. 262–283.

Nyers, Peter. *Rethinking Refugees: Beyond the State of Emergency*. New York: Routledge, 2006.

Owens, Patricia. "Reclaiming 'Bare Life'? Against Agamben on Refugees." *International Relations*, Vol. 23, No. 4 (2009), pp. 567–582.

Pittaway, Eileen and L. Bartolomei. *Welcome to Kakuma!—Field Trip Reports to Kakuma Refugee Camp, Kenya*. Sydney: UNSW Centre for Refugee Research Occasional Paper, 2003. http://www.crr.unsw.edu.au

Pittaway, Eileen and Emma Pittaway. "'Refugee Woman': A Dangerous Label: Opening a Discussion on the Role of Identity and Intersectional Oppression in the Failure of the International Refugee Protection Regime for Refugee Women." *Australian Journal of Human Rights*, Vol. 10, No. 2 (2004). http://www.austlii.edu.au/au/journals/AUJlHRights/2004/20.html

Pogge, Thomas. "'Assisting' the Global Poor." In Chatterjee, Deen ed. *The Ethics of Assistance: Morality and the Distant Needy*. Cambridge: Cambridge University Press, 2004.

———. *World Poverty and Human Rights*. 2nd Edition. New York: Polity Press, 2008.

———. *Politics as Usual: What Lies behind the Pro-Poor Rhetoric*. Cambridge: Polity Press, 2010.

Power, Samantha. *A Problem from Hell: America in the Age of Genocide.* New York: Basic Books, 2013.
Rancière, Jacques. "Who Is the Subject of the Rights of Man?" *South Atlantic Quarterly*, Vol. 103, No. 2/3 (Spring/Summer 2004), pp. 297–310.
Rawlence, Ben. *City of Thorns: Nine Lives in the World's Largest Refugee Camp.* New York: Picador, 2016.
Rawls, John. *Political Liberalism.* Cambridge: Harvard University Press, 1993.
———. *The Law of Peoples.* Cambridge: Harvard University Press, 2001.
Redclift, Victoria. *Stateless and Citizenship: Camps and the Creation of Political Space.* Florence, KY: Routledge, 2013.
Redmond, Ron. "Protracted Refugee Situations: Millions Caught in Limbo, with No Solutions in Sight." *United Nations Office of the High Commissioner for Refugees*, 2006. http://www.un.org/events/tenstories/06/story.asp?storyID=2600# (accessed April 27, 2012).
Rosenberg, Tina. "Beyond Refugee Camps, a Better Way." *New York Times*, September 6, 2011.
Roxström, Erik and Mark Gibney. "The Legal and Ethical Obligations of the UNHCR: The Case of Temporary Protection in Western Europe." In Steiner, Niklaus, Gibney, Mark and Loescher, Gill eds. *Problems of Protection: The UNHCR and Human Rights.* New York: Routledge, 2012, pp. 37–60.
Schaap, Andrew. "Enacting the Right to Have Rights: Jacques Rancière's Critique of Hannah Arendt." *European Journal of Political Theory*, Vol. 10, No. 1 (2011), pp. 22–45.
Scheffler, Samuel. *Boundaries and Allegiances: Problems of Justice and Responsibility in Liberal Thought.* Oxford: Oxford University Press, 2003.
———. "Immigration and the Significance of Culture." *Philosophy and Public Affairs*, Vol. 35, No. 2 (2007), pp. 93–125.
Schmeidl, Susanne. "Repatriation to Afghanistan: Durable Solution or Responsibility Shifting?" *Forced Migration Review*, Vol. 33 (September 2009), pp. 20–22.
Schuck, Peter. "Refugee Burden-Sharing: A Modest Proposal." *Yale Journal of International Law*, Vol. 222 (1997), pp. 243–297.
Shacknove, Andrew E. "Who Is a Refugee?" *Ethics*, Vol. 95 (January 1985), pp. 274–284.
———. "From Asylum to Containment." *International Journal of Refugee Law*, Vol. 5 (1993), pp. 516–533.
Singer, Peter. "Famine, Affluence and Morality." *Philosophy and Public Affairs*, Vol. 1, No. 3 (1972), pp. 229–243.
Singer, Peter and Renata Singer. "The Ethics of Refugee Policy." In Mark Gibney ed. *Open Borders? Closed Societies? The Ethical and Political Issues.* New York: Greenwood Press, 1988.
Smith, Merril. "Warehousing Refugees: A Denial of Rights, a Waste of Humanity." *Washington, DC: World Refugee Survey*, US Committee on Refugees and Immigrants, 2004, pp. 38–56.
Staples, Kelly. *Retheorising Statelessness: A Background Theory of Membership in World Politics.* Edinburgh: Edinburgh University Press, 2012.
Stemplowska, Zofia and Adam Swift. "Ideal and Nonideal Theory." In Estlund, David ed. *The Oxford Handbook of Political Philosophy.* Oxford: Oxford University Press, June 2012.
Stevens, Jacob. "Prisons of the Stateless: The Derelictions of the UNHCR." *New Left Review*, Vol. 42 (November–December 2006), pp. 53–67.

Ticktin, Miriam. "Where Ethics and Politics Meet: The Violence of Humanitarianism in France." *American Ethnologist*, Vol. 33, No. 1 (February 2006), pp. 33–49.

———. *Casualties of Care: Immigration and the Politics of Humanitarianism in France*. Berkeley: UC Press, 2011.

United Nations High Commissioner for Refugees (UNHCR). "OAC 1969 Convention Governing the Specific Aspects of Refugee Problems in Africa." 1969. http://www.unhcr.org/45dc1a682.html.

———. "Prevention and Response to Sexual and Gender-Based Violence in Refugee Situations, Interagency Lessons Learnt Conference Proceedings." 2001a. Geneva, Switzerland. March 27–29, 2001.

———. "Respect Our Rights: Partnerships for Equality." 2001b. Report on the Dialogue with Refugee Women, Geneva, Switzerland. June 20–22, 2001.

———. "UNHCR's Women Victims of Violence Project in Kenya: An Evaluation Summary, UNHCR." 2002.

———. "The State of the World's Refugees 2006 (Chapter 5: Protracted Refugee Situations: The Search for Practical Solutions)." 2006. http://www.unhcr.org/4444afcb0.pdf (accessed May 2015).

———. "Refugee Protection and Mixed Migration: A 10-Point Plan of Action." January 1, 2007. http://www.unhcr.org/4742a30b4.html (accessed May 2015).

———. "World Refugee Day: UNHCR Report Finds 80 Per Cent of World's Refugees in Developing Countries." June 20, 2011. http://www.unhcr.org/4dfb66ef9.html.

———. "Protecting Refugees and the Role of the UNHCR." 2014a. http://www.unhcr.org/509a836e9.html (accessed May 2015).

———. "World at War: Global Trends Forced Displacement in 2014." 2014b.

———. "Policy on Alternatives to Camps." 2014c. Date of entry into force: July 22, 2014. http://www.refworld.org/pdfid/5423ded84.pdf

———. "6 Steps towards Solving the Refugee Situation in Europe." Briefing Notes, March 4, 2016a. http://www.unhcr.org/56d96de86.html

———. "Figures at a Glance." June 2016b. http://www.unhcr.org/en-us/figures-at-a-glance.html

———. "Resettlement: A New Beginning in a Third Country." http://www.unhcr.org/pages/4a16b1676.html (accessed October 2015).

United States, Department of State. "Protracted Refugee Situations." http://www.state.gov/j/prm/policyissues/issues/protracted/index.htm#3 (accessed May 2015).

U.S. Committee for Refugees and Immigrants (USCRI). "Refugee Warehousing." http://www.refugees.org/resources/uscri_reports/refugee-warehousing-faq.html (accessed July 29, 2015)

Verdirame, Guglielmo and Barbara Harrell-Bond. *Rights in Exile: Janus-Faced Humanitarianism*. New York and Oxford: Berghahn Books, 2005.

Waldron, Jeremy. "Homelessness and the Issue of Freedom." *UCLA Law Review*, Vol. 39 (1991), pp. 295–324.

Walzer, Michael. *Spheres of Justice*. New York: Basic Books, 1983.

Ward, Jeanne. *If Not Now, When? Addressing Gender-Based Violence in Refugee, Internally Displaced, and Post-Conflict Settings: A Global Overview*. New York: The Reproductive Health for Refugees Consortium, 2002.

Weinstein, Liza. *The Durable Slum: Dharavi and the Right to Stay Put in Globalizing Mumbai*. Minnesota: University of Minnesota Press, 2014.

Weissbrodt, David. *The Human Rights of Non-Citizens.* Oxford and New York: Oxford University Press, 2008.
Wellman, Christopher Heath. "Immigration and Freedom of Association." *Ethics*, Vol. 119 (October 2008), pp. 109–141.
Wilde, Ralph. "Quis Custodiet Ipsos Custodes? Why and How UNHCR Governance of 'Development' Refugee Camps Should be Subject to International Human Rights Law." *Yale Human Rights and Development Law Journal*, Vol. 1 (1998), pp. 107–128.
Xenos, Nicolas. "Refugees: The Modern Political Condition." *Alternatives*, Vol. 18, No. 3 (Fall 1993), pp. 419–430.
Young, Iris. *Global Challenges: War, Self-Determination and Responsibility.* New York: Polity Press, 2007.
———. *Responsibility for Justice.* Oxford: Oxford University Press, 2011.
Zizek, Slavoj. "Against Human Rights." *New Left Review*, Vol. 34 (July–August 2005), pp. 115–131.

Index

abandonment 83, 90–3
Agamben, Giorgio 9, 83, 86–92, 95–7, 99, 105, 128–32
Agier, Michel 9, 29–31, 33–4, 77, 87–90, 128, 131–2, 139
Aleinikoff, Alexander 24–7, 37, 70, 145
alternatives to camps 42–3; UNHCR policy on 43–4
Arab Spring 37
arbitrary prolonged detention 31
Arendt, Hannah 6–7, 9, 11, 65, 68, 82–101, 112, 139–40
Ashford, Elizabeth 105, 108–10, 118, 127
Aristotle 87, 128
asylum seeker 25–6, 37, 62, 68, 84, 89, 92, 98, 136–7, 141; Australian policy on 38; Benhabib on 64–5, 68; Gibney on 72; legitimate *vs.* economic migrant 12, 24, 131; moral questions about 5–6, 18, 106; normative obligations for 21; Walzer on 56
Australia 3, 12, 29, 35, 38, 56

bare life 6, 83, 85–9, 91, 93–8, 100, 128–31, 140
Beitz, Charles 66, 76
Benhabib, Seyla 11, 51–2, 63–70, 74–6, 139
Betts, Alexander 42–3
bios 87, 128
Brock, Gillian 105, 118–20, 127
burden sharing 22, 73, 133–4

Canada 3, 10, 12, 74
Carens, Joseph 8, 10, 13, 51–2, 63, 70–6, 106, 139, 142
citizenship 5–6, 11, 18, 53–4, 58, 61, 64–70, 82–4, 85–90, 92, 98, 100, 129, 140, 143, 145
common humanity 72, 83, 85
common world 83, 86, 89–94, 98, 100, 131
communities of character 51, 53, 55–7
containment 3, 8, 17–18, 23–4, 26, 28–9, 37–8, 40, 58, 63, 75, 83, 99, 110, 115, 126, 139
continental (philosophy) 7, 9, 139
cosmopolitanism 33, 67–8, 72, 77, 114

Dadaab, Kenya 34, 37, 138
Declaration of the Rights of Man and Citizen 87
democracy 41, 53, 68
disaggregated citizenship 6, 67, 69–70
durable solutions 2–4, 20, 28

economic integration 6, 142
economic migrant 10–12, 54, 92, 131–2
emergency aid 2, 100
encampment 2, 7, 11, 13, 17–19, 27, 29, 39–42, 51, 55, 63, 68, 75–6, 78; as human rights violation 18, 32–3, 105–6, 121, 145–6; justification of 44; as moral harm 83, 100; ontological deprivation, and 85, 104, 140–1; as structural injustice 6, 110, 112, 120; as unofficial solution 3, 41,

158 Index

82–3, 137–8; Western support for and benefit from 36–7, 57–9, 115, 125–8
epistemic injustice 99
ethics of admissions 5, 51, 63–4, 75, 78
ethics of the temporary 52, 75, 104, 137, 139
Europe 1, 5, 7, 10, 19, 22, 25–6, 37–8, 65, 67–8, 125

Fassin, Didier 89, 98
forced displacement 1, 4–5, 7–8, 13, 17–18, 29, 37, 40, 52, 82, 100, 138–42, 145; philosophical perspectives on 63; responsibility for 83, 105, 107
freedom of association 51, 60–3
freedom of movement 31–3, 42–3, 101, 138
FRONTEX 37–8

gender based violence 34, 36
Gibney, Matthew 13, 37, 51–2, 63, 70, 72–6, 106, 139
global civil society 65, 69
Good Samaritan principle 54, 104, 106

Hamas 95, 97
Harrell-Bond, B. 29, 31–4, 36, 40, 77, 144
Hegel, G. W. 129–30
holding centers 29–30
humanitarian aid 11, 31, 38, 88
humanitarianism 25, 33, 52, 74–5, 77, 88
human rights 2, 4, 10, 11, 18, 20, 24–5, 28, 58–9, 68, 101, 109, 137–40, 144–6; Agamben on 129; Arendt on 82, 84–6, 89, 94, 96–7; institutional analysis of 76–8; in refugee camps 31–5; violations of 3, 6, 8, 13, 27, 39–41, 104–5, 124

identity 5–6, 10, 35, 57, 59, 65–6, 69–70, 82–6, 88–9, 91–8, 129–31, 140, 145
inclusive exclusion 83, 90, 92, 105, 128–9, 131, 133

Interahamwe 95, 97
interdependence 52, 64–8, 108, 124, 127
internally displaced people (IDPs) 13, 29–30, 36
International Committee of the Red Cross and Red Crescent (ICRC) 39, 42, 143, 145
involuntary migrants 18–19, 22–4, 26, 28, 40, 62, 106

Jordan 8

Lebanon 8
local integration 3–4, 27–8, 42–3, 57–9, 142–3
local integration, temporary 6, 42, 63, 100, 142–3

Miller, David 62–3, 139–40, 143; obligations to refugees 51, 58–9, 72, 74–5; on responsibility 7, 105–6, 116–20, 122–5
mutual aid 51–7, 72, 104, 106, 114

nationalism 2, 72
national responsibility 117
Nauru 38
NGOs (Non-Governmental Organizations) 20, 31, 35, 69, 88, 92, 97–8, 141–2
non-ideal theory 5
non-refoulement 6, 11, 21–4, 37, 70, 72–3, 85, 104

ontological deprivation 5–7, 45, 78, 83–5, 90–1, 93–6, 98–101, 104, 140, 142

participatory budgeting 41
permanent alienage 70, 143
phenomenology 9; of agency 105, 120
Pogge, Thomas 7, 9, 66, 76, 105, 107–10, 116–18, 120, 123, 127–8, 140
policy on alternatives to camps 43–4
political belonging 1, 5, 11, 24, 84, 100, 132
political membership 6, 54, 64–7, 83, 100, 140

poverty, global 9, 12, 25, 42, 61, 104, 107–11, 118–20, 123–4, 126, 127
prolonged detention *see* arbitrary prolonged detention
protracted refugee situation 2, 17, 82, 137

Rancière, Jacques 96, 99
Rawlence, Ben 34, 37, 138
Rawls, John 2, 9, 40–1, 54, 65–6
refugee camps 3, 5, 8, 23, 28–30, 39, 44, 63, 70, 78, 82–3, 85, 98–101, 137–9, 143; Agier on 88, 90, 131; Carens on 71–2; denial of rights in 2, 11–12, 31–7, 77, 96; Miller on 58–9; political violence, and 95, 97; UNHCR and 17, 19, 40–1; warehousing in 4
Refugee Convention (1951) 4, 10, 12–13, 17, 20, 31, 37, 39, 85, 101, 142
refugee regime 8–10, 12, 19–23, 39, 63, 69, 82, 89, 92, 114, 137–8, 144, 146; bare life, and 87; Carens on 70, 72, 74, 75; harms of 6, 13, 35; remedial responsibility 7, 105, 116–24, 132–3, 141; responsibility for 7, 52–3, 120–7; structural injustice, and 6–7, 105, 121–2, 133, 141; Walzer on 53, 58; Western support for 10, 18, 127–8
refugee women 35–6
repatriation 3, 18, 20, 23, 25–8, 37, 39–42, 52, 59, 82, 85, 100, 121, 128, 139–42
resettlement 8, 42, 58, 61, 63, 77, 82, 85–6, 100, 145; as durable solution 2–3, 18, 20, 23–8, 59, 128, 137; as duty or obligation 4–5, 39, 51–2, 70, 72–3, 75, 104, 139, 142; eligibility for 6, 33, 35, 110; programs and policies 7, 11–13, 126
responsibility 6–7, 14, 25, 43, 76, 104–7, 140–2; Ashford on 108–10; Benhabib on 66, 69; Brock on 119–20, 127; Carens on 71, 74; for displacement 120–2, 128, 133–4; Miller on 58, 116–19, 122–4; moral 3, 17; Pogge on 107–8, 127; of

Index 159

UNHCR 20, 77, 83, 86, 101; Young on 110–15, 124–6
rightlessness 84, 94
right to have rights 94

St Lewis, the 74
Sangatte 29
sans papiers 84
sexual violence 34–6, 141
Shire, Warsan 136
sovereignty 1–2, 18, 20–1, 24–7, 33, 58, 62, 87, 92, 126, 131, 132, 137–8, 144; bare life as source of 129; as relational 65–6, 69
statelessness 5–6, 9, 57, 76, 78, 82–6, 89, 90–1, 93–6, 99–101, 104, 140
stateless people 6, 65, 69–70, 77–8, 82–101, 112, 116, 123, 140
structural injustice 6–7, 105, 110–15, 118, 120–2, 124–6, 133, 140–1
sweatshops 110–11, 114, 119
Syria 1, 7, 19, 106, 137

temporary local integration *see* local integration, temporary
Turkey 1, 8

Uganda 32, 42–3, 142
UNHCR 17, 28–9, 41, 43–4, 100–1, 112, 121, 125, 141–2; critique of 32–4, 77; definition of refugees 12–13, 78; funding and budget 8, 22, 38, 128; purpose and role of 19–21, 23, 26–7, 44, 69, 92; reformation of 144–5; sexual violence, and 35–7
United Nations Convention Relating to the Status of Refugees *see* Refugee Convention (1951)
United States (U.S.) 3, 7, 12, 38

Verdirame, G. 29, 31–4, 36, 40, 77, 144

Walzer, Michael 51, 53–60, 63, 72, 75, 106, 132, 139, 143–4
warehousing 4, 7, 32, 42, 55, 57–9, 68, 105, 122, 124
Wellman, Christopher 51, 59–63, 76, 139

Woomera 29
worldlessness 91
World Trade Organization (WTO) 108
World War I 84
World War II 99

xenophobia 8, 73, 138

Young, Iris 7, 105, 109–16, 118, 120–7, 140

zoë 87, 128–9